COLLECTIVE SECURITY

Chandler Publications in
POLITICAL SCIENCE
VICTOR JONES, *Editor*

World Politics Series
PAUL SEABURY, *Editor*

Collective Security

Compiled and Edited by

Marina S. Finkelstein

and

Lawrence S. Finkelstein

Chandler Publishing Company, 124 Spear Street

San Francisco, California 94105

Library of Congress Catalog Card No. 66-11427
Printed in the United States of America

Contents

Acknowledgments

It would indeed be careless not to express our thanks to those who helped in the preparation of this collection. In particular, we should like to thank the following members of the staff of the Carnegie Endowment for International Peace: in the library, Vivian D. Hewitt, Jane Lowenthal, and Roberta Rothman; and in the administration, Kay de Wette, Fredric Busch, Ray Moran, Jesse Nesmith, and George Washington.

COLLECTIVE SECURITY

Introduction

Collective security is based on the principle that peace is indivisible: therefore, a threat to the peace anywhere is of *common concern* to the entire international community (as that is defined at any particular moment), which must agree *in advance* both *to react* against such a threat and *how* to react against it.

In a very simple kind of way, collective security may be seen as an effort to transfer to the international scene the "one for all and all for one" concept which guided Alexandre Dumas' d'Artagnan and his three doughty Musketeer friends. Actually, the comparison may be more revealing than appears at first glance, as it is the absence on the international scene of the qualities that the four friends shared—unswerving loyalties to the same overriding goals, deep friendship within their group, and an unflinching willingness to devote every resource of their skill, effort, and life itself to the carrying out of their loyalties and friendship—that goes far in explaining the spotty record so far achieved by systems of collective security.

"Collective security" is a term which arouses deep emotions—both for and against—and which lends itself to easy sloganeering. To be more precise about it, however, it should be pointed out that a collective security system is not the same as a system of collective defense. Thus, for example, NATO is not an example of collective security, since it is directed against threats to a specified area from an outside source and is intended as a system of self-defense, not as a system to keep the peace anywhere it happens to be threatened. The same can be said for SEATO and CENTO and the Warsaw Pact. All are self-defense organizations, not general international organizations designed to deal with peace as an indivisible entity.

We are accustomed to thinking of collective security as a comparatively modern development, dating mainly from the League of Nations and including the United Nations. But it is worth pointing out that the concept itself is of ancient origin. Thus, for example, the oath taken by the Greek city-states which belonged to the ancient Amphictyonic League provided an obligation not to destroy any city of the Amphictyons, "nor cut off their streams, in war or peace, and if any should do so, they would march against him, and destroy his cities, and should any pillage the property of the god, or be privy to or plan anything against what was in his temple at Delphi, they would take vengeance against him with hand and foot, and all their might."[1] Interesting practical developments took place also in the Middle Ages and during the nineteenth century. And there has been throughout modern history an abundance of plans and schemes designed to achieve the major goal of collective security: the preservation of the peace through common, predetermined, collective action.

Collective security is sometimes thought of solely in universal terms: certainly both the League of Nations and the United Nations were constructed to be, or to become, universal organizations. The fact that neither organization achieved universality remains a topic of lively debate, both in historical and contemporary terms. It is, however, perfectly possible to have a regional collective security organization, such as the Organization of American States is or as the Organization of African Unity may become. The essential point, the touchstone, is universality of membership for the region involved and the obligations that the members have assumed toward each other in the preservation of peace in their own area against threats emanating from within their area. The existence of regional organizations in a world which also has a well-nigh universal system obviously poses the difficult problem of meshing the activities of the regional and world organizations. It is also essential to point out that an organization may serve

---

[1] As cited in Elizabeth York, *Leagues of Nations, Ancient, Mediaeval, and Modern* (London: The Swarthmore Press, Ltd., 1919), p. 5.

both as a collective security system and as a collective defense system, as is the case with the Organization of American States.

For a realistic evaluation of collective security, it is essential to keep firmly in mind the following conclusions. First of all, collective security systems are not the only means to try to keep the peace. Historically speaking, there have been a number of other devices and other approaches. Furthermore, at any one time, governments will be using a number of other instruments for keeping the peace, such as traditional diplomacy and military power, expressed through a variety of means.

Finally, the effective expression of a common concern in keeping the peace through a system of collective security will depend not on its legal structure, its constitution, the cunning of its architects, but on the totality of the foreign policies and national goals and resources of those nations which "count" in a particular situation and which are in a position to take action of whatever nature is required, up to and including the use of force in support of the collective decision. As things are now, power rests in national hands and whether that power will be used for the collective goal will depend on national decisions and national calculations.

[1]

What Is Collective Security?

Is collective security a new way of conducting international affairs, based on a radical rearrangement of the international political structure? Or has it only, as the late Professor Nicholas J. Spykman put it, "changed the legal obligations of states" without basically altering "the organization of force in the international community."[1]

[1] Nicholas J. Spykman, *America's Strategy in World Politics* (New York: Harcourt, Brace and Co., 1942), p. 109. Reprinted by permission.

1. A New Name for an Old Reality

RICHARD N. CURRENT

. . . Until February of [1917] President Wilson had advanced toward a concept truly ecumenical in its essence and highly promising in its implications—the concept of an association of *all* the nations which was to be based upon a compromise to end the war with a "community" of power and without victors or vanquished. Wilson abandoned the distinctive elements of that idea when the final clash came between his interpretation of the free-

Richard N. Current, "The United States and 'Collective Security': Notes on the History of an Idea," in Alexander DeConde, editor, *Isolation and Security* (Durham: Duke University Press, 1957), p. 55. Reprinted by permission.

dom of the seas and the German use of the submarine. Thereafter, for the next forty years, whatever the phrase or the fervor with which it was expressed, the idea of collective security never amounted to much more than a new vehicle for old baggage. True, the League and the UN were more highly organized and more broadly inclusive in membership than old-fashioned alliances (and, incidentally, they performed valuable nonpolitical functions which those alliances did not). True also, the systems of collective security were designed for "police action" against an "aggressor," not for "war" against an "enemy." In these respects collective security was, perhaps, new. In fundamentals it was hard to distinguish from the timeworn statecraft of alliances designed to achieve for their adherents some kind of "balance," which usually meant predominance.

2. A Natural Evolution from the Balance of Power System

EDWARD V. GULICK

. . . One can see from the larger context that "collective security," far from being alien to the "age-old tradition of the balance of power," not only derives out of the latter, but also must be regarded as the logical end point of the balance-of-power system, the ideal toward which it has been moving, slowly and haltingly, for several hundred years. This contention leads to the hypothesis that the League of Nations and the United Nations, when considered as instruments for maintaining the "continued co-existence of independent governments in contact with one another," were merely further refinements in balance practice—namely, organizations representing a world-wide state system of sovereign, inde-

Edward V. Gulick, *Europe's Classic Balance of Power* (Ithaca: Cornell University Press, 1955), pp. 307-308.

pendent, and armed states, intent on preserving their security and independence and prepared to use an automatic coalition to prevent the dangerous expansion of any member state. Added to this were certain other embellishments of balance practice: the location of the organization in one city and the invention of a system of permanent representation there for the member states, an innovation which was to the new type of equilibrist organization what the system of permanent embassies was to the older types of balance practice. At bottom, however, the collective security of 1919 or 1945 was merely an elaboration and refinement of the coalition equilibrium of 1815, just as the latter was an elaboration and refinement of the alliance balance. . . .

3. A Planned Development from the Balance of Power System

QUINCY WRIGHT

. . . Policies of balance of power naturally lead to policies of collective security which become institutionalized through common organs, procedures, and rules of law to assure that aggression will be always confronted by insuperable force. International organization to promote collective security is, therefore, only a planned development of the natural tendency of balance of power policies. It is the natural tendency of states, when faced by an emergency, to gang up against the aggressor who, if successful against his first victim, will eventually turn on the others. Collective security seeks to supplement this natural tendency by positive obligations and convenient agencies and procedures to enlist common action. . . .

Quincy Wright, *The Study of International Relations* (New York: Appleton-Century-Crofts, 1955), p. 204. Reprinted by permission.

4. A Totally Different System for the Conduct of International Relations in Peace and War

WOODROW WILSON

. . . Repeated utterances of the leading statesmen of most of the great nations now engaged in war have made it plain that their thought has come to this, that the principle of public right must henceforth take precedence over the individual interests of particular nations, and that the nations of the world must in some way band themselves together to see that that right prevails as against any sort of selfish aggression; that henceforth alliance must not be set up against alliance, understanding against understanding, but that there must be a common agreement for a common object, and that at the heart of that common object must lie the inviolable rights of peoples and of mankind. The nations of the world have become each other's neighbors. It is to their interest that they should understand each other. In order that they may understand each other, it is imperative that they should agree to cooperate in a common cause, and that they should so act that the guiding principle of that common cause shall be even-handed and impartial justice.

This is undoubtedly the thought of America. This is what we ourselves will say when there comes proper occasion to say it. In the dealings of nations with one another arbitrary force must be rejected and we must move forward to the thought of the modern world, the thought of which peace is the very atmosphere. That thought constitutes a chief part of the passionate conviction of America. . . .

If it should ever be our privilege to suggest or initiate a movement for peace among the nations now at war, I am sure that the people of the United States would wish their Government to move along these lines: First, such a settlement with regard to their

Woodrow Wilson, Address before the League to Enforce Peace, May 27, 1916, *The Messages and Papers of Woodrow Wilson,* with Editorial Notes and introduction by Albert Shaw, 2 vols. (New York: The Review of Reviews Corp., 1924), Vol. I, pp. 273-275.

own immediate interests as the belligerents may agree upon. We have nothing material of any kind to ask for ourselves, and are quite aware that we are in no sense or degree parties to the present quarrel. Our interest is only in peace and its future guarantees. Second, an universal association of the nations to maintain the inviolate security of the highway of the seas for the common and unhindered use of all the nations of the world, and to prevent any war begun either contrary to treaty covenants or without warning and full submission of the causes to the opinion of the world—a virtual guarantee of territorial integrity and political independence.

But I did not come here, let me repeat, to discuss a programme. I came only to avow a creed and give expression to the confidence I feel that the world is even now upon the eve of a great consummation, when some common force will be brought into existence which shall safeguard right as the first and most fundamental interest of all peoples and all governments, when coercion shall be summoned not to the service of political ambition or selfish hostility, but to the service of a common order, a common justice, and a common peace. God grant that the dawn of that day of frank dealing and of settled peace, concord, and cooperation may be near at hand!

5. If Collective Security Is a Myth . . .

Robert E. Osgood

. . . But one may wonder what difference it makes if we console ourselves with a myth as long as we are compelled, in practice, to conduct our policies as the realities dictate. The only answer is that our longing for the myth may inhibit our adjustment to the

Robert E. Osgood, "Woodrow Wilson, Collective Security, and the Lessons of History," *Confluence,* Winter, 1957, pp. 341-354, at p. 354.

realities. The problems of the cold war, the problems of containment, cannot be resolved in terms of the general goals of opposing aggression and upholding collective security. They are concrete military and political problems which require the coherent management of national power according to an overall strategic plan for achieving specific security objectives. Our commitment to the ideal conception of collective security becomes a liability only when it conceals this necessary basis of action and leaves us straddled awkwardly between two worlds—the one, a world of aspirations; the other, a world of power politics—bridged only by a succession of pragmatic improvisations to meet a series of unanticipated crises. We shall be in a better position to avoid this liability when we can retain Wilson's conception as an ultimate aspiration but repay our debt to History with a candid acknowledgment that we live in a world he never envisioned.

[11]

The Principle of Common Concern

The principle of a common concern in preventing aggression is the taproot of collective security. If realized to the full through collective security, this principle would have a drastic impact on the conduct of foreign policy, as it would require states to pledge themselves ahead of time to act with determination and speed, according to common and predetermined plan, against any aggressor, no matter whether friend or foe in ordinary relations, and no matter how powerful or where located.

HISTORICAL EXAMPLES

For generations men have struggled to give this principle form, to make it the vehicle of concrete policy. The elaborate international organizations of what is to us the modern period have roots in the Concert of Europe of the nineteenth century and in various more or less "academic" plans which stretch back to much earlier times. The concentration of a certain type of power in the hands of the Papacy during part of the Middle Ages made possible a different expression of common concern. A brief glimpse of a very crowded field is shown by Stefan T. Possony (Reading 6).

After the Congress of Vienna in 1815, power in Europe was concentrated for a number of years in the hands of a few states. In varying ways these states sought to maintain and enforce the peace of the continent through the Concert of Europe, as discussed by Sir Charles K. Webster and Sidney Herbert (Reading 7).

THE WHY OF COMMON CONCERN

The ideas of collective security and of a common concern in the peace have old antecedents, it is true. It is also true that the burgeoning of collective security has taken place in the twentieth century. Our discussion of the basic concept underlying collective security will focus, therefore, on this period.

1. *Why should there be a common concern with preventing aggression, no matter where or how it may be threatened?*

The collective security answer may be summarized in the phrase "peace is indivisible."

This statement has certainly been made often enough. In his famous "Quarantine Speech" of October 5, 1937, President Franklin D. Roosevelt spoke of war as a "contagion" (Reading 8); on another occasion, Allen W. Dulles, head of the Central Intelligence Agency from 1953 to 1961, discussed the difficulties of remaining aloof from "world catastrophe" (Reading 9).

2. *If peace is indivisible, and if it is a matter of common concern to keep the peace, on what basis can collective action be justified?*

The absence of a body of law which is "sufficiently settled and sufficiently extensive to provide the sort of base which, in a nation state, gives precision and authority and consent to the operations of those who have to keep the peace . . ."[1] and does so in advance, has made the search for a basis for collective action a matter of very lively concern.

THE BASIS OF COMMON CONCERN

The classic defense of the position that collective action can be justified on the basis of international morality and international agreement was made by Emperor Haile Selassie of Ethiopia, when he came to speak before the League of Nations Assembly on June 30, 1936. His primitive land overrun by Italian troops in what the League itself had denounced as an act of aggression, the refugee ruler spoke with passionate dignity against the League's failure

---

[1] Peter Calvocoressi, *World Order and New States* (London: Chatto and Windus, 1962), p. 72. American edition published by Frederick Praeger, Inc. Reprinted by permission.

to punish aggression and to draw the lesson from his experience (Reading 10).

When Emperor Haile Selassie condemned the members of the League, it was for their failure to carry out obligations which he considered legal and just. Writing in 1945, while the San Francisco Charter was still in the making, Emery Reves denied that, in the absence of fully formulated and preexisting law, such obligations *can* be legal and just (Reading 11).

IS COMMON CONCERN REALISTIC?

3. *Is it realistic to expect that the principle of common concern will be accepted in international practice?*

In the sense that "common concern" is read to demand prior agreement by all or most states to action in the event of aggression anywhere, this principle has obviously not been accepted.

Nevertheless, the question persists as to whether it is realistic to expect significant changes in this regard under foreseeable conditions. Howard C. Johnson and Gerhart Niemeyer argue that such acceptance is impossible because of the conflict between prescription and reality (Reading 12), while F. P. Walters affirms that in somewhat modified and less definite form, the principle of common concern had already been accepted in the League of Nations period (Reading 13).

THE REGIONAL ASPECT OF COMMON CONCERN

4. *If peace is indivisible, does it follow that every threat of aggression requires the attention of the worldwide collective organization?*

If there is an operating regional collective security organization, in what relationship should it stand to the global organization? The issues involved in this question are always in process of adjustment and never finally adjusted. To take only one example in a long history, during the preparation of the United Nations Charter in 1944-1945, much acrimonious debate and much compromise took place before the United States and the Latin American countries could agree on a mutually satisfactory formula designed to strengthen the inter-American system without at the same time weakening the wider international organization.

The Charter provisions which resulted from the compromise were far from unambiguous (Reading 14). They left room for significant regional collective security arrangements, such as the Charter of the Organization of American States, based on the provisions of the Rio Treaty of 1947 (Reading 15). They left room also for a flexibility of interpretation according to political developments (Reading 16).

IS COLLECTIVE SECURITY TOO COSTLY?

5. *Even if peace is indivisible, is it reasonable to assume that nations will always give priority to the demands of collective security?*

As Viscount Halifax, British Secretary of State for Foreign Affairs, put it in a House of Lords debate on the fate of Czechoslovakia, on March 20, 1939, does collective security involve "dangerously indefinite commitments quite disproportionate to the real security that these commitments [give]?[2] In other words, is it logical to assume that national security and collective security are interchangeable and that what serves the one will serve the other?

This central problem has been much debated, some arguing that whatever the costs of collective action, they are less than the costs of not taking such action (Reading 17). Others have pointed out the difficulties involved in trying to carry out policies simultaneously through collective defense and collective security instrumentalities (Reading 18). For the policymaker, the problem comes down to a careful tailoring of policy according to a balance between resources and commitments. Thus, to cite one example, Mr. John D. Hickerson, Assistant Secretary of State, argued against the Douglas-Thomas Resolution, which proposed specific military commitments to use force against any nation adjudged to be an aggressor by a two-thirds vote of the General Assembly of the United Nations, including three of the five permanent members of the Security Council, in the event that body had been unable to reach a decision (Reading 19).

---

[2] Statement by the British Secretary of State for Foreign Affairs, Viscount Halifax, House of Lords, *Debates,* 5th ser., Vol. 112, March 20, 1939, coll. 310-319, at coll. 318.

CONSENSUS IN COLLECTIVE SECURITY

6. *Can the principle of common concern, and with it collective security, be realized if the major states do not share a significant similarity in world outlook and world goals?*

Even allies have been known to fall out when divergencies in goals and outlook appeared. What about nations which are basically hostile but which must nevertheless act together if there is to be an effective expression of common concern in the sense in which it is being discussed here?

Today, if there were to be collective security action on any broad scale, it could take place only if the United States and the Soviet Union could agree on such action. Yet the two nations are divided both in world outlook and world goals.

On his return from his Vienna meeting with Soviet Premier Nikita S. Khrushchev in 1961, President John F. Kennedy explained his evaluation of the differences in goals between the two nations (Reading 20).

The same year, Khrushchev explained Soviet policies of "peaceful coexistence" and support for so-called "wars of national liberation" (Reading 21).

Nevertheless, given the high stakes which are involved, it is important to try to find out whether there are any interests in common between the United States and the Soviet Union which may, in certain circumstances, form a basis for a degree of consensus, even though a limited one (Reading 22).

"JUST WAR" AND NEUTRALISM

7. *Does the principle of common concern, if adequately realized, mean the revival of the concept of the "just war" and the elimination of the possibility of neutrality in a conflict condemned by an international collective security organization.*

Put in the simplest way, the concept of the "just war" means that war is justified only in response to an injury; that is, it must be fought in a just cause, in response to certain unjustified actions. In the Middle Ages, St. Augustine, St. Thomas Aquinas, and the Scholastic writer Vittoria were leading exponents of the doctrine of just war. Hugo Grotius, often called the father of modern international law, attempted to revive the concept after the Thirty

Years' War. In his famous treatise, *De Jure Belli ac Pacis,* Grotius stated that "right reason . . . and the nature of society" do not prohibit all use of force "but only that use of force which is in conflict with society, that is which attempts to take away the rights of another. . . ."[3]

This concept was largely abandoned in the nineteenth century, war being considered a fact of life in which justice and injustice were not involved. "The right of war, for whatever purposes, was a prerogative of national sovereignty. Thus conceived, every war was just. . . ."[4] It always lay within the power of a state "to gain political or other advantages over another, not merely by the employment of force, but also by direct recourse to war . . .[5] (Reading 23).

It is clear that strict, traditional neutrality is not compatible with full membership in an organization with collective security goals, as a member must accept certain obligations which may cut down on his freedom to maintain such neutrality in a given situation (Readings 24 and 25).

WAR AND COLLECTIVE SECURITY

8. *Is collective security synonymous with major war?*

Readings 26, 27, and 28 discuss this question.

---

[3] Hugo Grotius, *De Jure Belli ac Pacis,* J. B. Scott, editor, *The Classics of International Law* (London: Oxford, at the Clarendon Press, 1925), Book I, Ch. II, i, 5, p. 53. (Reprinted in 1964 by Oceana Publications, New York, U.S.A.) Reprinted by permission.

[4] L. F. L. Oppenheim, *International Law, A Treatise,* Vol. II, *Disputes, War and Neutrality,* 7th ed., edited by H. Lauterpacht (New York: Longmans, Green and Co., 1952), p. 223. Reprinted by permission of David McKay, Inc., New York City.

[5] Charles Cheney Hyde, *International Law, Chiefly as Interpreted and Applied by the United States,* 2nd ed. (Boston: Little, Brown and Co., 1951), Vol. III, p. 1686. Reprinted by permission.

HISTORICAL EXAMPLES

6. A Historical Survey

STEFAN T. POSSONY

Almost 1000 years ago, the now forgotten Bishop Gui d'Anjou initiated one of history's great attempts to secure peace. He proclaimed a truce of God and issued instructions limiting the use of arms. At the same time, he mobilized the spiritual power of the Christian religion against the scourge of war. To the surprise of many, the Bishop succeeded in curbing violence in his diocese; so impressive was his success that other French Bishops emulated his example. In the year 1000, a council at Poitiers adopted the motto *"Guerre à la guerre"* and passed a resolution which obligated the princes of the Church to oppose war by forceful means, that is, by the intervention of troops under religious leadership. At a synod in Limoges in 1031, it was resolved to excommunicate violators of the peace. It was also decided that, should moral coercion prove insufficient, military force was to be used against any breakers of God's truce. The participants of the synod of Bruges in 1038 swore to take military measures against violators of ecclesiastic peace laws. Under the energetic leadership of Archbishop Aimon of Bourges several punitive expeditions were carried out against rebellious knights; the Archbishop may, in fact, be considered as the earliest predecessor of the commander of a modern international armed force. Priests in large numbers fought

---

Stefan T. Possony, "Peace Enforcement," *The Yale Law Journal,* Vol. 55, No. 5, 1946, pp. 910-949, at pp. 910-918. Reprinted by permission of the copyright holder. Single issues, as well as back issues, available at $2.50 from F. B. Rothman, 57 Leuning Street, South Hackensack, New Jersey. Subscriptions, $10.00 per volume, available from Business Office, *Yale Law Journal,* 401-A Yale Station, New Haven, Conn. 06520.

in his peace enforcement army to safeguard the inherent justice and the disinterested nature of the intervention. Unfortunately, Aimon's peace force was soon annihilated by a group of knights who were more expert in the art of war than the 700 clerks whom they killed.[1]

During the 11th and 12th centuries, many French and German dioceses adopted laws and institutions to impose the truce of God. The *iudices pacis* determined whether or not the truce had been violated, while the *communitas pacis,* a medieval security council, enforced the decisions of the judicature. The principle of *active* maintenance of God's truce was proclaimed time and again. Pope Urban II, in preparation of the Crusade, decreed a general pacification of the Occident to be imposed by associations of nobles; the Crusade was to unite Christendom and create the essential prerequisites of perennial world peace (Council of Clermont, 1095). Pope Alexander III (1159-1181) decreed that *"pacem et concordiam . . . praedicari ac seminari oportet,"* the word *seminari* being a euphemism for "to coerce."[2] In the Council of Avignon (1209) a resolution was passed that peace was to be forced upon knights and towns. A few years later, the Council of Toulouse perfected the legal framework for the maintenance of the truce of God; it was ordered that

(a) every person over fourteen years of age was to pledge himself with a solemn oath not to violate the truce of God and not to assist any violator of the peace;

(b) this oath was to be repeated every three years, and a person refusing to renew the pledge was to be treated as a breaker of the law;

(c) alliances between nobles were forbidden;

(d) any violator of the peace was to be attacked forthwith by all the others who had pledged themselves to maintain peace; his territory was to be cut off from communications and traffic; his

---

[1] HUBERTI, *Studien zur Rechtgeschichte des Gottesfrieden und Landfrieden* in 1 DIE FRIEDENSORDNUNGEN IN FRANKREICH, (1892) 216 *et seq.* Contains bibliography.

[2] "Peace and concord . . . must be proclaimed and begotten." 1 SÉMICHON, LA PAIX ET LA TRÊVE DE DIEU (2d ed. 1869) 35 *et seq.*

stronghold was to be besieged and stormed; the aggressor and his men were to be punished severely and their property confiscated;

(e) the violator of the peace was to be excommunicated (a sanction which frequently entailed economic ruin and even physical destruction);

(f) the subjects of the aggressor were formally ordered to revolt against their master and to obstruct his aggression.[3]

In some regions of France, it also became customary for the knights who had obligated themselves to protect the truce of God to accept personal responsibility for any breaches of the peace. Out of his own pocket, the knight paid, or was expected to pay, an indemnity to those persons who had suffered from illegal warfare which he had been unable to prevent.[4]

The overall success of these various measures was by no means small. On the whole, fighting was limited to the period between Monday morning and Thursday evening; the truce of God reigned on Fridays, Saturdays, and Sundays. Certain groups of persons and institutions enjoyed a perpetual peace of God—clerics, monks, nuns, pilgrims, women, children, and workers, as well as churches, monasteries, cemeteries, and tools of work.

We do not know whether the frequency and intensity of war was reduced between 1000 and 1250. We know that powerful princes often disregarded the limitations imposed upon them and that they observed the law only when it was in their interest to do so. But we also know that the truce and peace of God were strictly observed in many regions. Peace was enforced by the spiritual power of the Church, accompanied by strong economic and sometimes military sanctions. But later the church's power declined, and it was no longer able to impose its law. In France wars tended to become perpetual; in Germany the *interregnum* created conditions wherein everybody was everybody else's enemy. Secular power then assumed the task of pacification. In France, Saint Louis IX issued his famous *ordonnance* which outlawed "private warfare"; an edict enforced by the power of his sword. In Ger-

[3] 2 *id.* at 62-7.
[4] *Id.* at 251.

many, Rudolph of Habsburg ended the lawless chaos by declaring the *Landfrieden.* The maintenance of internal peace had become the duty as well as the *raison d'être* of the secular state.[5]

DANTE AND DUBOIS

At the beginning of the 14th century, the question arose whether international war could not also be limited. While the ideal of peace was, of course, known to previous centuries, it is nevertheless correct to say that the roots of modern pacifism go back to that period. Scholastic philosophy, under the leadership of Thomas of Aquinas, had insisted on the difference between just and unjust war. But now the idea was pronounced that war is always an evil; Pierre Dubois said explicitly, *"Omne bellum in se malum et illicitum."*[6] It was also stated that permanent peace is the greatest of all blessings, and that society thrives best in the tranquillity of universal peace; in the words of Dante, *"Genus humanum optime se habens quaedam concordia."*[7]

Yet how should peace be preserved? Dante wanted to gain universal peace through the establishment of a universal monarchy. Pierre Dubois rejected this idea, asserting that advocates of universal monarchy were of unsound mind, but proposed instead a congress of princes to rule the affairs of Europe. Union and federation still compete as alternative patterns of world organization; the political inventiveness of mankind is undeniably small.

Dante pointed out that disputes between princes cannot be settled because the litigants are equal in rank,[8] whereas the monarch is most powerful and can impose his will to maintain peace. The idea of international military coercion was implicitly argued by Dante; there would be no point in establishing a universal monarchy unless the monarch has the power to eliminate aggression. He would preserve peace by virtue of his authority, to be sure,

---

[5] EGGERT, STUDIEN ZUR GESCHICHTE DER LANDFRIEDEN (1875) *passim.* For precedents in ancient Greece, Rome, and the early Middle Ages, see DAVIES, THE PROBLEM OF THE TWENTIETH CENTURY (1938) c. 2, and the literature quoted therein.

[6] DUBOIS, DE RECUPERATIONE TERRE SANCTE, TRAITÉ DE POLITIQUE GÉNÉRALE (Langlois' ed. 1891) 4.

[7] DANTE, DE MONARCHIA (Moore's ed. 1916) c. 1, § 15.

[8] *Id.* § 10.

but this authority was to be based on material strength superior to that of any other prince.

While Dubois argued that universal monarchy[9] could not lead to peace—continuous wars would have to be waged to establish and maintain the universal system—he recognized that the establishment of his system in the contemporary world also would require a series of preventive wars in the Holy Land, Italy and Germany. After pacification, international cooperation was to be achieved by a lucrative association of the states in common enterprises for the colonization of the Holy Land.

Within the league, peace was to be settled by arbitration, the Pope being the supreme arbiter; the judges were to be appointed by papal council. If peace was violated, the aggressor, called *"bellum ferens,"* was to be subdued by an international army formed from the troops of all confederate states. Economic blockade was to be used as one of the chief weapons.[10] No help was to be given to the aggressor populace which, after repression of its rebellion, was to be expropriated and expelled from its territory and used for conquest and colonization of the Holy Land. The aggressor was to be outlawed and prevented from resuming the attack. Thus, universal peace was to be preserved through four devices: confederation, economic association, arbitration and military coercion.

THE LATE MIDDLE AGES

The writings of Dante and Dubois had virtually no effect. Dubois was soon forgotten, and even Dante whose treatise could have served as a program for an expanding Imperial institution was almost totally neglected. In the ideology of the medieval Imperium, the idea of peace was little emphasized. The Holy Roman Empire became a mere symbol for the unity of the Christian world. For short moments the Empire took charge of the common defense of the Christian world against the assaults of Arabs, Mongols, and

---

[9] On Dubois, see MEYER, DIE STAATS- UND VOELKERRECHTLICHEN IDEEN VON PETER DUBOIS (1908); Barroux, *Pierre Dubois et la Paix perpétuelle* (France, 1933) 47 REVUE D'HISTOIRE DIPLOMATIQUE 232; Knight, *A Mediaeval Pacifist—Pierre Du Bois* (1924) 9 GROTIUS SOCIETY TRANSACTIONS 1.

[10] DUBOIS, *op. cit. supra* note 6, c. 5, at 8. His ideas on enforcement were also developed in DE ABREVIATIONE which was not available to the author.

Turks. But the eternal struggle between the spiritual and temporal leader weakened both to such an extent that both lost their authority. The Pope, depending on the fluctuations of the *Zeitgeist,* was from time to time able to arbitrate and mediate international disputes, but when Emperor Sigismund tried, during the Council at Constance (1415), to rejuvenate the Emperor-institution by transforming it into a supreme arbitration authority and to mediate peace between France and England, he failed completely. Nevertheless, the Emperor ideology did not die; as late as 1688, for example, Charles V, Duke of Lorraine, proposed that the Emperor should arbitrate the disputes of Germany and Italy.

In the sphere of theoretical writings, there was for a long time no development of the idea of peace enforcement, except in Marsiglio di Padua's *Defensor pacis* which showed the connection between "democracy" (or, more generally, society) and peace.

In 1462, George Poděbrad, King of Bohemia, under the influence of the otherwise obscure pamphletist Antonius Marinus, proposed the establishment of a European league.[11] The nucleus of this league was to be an alliance against the Turks between France under Louis XI, Venice and Bohemia. (Constantinople had fallen nine years earlier.) The suggested treaty authorized sanctions against the aggressor; the victim of aggression was to be helped by all members of the confederation, which was to assume the initiative to settle disputes even among states not belonging to it. Article VI stipulated the outlawing of any individual who disturbed the peace; every aggressor was to be punished as a "violator of general peace." The right to declare war was no longer to be exercised by individual states, but devolved upon the confederation as a whole.

Another abortive attempt to preserve peace was made during the early years of the 16th century. In 1517, Pope Leo X published a bull ordering a general truce of five years.[12] Trying to

---

[11] SCHWITZKY, DER EUROPAEISCHE FUERSTENBUND GEORGS VON PODEBRAD. EIN BEITRAG ZUR GESCHICHTE DER WELTFRIEDENSIDEE (1907) *passim*. See also Darby, *Some European Leagues of Peace* (1919) 4 GROTIUS SOCIETY TRANSACTIONS 169.

[12] 1 LANGE, HISTOIRE DE L'INTERNATIONALISME, JUSQU'À LA PAIX DE WEST PHALIE, 1648 (1919) 118; TER MEULEN, DER GEDANKE DER INTERNATIONALEN ORGANISATION IN SEINER ENTWICKLUNG, 1300-1800 (1917).

follow the papal recommendation, François I of France, Henry VIII of England, and Charles I of Spain (later Emperor Charles V) concluded, in October 1518, a convention to establish "universal peace." The Papal State and the Church adhered to this alliance. If an aggression should occur, diplomatic means were to be employed; if peaceful means should fail, the confederates would, after the lapse of one month, declare themselves to be the enemies of the aggressor, and after the delay of a second month, invade the aggressor's country. Every confederate was to pay for his own expenses; the right of free passage was guaranteed. Moreover, the federation was open to everybody. Although conceived for all future times, it fell apart one year after its conclusion when the death of Emperor Maximilian secured Charles' ascension to the Imperial throne. It ended legally in 1521 when Cardinal Wolsey, one of the fathers of the confederation, concluded a secret alliance with Charles against France. There followed a series of devastating wars between Charles and François, two former "confederates."

In 1544, after the last war between Charles and François, Guillaume Postel published his book *De Orbis Terrae Concordia Libri IV* in which he proposed a universal monarchy under France.[13]

FROM CAMPANELLA TO JAMES MADISON

The 17th century witnessed the publication of a number of peace projects. The series was opened by Campanella's *De Monarchia Hispanica Discursus,* a treatise which resumed Dante's and Postel's fundamental argument but placed the burden for the enforcement of universal peace on Spain, then the most powerful country. (In *Monarchia Messiae,* published in 1633, the Pope was chosen for the task.) Spain should establish unity of faith and a united government—a republic of all states with the Pope as its chief; if this were done, there would be no schism, no heresy, no famine and no war.

In 1625, an anonymous statesman submitted to the Chancellor of France, Etienne d'Aligre, a book titled *"Le Caton du Siècle, un conseil salutaire d'un ancien ministre d'Etat pour la conservation*

[13] *Id.* at 378.

de la paix universelle." In this book, the anonymous Frenchman, realizing that one country will always be too weak to establish a universal system, advocated a sort of a federal union between France and Spain.[14]

In the same year, Grotius published *"De jure belli ac pacis,"* where a paragraph was devoted to our problem. It reads as follows:

> . . . It would be useful and in some fashion necessary that the Christian powers should make between themselves some sort of body in whose assemblies the troubles of each should be determined by the judgment of others not interested, and there should be sought means of constraining the parties to come to an agreement under reasonable conditions.[15]

In his *Mémoires,* written between 1617 and 1638, the Duc de Sully alleged that Queen Elizabeth of England and King Henry IV of France had elaborated a scheme for the maintenance of peace in Europe. Whether Sully's report was historically accurate is immaterial.[16] Some of the thoughts expressed in the scheme were probably not unfamiliar to the two princes; it is certain that most European statesmen of later periods were familiar with the project. The "Grand Design" suggested that Europe should be divided equally among the powers in such a manner that none of them could impose his will upon the others; no state was to seek aggrandizement by conquest. The reallocation of land was to eliminate causes of international friction; this is an idea which, 200 years later, was developed in its economic aspects by Fichte in *"Der geschlossene Handelsstaat."* The European states were to be ruled by a general council, to be named by the princes, including the Emperor and the Pope. The council would have at its command military and naval contingents to enforce its decisions and to preserve the peace. "I dare maintain," wrote Sully, "that peace is the great and common interest of Europe . . . The greater powers should force the lesser into it, if necessary, by assisting

---

[14] *Id.* at 397.

[15] Quoted from RALSTON, INTERNATIONAL ARBITRATION FROM ATHENS TO LOCARNO (1929) 118-9.

[16] *Ibid.;* also DAVIES, *op. cit. supra* note 5, at 72-6. THE GRAND DESIGN, in the version by the Abbé de l'Ecluse des Loges, was reprinted by the Grotius Society.

the weak and oppressed; this is the only use they ought to make of their superiority."[17] This statement could have served as a motto of the Dumbarton Oaks Conference.

In the period of the Thirty Years War, the organization of peace was a widely discussed subject. Since that time, each major conflagration was accompanied by a flood of ideas about the art of "peacefare." The treaties of Osnabrueck and Muenster reflected this tendency and contained provisions to assure the stability and permanence of peace. Paragraphs 114-116 of the Treaty of Muenster determined that any person breaking the convention or public peace, either intentionally or in fact, would incur the punishment prescribed for such violations. Despite violations, the peace would remain in force; all signatories to the treaties were obligated to defend and protect each other as well as the laws or conditions of the peace against whomever it might be, without distinction of religion. If violations occurred, it was to be attempted to settle the dispute by friendly means or legal procedures; if, however, after three years (sic) the dispute could not be settled by peaceful means, all the interested parties were bound to help the victim.[18] No attempt was ever made to apply these provisions in practice.

In 1693, William Penn, in his *"Essay towards the Present and Future Peace of Europe, by the Establishment of an European Diet, Parliament or Estates,"* suggested the organization of an international tribunal and a diet of the European Sovereigns.[19] This tribunal was to settle disputes which could not be resolved by diplomacy. "Refusal to refer by one party or refusal to respect the decision subjected the offender to the exercise of force by the others."[20] All the members of the European Parliament were to unite against the aggressor to "compel the submission and performance of the sentence."

The end of the War of the Spanish Succession brought forth the publication of one of the most renowned peace projects, the

---

[17] SULLY, MEMOIRS, Book XIV. Quoted from VESTAL, THE MAINTENANCE OF PEACE (1920) 288.

[18] 1 LANGE, *op. cit. supra* note 12, at 497.

[19] DAVIES, *op. cit. supra* note 5, at 77.

[20] RALSTON, *op. cit. supra* note 15, at 120.

"Projet de Paix Perpetuelle," by the Abbé de Saint-Pierre.[21] The Abbé was secretary of one of the French plenipotentiaries to the peace negotiations, and since his book was published at Utrecht, it may be assumed that he, or high persons behind him, tried to influence the proceedings. In fact, copies of the book were distributed to members of the conference. Saint-Pierre envisaged, like others before and after him, a European senate or council, yet his project is interesting for the methods of coercion it suggested. In his Fundamental Article VIII we read the following sentences:

> The Sovereign who shall take up arms before the Union has declared war, or who shall refuse to execute a regulation of the society, or a judgment of the Senate, shall be declared an enemy to the society, and it shall make war upon him, 'till he be disarmed, and 'till the judgment and regulations be executed. . . . If after the society is formed . . . , a Sovereign shall refuse to enter into it, it shall declare him an enemy to the repose of Europe, and shall make war upon him 'till he enter into it, or 'till he be entirely dispossessed.[22]

Saint-Pierre also attempted to determine the aggressor by defining him as the sovereign who attacks suddenly or who refuses to conform to the decisions of the Union. In his Fundamental Article IV, the Abbé linked peace clearly and unequivocally to the maintenance of the status quo:

> All the sovereignties of Europe shall always remain in the condition they are in, and shall always have the same limits that they have now.

While Leibnitz commented favorably upon the project and considered it feasible, Frederick II of Prussia, writing to Voltaire, said, "The thing is most practicable, for its success all that is lacking is the consent of Europe and a few similar trifles."[23]

There may have been no "consent" on the part of Europe, yet Saint-Pierre's scheme became very well known during the 18th century. It was known to Benjamin Franklin who may have had

---

[21] *Ibid.* This project was also reprinted by the Grotius Society.

[22] Quoted from DAVIES, *op. cit. supra* note 5, at 81.

[23] ALDINGTON, LETTERS OF VOLTAIRE and FREDERIC THE GREAT (1927) 160 (Letter of Apr. 12, 1742).

it in mind when he proposed his Albany plan. During the Seven Years War, Rousseau used the *"Projet"* to work out a peace plan of his own, calling it *"Lasting Peace through the Federation of Europe,"* published between 1761 and 1782. Rousseau proposed that the powers should conclude a perpetual and irrevocable alliance[24] and settle their differences by arbitration or judgment; there was to be mutual guaranty of possessions on the basis of the status quo; violators were to be put under the ban of Europe as common enemies, and the confederation would be entitled to enforce its rights. Rousseau's plan also contained a veto provision; the diet was to vote by majority, but the five fundamental articles of the European constitution were not to be changed without the unanimous consent of all parties.

In America, the problem of coercion was thoroughly discussed by the drafters of the Constitution. Both the so-called Virginia and New Jersey plans contained provisions for enforcement against recalcitrant states and against those members of the Union who should fail to fulfill their duty under the articles of the Constitution.[25] These proposals met, however, the strenuous opposition of Madison and Hamilton. Madison thought that force should not be applied to people collectively but individually, and pointed out that enforcement would lead to war and to the destruction of the Union. Speaking militarily, he observed,

> Could the national resources, if exerted to the utmost, enforce a national decree against Massachusetts abetted perhaps by several of her neighbors? It would not be possible. A small proportion of the Community in a compact situation, acting on the defensive, and at one of its extremities might at any time bid defiance to the National authority.[26]

He called the idea that the central government could force its will upon the states "visionary and fallacious." Hamilton added that

---

[24] RALSTON, *op. cit. supra* note 15, at 121.

[25] LOWE, THE ORIGINS OF AMERICAN DIPLOMACY (unpublished manuscript) c. 1. See also SCOTT, THE UNITED STATES OF AMERICA: A STUDY IN INTERNATIONAL ORGANIZATION (1920) 203 *et seq.* Compare THE FEDERALIST Nos. 15 and, especially, 16. These same arguments later played a major role in the Senate debate of 1919 concerning the League. See FREEMAN, COERCION OF STATES IN INTERNATIONAL ORGANIZATIONS (1944).

[25] LOWE, THE ORIGINS OF AMERICAN DIPLOMACY (unpublished manu-

foreign powers would "not be idle spectators" during enforcement operations, and summed up his opinion,

> To coerce the states is one of the maddest projects that was ever devised. A failure of compliance will never be confined to a single state. This being the case, can we suppose it wise to hazard a civil war?[27] . . .

[27] *Ibid.*

7. The Concert of Europe: Its Relevance to the League of Nations

CHARLES K. WEBSTER AND SIDNEY HERBERT

. . . The main lines of development were four, and as they are all to be seen in the League system to-day they merit some consideration. In the first place, there were the meetings of the representatives of the Great Powers which came to be known as the "Concert of Europe." These were not meetings of the principal statesmen. Such meetings only occurred twice after the European Alliance had ceased to function. In 1856 at Paris and 1878 at Berlin the Powers were thus represented, but on these occasions they had met to draw up or revise a treaty of peace. The other meetings were composed of the diplomatic representatives of the Great Powers, meeting in the capital of one of them (occasionally at some other place) under the presidency of the Foreign Minister of the country to which they were accredited. Of these meetings, great and small, there were about thirty in the course of the century. . . .

. . . [The] "Concert" remained a machine to settle problems, for the most part, of secondary importance and attended only by diplomatic representatives and not by those who held the real

Sir Charles K. Webster and Sidney Herbert, *The League of Nations in Theory and Practice* (London: Allen and Unwin, Ltd., 1933), pp. 19-21. Reprinted by permission.

power of nations in their hands. Nevertheless, they were of great service, for some of these questions might have led to war between the Great Powers, if some such machinery for reconciling conflicting interests had not been used—notably in the Near Eastern Question.

The device was, however, never systematized. It had no continuity, and no Power was bound to accept it. When any one Power wished to block a conference it made conditions before accepting which it knew some other Power would refuse. On many occasions, and especially where the interests of a Great Power were vitally concerned, the machinery could not function, and there was thus no contact between the Powers as a body. The idea unfortunately arose that there was a loss of prestige for a Great Power to accept such a discussion on any matter in which it was vitally interested, even though other Powers had obvious interests also. The system of alliances also made it necessary for the members of the competing systems to support one another at the Conferences irrespective of the rights of the question.

Nor had the small Powers any right of representation. At the Conference of Aix-la-Chapelle (1818), it is true, it had been agreed that they should be summoned to any meeting at which their rights and interests were under discussion. This had been used as the basis of the invitation to Holland and Belgium to the Conference in 1830, which resulted in the establishment of the Belgian state. But neither at this Conference nor at the few subsequent ones at which they were present were the small Powers given an equal position, and for the most part they were simply ignored and the matter arranged without them.

The machinery of the Great Power Conference was executive, legislative, and mediatory. It took executive action in the sense of ordering sometimes armed forces to produce certain results. It was legislative by reason of its pronouncements on general questions of international law, and it was sometimes a judge between the conflicting interests of its own members or of other Powers. In all these functions it anticipated part of the machinery of the League of Nations. But it was so inchoate and so little elaborated that it depended almost entirely on the personal disposition of the statesmen of Europe. One malevolent or stupid man could easily prevent it from functioning. It never became, therefore, the normal and obvious method of procedure. The experience of one Conference was not handed on by any permanent machinery to the next. It must also be admitted that, strangely enough, it never attracted much attention from theorists or lawyers. It met in secret, and though records of its decisions were published, the processes by which they had been produced were for the most part not known. The statesmen themselves were incapable of analysing or understanding the machinery which they were using, and neither historians nor publicists gave them much assistance. A device, therefore, which contained in itself the germ of an international body such as was obviously necessary for the problems of the age was allowed to remain undeveloped and Lord Grey appealed to it in vain in 1914. . . .

THE WHY OF COMMON CONCERN

8. The "Quarantine Speech"

FRANKLIN D. ROOSEVELT

. . . It seems to be unfortunately true that the epidemic of world lawlessness is spreading.

When an epidemic of physical disease starts to spread, the

Peace and War, United States Foreign Policy, 1931-1941, Department of State Publication 1983 (Washington, D.C.: Government Printing Office, 1943), pp. 383-387, at pp. 386-387.

community approves and joins in a quarantine of the patients in order to protect the health of the community against the spread of the disease.

It is my determination to pursue a policy of peace and to adopt every practicable measure to avoid involvement in war . . .

War is a contagion, whether it be declared or undeclared. It can engulf states and peoples remote from the original scene of hostilities. . . .

9. A Form of Insurance

ALLEN W. DULLES

. . . I believe, however, that even in the case of a country as fortunately situated as the United States, it is unlikely that we can be more successful in the future than we have been in the past in remaining outside and unaffected by any world catastrophe. It is from this point of view that an American citizen can and should realistically approach the question of Collective Security, namely, that we should have a part in the system not because of our interest in other nations or even because of our interest in the preservation of world peace in the abstract, but because any disturbance to the peace is of vital concern to us.

Participation in a programme for Collective Security is a form of insurance. The nature of the participation may vary according to the respective needs and positions of different countries. Each country must decide the method of taking out this insurance and the amount of its contribution, but no country can safely disregard the problem or find salvation in isolation.

Allen W. Dulles, A Lecture, *Collective Security, A Record of the 7th and 8th Studies Conferences, London, 1935, League of Nations, International Studies Conferences,* Maurice Bourquin, editor (Paris: International Institute for Intellectual Co-operation, 1936), p. 44. See also Readings 26, 27, and 28.

THE BASIS OF COMMON CONCERN

10. Collective Action on the Basis of International Morality and International Agreement

HAILE SELASSIE

. . . I assert that the issue before the Assembly to-day is a much wider one. It is not merely a question of a settlement in the matter of Italian aggression. It is a question of collective security; of the very existence of the League; of the trust placed by States in international treaties; of the value of promises made to small States that their integrity and their independence shall be respected and assured. It is a choice between the principle of the equality of States and the imposition upon small Powers of the bonds of vassalage. In a word, it is international morality that is at stake. Have treaty signatures a value only in so far as the signatory Powers have a personal, direct and immediate interest involved?

No subtle reasoning can change the nature of the problem or shift the grounds of the discussion. It is in all sincerity that I submit these considerations to the Assembly. At a time when my people is threatened with extermination, when the support of the League may avert the final blow, I may be allowed to speak with complete frankness, without reticence, in all directness, such as is demanded by the rule of equality between all States Members of the League. Outside the Kingdom of God, there is not on this earth any nation that is higher than any other. If a strong Gov-

---

League of Nations Official Journal, Records of the 16th Ordinary Session of the Assembly, Special Supplement 151, Text of Debates, Part II, pp. 22-25, at p. 25.

ernment finds that it can, with impunity, destroy a weak people, then the hour has struck for that weak people to appeal to the League of Nations to give its judgment in all freedom. God and history will remember your judgment.

I have heard it asserted that the inadequate sanctions already applied have not achieved their object. At no time, in no circumstances, could sanctions that were intentionally inadequate, intentionally ill-applied, stop an aggressor. This is not a case of impossibility, but of refusal to stop an aggressor. When Ethiopia asked—as she still asks—that she should be given financial assistance, was that a measure impossible to apply? Had not the financial assistance of the League already been granted—and that in time of peace—to two countries, the very two countries which in the present case refused to apply sanctions against the aggressor?

In presence of the numerous violations by the Italian Government of all international treaties prohibiting resort to arms and recourse to barbarous methods of warfare, the initiative has today been taken—it is with pain that I record the fact—to raise sanctions. What does this initiative mean in practice but the abandonment of Ethiopia to the aggressor? Coming as it does on the very eve of the day when I was about to attempt a supreme effort in the defence of my people before this Assembly, does not this initiative deprive Ethiopia of one of her last chances of succeeding in obtaining the support and guarantee of States Members? Is that the guidance that the League of Nations and each of the States Members are entitled to expect from the great Powers when they assert their right and their duty to guide the action of the League?

Placed by the aggressor face to face with the accomplished fact, are States going to set up the terrible precedent of bowing before force?

The Assembly will doubtless have before it proposals for reforming the Covenant and rendering the guarantee of collective security more effective. Is it the Covenant that needs reform? What undertakings can have any value if the will to fulfill them is lacking? It is international morality that is at stake, and not the articles of the Covenant.

On behalf of the Ethiopian people, a Member of the League of Nations, I ask the Assembly to take all measures proper to secure respect for the Covenant. I renew my protest against the violations of treaties of which the Ethiopian people is the victim. I declare before the whole world that the Emperor, the Government and the people of Ethiopia will not bow before force, that they uphold their claims, that they will use all means in their power to ensure the triumph of right and respect for the Covenant.

I ask the fifty-two nations who have given the Ethiopian people a promise to help them in their resistance to the aggressor: What are they willing to do for Ethiopia?

I ask the great Powers, who have promised the guarantee of collective security to small States—those small States over whom hangs the threat that they may one day suffer the fate of Ethiopia: What measures do they intend to take?

Representatives of the world, I have come to Geneva to discharge in your midst the most painful of the duties of the head of a State. What answer am I to take back to my people?

11. Collective Action and a Preexisting System of Law

EMERY REVES

. . . Whether the application of force is an act of war or a police action depends upon one single criterion: whether or not the force is being used to execute the judgment of a court, applying established law in a concrete case.

If force is used without previously enacted law, defining clearly

Emery Reves, *The Anatomy of Peace* (New York: Harper & Bros., 1945), pp. 216-218. Reprinted by permission of the author.

the principles of human conduct and the norms determining such conduct, then the use of force is arbitrary, an act of violence, war—whether the decision to resort to it be made by a national representative as a member of an inter-national council, by a national legislative assembly, or even by national referendum.

In the proposals for the new world organization, there is no provision for the creation of law regulating the relations of the nations. On the contrary, it is clearly stated that sovereign power to create law is the exclusive appanage of the individual nation-states, and that the international organization is an association of such sovereign nation-states.

There being no law to define human conduct in inter-national relations, any use of force is arbitrary, unjustified, an act of war. Such an international organization may succeed in unimportant issues when force can be used by a major power or by a combination of powers against a weak and small nation. It is bound to fail whenever such use of force has to be resorted to by one power or group of powers against another power or group of powers with equal or approximately equal military strength. The application of force against a great power by a small nation in case the great power commits the aggression is, *ab ovo,* unthinkable and need not be discussed.

Such a state of affairs has absolutely nothing to do with the functioning of a police force in society. Such an organization as was the League and as the new international organization proposed at Dumbarton Oaks and San Francisco does not differ in any except external and formal aspects from the state of affairs that has always and at all times existed, without a league or any world organization. . . .

But without previously enacted laws for international conduct, any proposal to use force is immoral and dangerous in the highest degree. It is an unforgivably false conception to believe that force without the pre-existence of law can maintain peace and prevent war, if the decision as to its application rests in the individual sovereign nation-states forming the inter-national society, no matter which department of the sovereign nation-states may be endowed with that power. . . .

IS COMMON CONCERN REALISTIC?

12. A Reliance on Universals

HOWARD C. JOHNSON AND GERHART NIEMEYER

. . . As modern war became more and more fearful to contemplate, people increasingly compared the chaos of international relations with the kind of peace that is found within states and empires—a peace which, so it was often alleged, is ordered by police, and in which the normal conduct of people is not motivated by the expectation of armed conflict. This comparison usually inspires both the hope and expectation that international politics can be *transformed* from its present anarchic state into something resembling a peaceful commonwealth, a world of law and order in which violence would be discounted in the normal behavior of states and in which conflicts would be settled by nonviolent procedures. Since the days of Woodrow Wilson, both the hope and the expectation have come to rest in the concept of collective security which is the object of the present inquiry. For the purposes of this paper, we may define collective security as a system based on the universal obligation of all nations to join forces against an aggressor state as soon as the fact of aggression is determined by established procedure. In such a system, aggression is defined as a wrong in universal terms and an aggressor, as soon as he has been identified, stands condemned. Hence, the obligation of all nations to take action against him is conceived as a duty to support *right* against *wrong*. It is equally founded upon the practical expectation that the communal solidarity of all nations would from the outset make it clear to every govern-

Howard C. Johnson and Gerhart Niemeyer, "Collective Security: The Validity of an Ideal," *International Organization*, February, 1954, pp. 19-35, at pp. 20-21 and 35. Reprinted by permission.

ment that "aggression does not pay". The question of force is held to be solved in the sense that the world coalition against the aggressor would presumably possess overwhelming military strength, so much so that the assured prospect of such a coalition would deter any nation from attempting aggression. Thus force would be used only according to a universal system of law and in the service of the law, and within the community thus established nations would be expected to conduct themselves according to legal and moral community principles. The concept implies the vision of a future condition of enduring peace in which nations, though still armed and capable of making war, would have shed their previous fears and selfish attitudes and adopted enlightened habits of self-restraint, law-abiding discipline, cooperation and goodwill. In a system of nations in which governments could feel assured of the good citizenship if not the goodwill of other countries, resort to violence would be unnecessary except when an occasional lawless element needed to be repressed.

Even though one may have difficulty in finding the fullness of this concept embodied in any single speech, treaty or other document, it is certainly not unfair to say that the above definition renders an accurate picture of one of the principal bases, if not the principal basis, upon which collective security has been represented to the public over a period of many years. This is the ideal that has been held before our eyes. Along with it, we have usually been offered one or another practical scheme of bringing the ideal closer to reality. Mostly, these schemes contemplate a gradual evolution of policies, principles and institutions, or rather a process of education of governments with the help of international institutions. In this process the traditional self-centered power motives of governments would be experimentally and progressively supplanted by more enlightened conduct looking toward the common good. Little by little, the international system would change its character, as governments would (a) develop and demonstrate goodwill by faithful observation of agreements, reduction of armed forces, non-intervention in each other's affairs, mutual assurance through appropriate pacts, etc., (b) create international legal principles and procedures—for the pacific settlement of disputes, collective action against an aggressor, mutual assistance, etc.—to which their attitudes would more and more conform, and (c) support and strengthen international organizations and their collective purposes.

The significant characteristic of this concept is its reliance on universals. It approaches international politics from the point of view of general and ideal concepts rather than concrete political circumstances, largely ignoring power relations, particularly interests and commitments of nations, and specific responsibilities stemming from geographic location, resources and capabilities. The emphasis is on global community, universal concepts of right and wrong, universal application of legal procedures, general interest supposedly common to all nations, and an abstract notion of peace. While never fully realized, this concept to a considerable degree has influenced international reality, and it is useful that we ask ourselves what the results of this influence have been. It has set before us a vision of future possibilities to which allusion is constantly made in the statements of many of our leaders. The idea of a gradual education of governments into citizen-agencies of the world community has been widely hailed as an objective to which we should pledge our foreign policy. We have been assured that it would be beneficial for us and for the entire world to conduct our foreign relations on the assumption that world law, world community, world peace, and world force are emergent realities. Since all of these premises, on their own showing, presumably call for foreign policies different from those based on other premises, it is pertinent and important to examine the idea of collective security as such with the utmost care. . . .

The following findings, therefore, seem to be justified:

a. In the present international order of armed states great powers, according to their pattern of behavior, cannot be expected to accept clearly defined legal commitments of universal collective security.

b. Judging from the actual behavior of states in response to general principles of collective security the policies of states cannot be expected to measure up to what, according to the concept, would be necessary if universal collective security were to become a working reality.

c. As far as our present experience goes, there do not appear to be habit-forming effects from attempts to invoke collective security or permanent advances in the attitudes and policies of governments toward the ideal standards of collective security.

d. Collective security, conceived in universal terms, is not actually considered by the great powers as a remedy for the basic insecurity of the present international system.

From these findings, we would venture to draw these conclusions: It is (and has been) a mistake to work for an improvement of international relations by starting from universal concepts and seeking to impose them, intellectually or otherwise, on national policies. Collective security, in the definition here employed, is such a concept; its elements (world-wide obligation, a global common interest, a community of nations, world law, world security, aggression conceived as a universal crime, indivisibility of peace, world solidarity against aggression) represent universal standards and fail to allow for the particular situations that make up the reality of international politics. Collective security has actually been possible in certain historical instances when those universal concepts and standards happened so to coincide with configurations of the political forces that some concrete action required in the interests of a number of nations could be taken in the name of the universal principle. We should in soberness be aware of the concrete conditions that govern the use and action of national power; we should continue to employ national power, in the concrete setting of political forces, for the promotion of those human values for the sake of which governments enjoy allegiance. Any further contribution that international organization may make to the problem of security on a global scale will have to stem from new and deeper insights into the problem of causation in international politics, and the ways in which common values and interests relevant to the use of force could actually take global shape. This would suggest the importance of providing the United Nations with a new conceptual foundation if it is to develop its greatest potential under present conditions as well as under more auspicious circumstances which it is hoped history will provide in the future.

13. . . . Everywhere Taken for Granted

F. P. WALTERS

. . . Before the League, it was held both in theory and practice that every State was the sole and sovereign judge of its own acts, owing no allegiance to any higher authority, entitled to resent criticism or even questioning by other States. Such conceptions have disappeared for ever: it is not doubted, and can never again be doubted, that the community of nations has the moral and legal right to discuss and judge the international conduct of each of its members. The belief that aggressive war is a crime against humanity and that it is the interest, the right, and the duty of every State to join in preventing it, is now everywhere taken for granted.

True, the acceptance of that principle is only a first step towards the actual abolition of war; but it brought with it consequences which have deeply and permanently affected the relations of States between themselves and the attitude of individual citizens towards all questions of foreign policy. A new respect for the rights of small nations; a new understanding of the need for co-operation in social and economic affairs; the habit of public debate on even the gravest diplomatic issues; the formation of an international civil service—these are examples of the immense innovations brought about in a period of less than twenty years. They have not yet exhausted their effects. The League, as a working institution, is dead; but the ideas which it sought to promote, the hopes to which it gave rise, the methods it devised, the agencies it created, have become an essential part of the political thinking of the civilized world, and their influence will survive until mankind enjoys a unity transcending the divisions of States and nations. . . .

F. P. Walters, *A History of the League of Nations,* 2 vols. (London: Oxford University Press, under the auspices of the Royal Institute of International Affairs, 1952), pp. 1-2. Reprinted by permission.

THE REGIONAL ASPECT OF COMMON CONCERN

14. The Ambiguity of the Charter Provisions: Articles 33, 51-54

CHARTER OF THE UNITED NATIONS

CHAPTER VI. PACIFIC SETTLEMENT OF DISPUTES

Article 33. 1. The parties to any dispute, the continuance of which is likely to endanger the maintenance of international peace and security, shall, first of all, seek a solution by negotiation, enquiry, mediation, conciliation, arbitration, judicial settlement, resort to regional agencies or arrangements, or other peaceful means of their own choice.

2. The Security Council shall, when it deems necessary, call upon the parties to settle their dispute by such means.

Article 51. Nothing in the present Charter shall impair the inherent right of individual or collective self-defense if an armed attack occurs against a Member of the United Nations, until the Security Council has taken the measures necessary to maintain international peace and security. Measures taken by Members in the exercise of this right of self-defense shall be immediately reported to the Security Council and shall not in any way affect the authority and responsibility of the Security Council under the present Charter to take at any time such action as it deems

---

Charter of the United Nations together with the Statute of the International Court of Justice, signed at the United Nations Conference on International Organization, San Francisco, California, June 26, 1945, Department of State Publication 2353, Conference Series 74 (Washington, D.C.: Government Printing Office, 1945).

necessary in order to maintain or restore international peace and security.

CHAPTER VIII. REGIONAL ARRANGEMENTS

Article 52. 1. Nothing in the present Charter precludes the existence of regional arrangements or agencies for dealing with such matters relating to the maintenance of international peace and security as are appropriate for regional action, provided that such arrangements or agencies and their activities are consistent with the Purposes and Principles of the United Nations.

2. The Members of the United Nations entering into such arrangements or constituting such agencies shall make every effort to achieve pacific settlement of local disputes through such regional arrangements or by such regional agencies before referring them to the Security Council.

3. The Security Council shall encourage the development of pacific settlement of local disputes through such regional arrangements or by such regional agencies either on the initiative of the states concerned or by reference from the Security Council.

4. This Article in no way impairs the application of Articles 34 and 35.

Article 53. 1. The Security Council shall, where appropriate, utilize such regional arrangements or agencies for enforcement action under its authority. But no enforcement action shall be taken under regional arrangements or by regional agencies without the authorization of the Security Council, with the exception of measures against any enemy state, as defined in paragraph 2 of this Article, provided for pursuant to Article 107 or in regional arrangements directed against renewal of aggressive policy on the part of any such state, until such time as the Organization may, on request of the Governments concerned, be charged with the responsibility for preventing further aggression by such a state. . . .

Article 54. The Security Council shall at all times be kept fully informed of activities undertaken or in contemplation under regional arrangements. . . .

15. Collective Security and the Organization of American States

CHARTER OF BOGOTÁ

. . . e) The American States condemn war of aggression: victory does not give rights;

f) An act of aggression against one American State is an act of aggression against all the other American States;

g) Controversies of an international character arising between two or more American States shall be settled by peaceful procedures; . . .

Art. 15. No State or group of States has the right to intervene, directly or indirectly, for any reason whatever, in the internal or external affairs of any other State. The foregoing principle prohibits not only armed force but also any other form of interference or attempted threat against the personality of the State or against its political, economic and cultural elements. . . .

Art. 24. Every act of aggression by a State against the territorial integrity or the inviolability of the territory or against the sovereignty or political independence of an American State shall be considered an act of aggression against the other American States.

Art. 25. If the inviolability or the integrity of the territory or the sovereignty or political independence of any American State should be affected by an armed attack or by an act of aggression that is not an armed attack, or by an extra-continental conflict, or by a conflict between two or more American States, or by any other fact or situation that might endanger the peace of America, the American States, in furtherance of the principles of continental solidarity or collective self-defense, shall apply the measures and procedures established in the special treaties on the subject. . . .

Ninth International Conference of American States, Bogotá, Colombia, *Report of the Delegation of the United States,* Department of State Publication 3263 (Washington, D.C.: Government Printing Office, 1948), pp. 166-186, at pp. 168-170.

16. Cold War Has Prevailed over the Charter

INIS L. CLAUDE, JR.

This analysis of the episodes in which the status of the OAS has been heated by argument and hammered into shape at the United Nations forge demonstrates above all the malleability of the Charter under the impact of political considerations and political forces. For an understanding of what has happened, the analytical skill of the student of international politics is vastly more relevant than that of the international lawyer. The cold war has prevailed over the Charter; the latest adaptation of the Monroe Doctrine has relegated Article 53 to the ash heap of politically charred legal provisions; the fear of the Soviet veto has taken precedence over the principle that regional agencies should be subordinated to the United Nations.

Most of the political impetus for this transformation of the status of the OAS has been provided by the United States, which lagged behind and held back its fellow members of the Inter-American system in their drive for regional autonomy during the formative stages of the United Nations. The record shows a mixed pattern of victories and defeats for the United States in the pro-OAS campaign. The effort to establish the mandatory "Try OAS first" principle came to naught and was abandoned, in part because of the gradual diminution of Latin American support; after the Guatemalan case, the United States could find few friends, in the OAS or elsewhere, willing to endorse the view that American states were prohibited from appealing to the Security Council, and the Council was barred from heeding their appeals, until the OAS had completed its action or inaction on their complaints. On the other hand, the United States succeeded, thanks largely to the steady growth of Latin American support, in eman-

Inis L. Claude, Jr., "The OAS, the UN, and the United States," *International Conciliation*, No. 547, March, 1964, pp. 3-67, at pp. 61-63.

cipating OAS enforcement activity from United Nations control; after the Dominican case, the United States found an increasing number of friends, both in the OAS and outside, willing to endorse the view that Article 53 should not be so construed as to inhibit OAS activities against communist intrusions in the hemisphere. In the one case, the Latin American states refused to accept the restriction of their rights; in the other, they rallied to support the expansion of their rights as a regional group.

Fundamentally, this entire struggle over the OAS must be regarded as but a chapter in the larger volume of the cold war. A major feature of the general history of the United Nations is the persistent effort of the United States to deprive the Soviet Union of an effective veto power and of the Soviet Union to retain that power. In this instance of the conflict over the veto, as in many others, the United States has succeeded. It may well be that the United States was able to attract greater support for releasing the OAS from the restriction of Article 53 than for expanding its jurisdictional rights under Article 52, precisely because the former did, and the latter did not, involve an attack upon the Soviet veto power. The Soviet Union's position in regard to the "Try OAS first" issue supported the competence of a majority in the Security Council to take action; its position with respect to Article 53 represented its claim of competence to veto action by the Council, and implied that all regional organizations were subject to the paralyzing impact of the veto power. Hence, it is not surprising that the Soviet Union was rebuffed in the latter case, rather than the former.

Throughout these cases, the Soviet Union appeared in the unusual role of champion of the rights and competence of the United Nations, while the United States was cast, in equally significant deviation from normal character, as the prime opponent of a strong and active world organization. No more striking demonstration can be found of the inexorable subordination of principle to policy in the operations of statesmen than was revealed by the United States in this set of cases. The United States did not repudiate the principle of the paramountcy of the United Nations in the international system, but it subordinated that principle to the necessity of gaining a free hand for combating communist infiltration in the Western Hemisphere. It did not renounce the principle of nonintervention, or of nonviolence except in self-defense, but it made these yield to what it regarded as vital policy considerations. It did not deny the principle of truthfulness and good faith, but, under the pressure of policy commitments, it misstated both its acts and its intentions with respect to communist-oriented regimes in the Caribbean area. It did not renounce the principle of the rule of law, but it protected its policy by constricting the provision of Article 53 that expressed the authority of the Security Council over the OAS, and insisted upon avoiding a judicial inquiry into the meaning of that provision.

The development of the relationship between the OAS and the United Nations confirms the proposition that the original project of permitting and encouraging regional agencies to operate within a framework of United Nations supervision and control has broken down. The OAS has failed to achieve a monopolistic jurisdiction over disputes within its area, but, more importantly, the Security Council has lost any meaningful capacity to regulate or restrict the enforcement operations of the OAS. Broadly, these observations apply as well to other regional organizations dealing with political and security problems. These organizations have exhibited little interest in establishing jurisdictional priority over local disputes, and their members would probably resist any effort to restrict the right of access to the United Nations, just as the Latin Americans have done. With regard to enforcement measures, however, members of all regional agencies have an interest in escaping the control of the Security Council, and it is unlikely that the superior authority of the Council can be effectively applied to any regional body. In the era of the cold war, regional organizations are the chosen instruments of the great antagonists locked in political conflict. Those antagonists will not permit their instruments to be held in check by the United Nations.

IS COLLECTIVE SECURITY TOO COSTLY?

17. The Alternative to Accepting the Law of the Community

Clyde Eagleton

We want law and order in the world, we say; and to the average citizen this desire is sharply pointed, by the roar of war all around him, into a more specific demand: we want to get rid of war. Probably neither can be done without the other; and certainly, international organization is required to accomplish either. This conclusion would be accepted by most persons; but, having gone thus far, they are then faced with the question: must this international system have behind it sufficient coercive power to compel acceptance of its authority?

After the experience of the past eight or nine years, it would be hard to give other than an affirmative answer to this question; and all of history gives the same answer. Law has always been maintained by force. A nation, today, like individuals in the past, must choose between continuous and probably incompetent self-defense against aggressors, or collective action against them. In the former case, it may claim complete freedom, but will probably not be able to maintain it; in the latter case, it must give up some of its freedom in order to secure collective support for the rights which the community agrees that its members should have. This is the explanation of law and government among human beings;

Clyde Eagleton, "Peace Enforcement," in *Preliminary Report and Monographs,* Commission to Study the Organization of Peace, *International Conciliation,* No. 369, April, 1941, pp. 193-525, at pp. 499-501.

and it is through law and government that order has been maintained among human beings. . . .

It is idle to waste time on such a point; and it cannot be doubted that it is to the interest of every member of the community of nations to make sacrifices in order to prevent the use of violence between members. The chief concession which must be made is some surrender of the complete freedom of action claimed by sovereign States; and this is no great concession since, as the record of history shows, the chances are that it will, in any case, be unable to uphold its freedom against unprincipled and selfish competitors. . . .

Participation in military sanctions may involve risk and expense; but that risk and expense is manifestly less when security is backed by all, and when the money and man power necessary to achieve it is divided among all. It is probably true that the cost of an armed force sufficient to maintain order among nations, once it was established, would be less than what the United States alone spends in fearful preparation for war. No imaginable system could cost more than the present one, or offer less security! The alternative to accepting the law of the community and receiving its protection is submitting to the selfish and lawless direction of a mightier nation or combination—that, or living in costly preparedness and constant nervous anxiety. The fear of government made many persons hesitate in the days when our federal union was being established; there are few today who would regret that the American Union was set up over the sovereign States.

All the lessons of human experience point toward the necessity of an international organization which would reserve to itself the monopoly of the use of force, and forbid to any nation the right to use force for its own purposes. To do this requires overwhelming force, a force which can only be supplied by the combination *omnium contra unum*—of all law-abiding States against the lawbreaker. The experience of the League of Nations shows—as does also, of course, that of domestic government—that halfway measures are not enough. . . .

18. Collective Defense versus Collective Security

ARNOLD WOLFERS

. . . Soon after the Korean war had rekindled the hope that collective security under the United Nations would of necessity be directed against nondemocratic countries belonging to the Soviet bloc—the same countries, therefore, against which all Western collective defense arrangements were directed—the Suez crisis brought a rude awakening. The "aggressors" on this occasion were two of the leading democracies of Europe, and democratic Israel. The three countries resorted to war against Egypt in the very fashion that their own leaders and publicists, no less than those of other countries, had persistently labeled as "aggression" and condemned as a crime. No longer was there any necessity for proof that action "against any aggressor anywhere" might mean action against closest friends or allies even though they be democratic. Instead of supplementing each other, the two policies of collective defense and collective security crashed head-on as far as the West was concerned: countries committed to both had to choose between their conflicting commitments.

But the clashes that may occur between the two types of commitments to collective action are not limited to the kind of clash illustrated by the Suez or Abyssinian crises. Instead, there are three different kinds, all of which pose serious problems for countries caught in the dilemma.

So far, both under the League and under the United Nations, only the one just mentioned has actually occurred: the case in which nations are called upon to participate in collective security action—even in the mild form of condemnation—against a friendly or allied country on whose support they depend for defense against a recognized national enemy. When faced with the choice of either losing the support of Italy or defaulting on col-

---

Arnold Wolfers, "Collective Defense versus Collective Security," in Arnold Wolfers, editor, *Alliance Policy in the Cold War,* (Baltimore: Johns Hopkins Press, 1959), pp. 49-74, at pp. 55-58 and 74. Reprinted by permission.

lective security, France chose the latter course. In the Suez crisis, the United States took the opposite line, upholding the principles of collective security despite the damage that might have resulted for two of her most essential alliances. Fortunately for the United States, the outcome was not calamitous because the three "aggressors" did the exceptional thing of restoring the *status quo ante* despite the absence of collective military sanctions. The members of the United Nations can hardly expect to resolve the dilemma as easily on every occasion.

A second type of clash may arise from the participation of a country's national enemy in collective security action against a third power. To take a fictitious example: if Greece were condemned for committing an act of aggression against Turkey and punitive action were recommended by the General Assembly of the United Nations, Bulgaria, as a member of the United Nations, would have the right to participate in "police action" against Greece and might do so with enthusiasm. In the course of such collective action, her troops might occupy Thrace, thereby upsetting the balance of power between East and West in the vital area of the Eastern Mediterranean. Who would venture to predict that the Bulgarians in such a case would withdraw from territory they had long coveted once the United Nations decided to call a halt to collective action and invited its members to restore the *status quo ante?* Instead, it would be in line with historical experience to expect that the military situation at the close of hostilities would profoundly affect the territorial provisions of any subsequent settlement. The results of initiating collective security measures in this hypothetical case, therefore, would probably be favorable to Bulgarian interests and damaging to the West. This example illustrates one of the dangers a country might face at a time of serious tension if the universal collective security system led national opponents to take part in common military action against a third power.

The third type of clash will not appear serious to people who are confident that their own country will never commit an act that many nations would condemn as aggression. Surely, few American statesmen have been worried that they were restricting their own freedom to act in defense of American security either by their constant efforts to strengthen and broaden the scope of collective security under the United Nations or by their success in popularizing the idea of "police action" against every aggressor. Yet, as Britain—once an equally staunch proponent of collective security—discovered to her sorrow in 1956, a policy that emphasizes the principles of collective security can, under certain conditions, prove a dangerous trap. If what is condemned as aggressions were necessarily an act similar to Hitler's military invasion of Poland in 1939 or even to Britain's initiation of war against Egypt in 1956, some countries might well feel satisfied that they will never commit such follies or crimes nor risk, therefore, being accused of aggression. But if earlier events under the League of Nations were not enough to prove that the definition of aggression and the identification of the aggressor are most difficult problems and may often become highly controversial political issues, recent developments under the United Nations should be driving the point home. . . .

Despite the possibilities of such clashes between the policies of collective defense and collective security, it cannot be concluded, as a general proposition, that nations would do well to give up their commitments to one or both of these policies. Many states cannot forego collective defense because they lack the power of defending themselves without outside assistance; many may find that withdrawal from the collective security system in order to avoid the possible future embarrassment of conflicting commitments would cause them losses they dare not take. Because there is not likely to be any general answer that would fit the best interests of all countries, the possible solutions to the problem will be discussed in relation to the particular situation of the United States. . . .

. . . The United States will have done all it can for both its own protection and that of its friends and allies if it succeeds in maintaining a reliable collective defense network backed by adequate national armaments and if, in addition, it gives strong support to United Nations mediatory and conciliatory efforts within the non-Soviet world while preserving United Nations collective security as a last resort.

19. An Argument for Balance between Resources and Commitments

JOHN D. HICKERSON

. . . Conclusion of the pact proposed in the resolution, however, would formalize and freeze the operation of this machinery in a rigid pattern. Such a pact looks toward maximum solidarity in support of the purposes and principles of the United Nations and against aggression. We certainly support this objective. But here we must distinguish clearly between the obligations to support the purposes and principles of the Charter by assisting the victim of an armed attack, and an ironbound agreement to do so in every case with our armed forces.

There are limitations to our military capabilities. We cannot now guarantee to assist every corner of the globe at once with our armed forces. We must be careful not to confuse and perhaps mislead the world by promising military assistance beyond our ability.

This resolution not only calls upon members to support majority decisions, but it also may place practical limitations on the freedom of action of members in supporting a victim of attack in the absence of necessary General Assembly action. We may find it necessary to take action immediately under Article 51, and such action is, of course, authorized.

Complete solidarity of United Nations members against aggression must be our goal. I believe that the American people and the Congress support our working toward the establishment of an international community both through strengthening the United Nations and through progressively closer association within the free world.

In my opinion, however, it is highly doubtful if any of the great powers or a large number of the smaller and middle powers in the United Nations would be prepared at this time to accept the

---

Revision of the United Nations Charter, Hearings before a Subcommittee of the Committee on Foreign Relations, United States Senate, 81st Congress, 2nd Session (Washington, D.C.: Government Printing Office, 1950), pp. 415-416.

obligations involved in this resolution. We must recall the difficulties that Senator Austin had in his efforts to obtain the assent of the other permanent members of the Security Council to the elimination of the veto in matters affecting the pacific settlement of disputes. I know of no evidence that these countries are prepared to give up their veto on matters within the area covered by this resolution. Furthermore, there are still many nations outside the Soviet orbit which have probably not yet reached a point in their thinking which would permit them to participate in the proposed pact. . . .

CONSENSUS IN COLLECTIVE SECURITY

20. A President Reports

JOHN F. KENNEDY

. . . the facts of the matter are that the Soviets and ourselves give wholly different meanings to the same words—war, peace, democracy, and popular will.

We have wholly different views of right and wrong, of what is an internal affair and what is aggression, and, above all, we have wholly different concepts of where the world is and where it is going. . . .

. . . But both of us were there, I think, because we realized that each nation has the power to inflict enormous damage upon the other, that such a war could and should be avoided if at all

Report to the American People, June 6, 1961, *Public Papers of the Presidents of the United States, John F. Kennedy, 1961* (Washington, D.C.: Government Printing Office, 1962), pp. 443-444.

possible, since it would settle no dispute and prove no doctrine, and that care should thus be taken to prevent our conflicting interests from so directly confronting each other that war necessarily ensued. We believe in a system of national freedom and independence. He believes in an expanding and dynamic concept of world communism, and the question was whether these two systems can ever hope to live in peace without permitting any loss of security or any denial of the freedom of our friends. However difficult it may seem to answer this question in the affirmative as we approach so many harsh tests, I think we owe it to all mankind to make every possible effort. That is why I considered the Vienna talks to be useful. . . .

21. An Explanation of Soviet Policies

NIKITA S. KHRUSHCHEV

. . . Now a word about national liberation wars. The armed struggle by the Vietnamese people or the war of the Algerian people, which is already in its seventh year, serve as the latest examples of such wars. These wars began as an uprising by the colonial peoples against their oppressors and changed into guerrilla warfare. Liberation wars will continue to exist as long as imperialism exists, as long as colonialism exists. These are revolutionary wars. Such wars are not only admissible but inevitable, since the colonialists do not grant independence voluntarily. Therefore, the peoples can attain their freedom and independence only by struggle, including armed struggle. . . .

Can such wars flare up in the future? They can. Can there be such uprisings? There can. But these are wars which are national uprisings. In other words, can conditions be created where a

---

Report by Premier Khrushchev on the Moscow Conference of Communist Parties (Extracts), January 6, 1961, *Documents on Disarmament, 1961* (Washington, D.C.: Government Printing Office, 1962), pp. 1-15, at pp. 7-8 and 11.

people will lose their patience and rise in arms? They can. What is the attitude of the Marxists toward such uprisings? A most positive one. These uprisings must not be identified with wars among states, with local wars, since in these uprisings the people are fighting for implementation of their right for self-determination, for independent social and national development. These are uprisings against rotten reactionary regimes, against the colonizers. The communists fully support such just wars and march in the front rank with the peoples waging liberation struggles. . . .

Thus, the policy of peaceful coexistence, as regards its social content, is a form of intense economic, political, and ideological struggle of the proletariat against the aggressive forces of imperialism in the international arena.

The struggle against imperialism can be successful only if its aggressive acts are resolutely rebuffed. Verbal exhortations will not contain the imperialist adventurers. There is only one way of bringing imperialism to heel, the unflagging consolidation of the economic, political, and military might of the socialist states, an all-out unification and consolidation of the world revolutionary movement and the mobilization of the broad popular masses for the struggle to prevent the danger of war. . . .

22. A "Limited Adversary" Relationship

MARSHALL D. SHULMAN

. . . we are engaged in an extremely serious conflict, but it is neither total nor absolute.

In certain aspects of our confrontation, the security of each side is interlocked with the security of the other. It is therefore possible to have some measures which the Soviet leaders feel may serve

Testimony of Marshall D. Shulman, *Nuclear Test Ban Treaty,* Hearings before the Committee on Foreign Relations, United States Senate, 88th Congress, 1st Session, on Executive M (Washington, D.C.: Government Printing Office, 1963), pp. 798-799.

their interests, and which we, for reasons of our own, regard as in our interests as well.

This situation arises not only because of a difference of evaluations in Moscow and Washington, but because some overlapping of mutual interests does exist, based on the mutual interests of survival.

It should be possible for us to recognize, without in the slightest minimizing the seriousness of our conflict with the Soviet Union or diminishing the vigor of our prosecution of this effort, that this does not preclude the search for some safeguards, although perhaps at this stage only marginal ones, which can be mutually advantageous.

5. Although the present period does not afford much encouragement for an early settlement of major issues with the Soviet Union, or for substantial advances toward disarmament, it appears possible that the Soviet leadership can be brought to perceive a mutual self-interest in some limited safeguards in the arms race.

It is worth noting, I think, since 1954 there has been a very considerable evolution of the Soviet appreciation of the effect of nuclear war, a sobriety, an increasing sobriety, and this has a deep effect on the Soviet attitude. Within the past year and a half there has been a substantial increase in the discussion in Soviet journals of what is in this country called arms control, and what the Soviets call partial measures of disarmament.

An increasing number of Soviet specialists have appeared, who demonstrate a competence in the arms control literature. We have an interest in this exploration, against the time when the Soviet political leadership reaches the realization that its [own] self-interest requires moving from the slogan of "general and complete disarmament," which now serves to block progress in this field, to more modest and attainable measures of introducing some stability, some moderation in the military side of our confrontation, without requiring millennial changes in the Soviet system.

6. And last, one of the lessons to be gained from a study of Soviet policy since the war is a realization that there is a substantial amount of interreaction between Soviet policy and our own, and that the condition which has most favored the evolution

of Soviet policy in the direction of moderation has been a firm resistance to Soviet probes, combined with demonstrated political and economic vitality on the part of the non-Communist nations. . . .

"JUST WAR" AND NEUTRALISM

23. A Reversion to Earlier Concepts after World War I

MORTON A. KAPLAN AND NICHOLAS DEB. KATZENBACH

. . . The Versailles Treaty represents a return to the concept of war as an instrument for law enforcement—for punishing the guilty state—and thus represents a reversion to earlier concepts. Germany had to give up parts of its territory in retribution for its wrongs, and to answer with monetary damages for civil claims. The League of Nations was envisioned prospectively as the instrumentality whereby force could be brought within a legal framework by collective sanctions to insure the punishment of violators, a method of enforcing community policy laid down by the Treaty and by the League as a body to implement its principles. That, hereafter, force was to be confined to law enforcement in support of League decisions was reconfirmed by the Kellogg-Briand Pact of 1928 renouncing war "as an instrument of national policy" and pledging to settle disputes exclusively by "pacific means." The Treaty was ratified or acceded to by some sixty-three states. The only exception to this sweeping renunciation of

Morton A. Kaplan and Nicholas deB. Katzenbach, *The Political Foundations of International Law* (New York: John Wiley and Sons, Inc., 1961), pp. 211-213. Reprinted by permission.

war was the understanding, clarified in the course of the Treaty's negotiation, that the "inherent right of self-defense" was not restricted or impaired, and, to quote the Secretary of State, "every nation is free at all times to defend its territory from attack or invasion and it alone is competent to decide whether circumstances require recourse to war in self-defense."

Apart from the fact that saying so did not make it so, there was room for technical argument about what the Covenant and the Kellogg-Briand Pact said. In the first place, both instruments talked of war, leaving room for doctrinal niceties of the kind which had occurred in the previous century. Was "war" to be understood as excluding other uses of violence such as "reprisals" and "hostile measures short of war"? Certainly the Kellogg Pact, by renouncing only "war as an instrument of national policy" was open to the interpretation that it did not prohibit the use of force by states as a sanction, to enforce "rights"—the classic *bellum iustum,* which, as we have seen, was always conceived as a sanction for community policy—but only wars of "aggression." This interpretation was to some extent reinforced by the fact that the Covenant itself did not prohibit war altogether, but simply prohibited resort to war where the Covenant provided (in theory) effective substitutes in the way of substitute procedures. Sanctions were provided against those states who "resort to war in disregard of their covenants under Articles XII, XIII or XV." In the event of failure of these peaceful settlement methods, or on matters not covered by them (if any), a good argument for "self-help" as lawful could be made—that is, argument in favor of the just war or lesser forms of sanction.

Efforts to remedy these technical defects, as well as the gaping exception of self-determined "self-defense," were made at San Francisco following the Second World War. The ambiguous term "war" is replaced, in the key section (Article 2, paragraph 4) of the United Nations Charter by prohibiting Members "from the threat or use of force against the territorial integrity or political independence of any state." The only important exception to this seemingly sweeping prohibition of violence is Article 51, which permits a state—or states, collectively—to use armed force against an armed attack "until the Security Council takes the necessary measures to restore international peace and security." Conceived as an interim measure of short duration, Article 51, along with NATO, SEATO and other alliances of less importance, became a cornerstone of the Western security system. . . .

24. A Swiss Examination of the Dilemma of a Permanently Neutral State

JACQUELINE BELIN

. . . In its legal effects, permanent neutrality affects the entire life of a state; there is no vacuum but an absolute and perfect legal continuity. In peacetime, the neutral state must guard against any appearance of belonging to a political bloc, so as not to be drawn into participating in a conflict, and thus into losing its status of permanent neutrality. . . .

As far as the organization of collective security is concerned, there is an incompatibility between the concepts of solidarity and of neutrality, the obligations flowing from permanent neutrality and those flowing from the statutes of an international political organization being in fact almost irreconcilable. A state which is permanently neutral cannot carry out collective sanctions without moving away from its neutrality, and the international organization cannot free a state from executive measures without abdicating some of its effectiveness. . . .

In conclusion, one may state again that Switzerland remains faithful to the political line which she will soon have followed for a century and a half. She reserves her attitude toward international organizations whose political character could lead her away from her permanent neutrality without offering her real compensation along security lines. On the other hand, Switzerland is always ready to cooperate with technical or humanitarian institutions, thinking

Jacqueline Belin, *La Suisse et les Nations Unies* (New York: Manhattan Publishing Co., for the Carnegie Endowment for International Peace, 1956), pp. 65 and 80-81. Editors' translation. Reprinted by permission.

in this way to be faithful to her special spirit and to contribute to international collaboration in a tangible way but without involving her political future. In the realm of international collaboration, the limits beyond which Switzerland cannot go are thus equally delimited by the law of neutrality and by the policy of neutrality. . . .

25. The Complexities of Neutrality and Collective Obligation

WESLEY L. GOULD

. . . As opinions expressed during the Korean War pointed out, the question fundamental to the thinking of national politicians was bound to be that of whether collective action under the United Nations banner was not in reality the political action of one alliance against another. If so, there could hardly be a duty for Members to participate in collective measures, for such measures would not then be in support of the principles of the United Nations. While Members of the United Nations have a duty to thwart aggression, they have no duty to promote the political ambitions of one bloc or another. In so far as self-interest does not align individual Members with one political group in conflict with another, neutrality is not out of order for the Members[100] unless they should by chance—a most unlikely chance in the event of a Soviet-American war—be in a position to wedge themselves between the warring sides and compel a settlement.

Article 2, paragraph 5, of the United Nations Charter reads as follows:

All Members shall give the United Nations every assistance in any action it takes in accordance with the present Charter, and shall refrain

[100] For a survey of areas of neutrality under the United Nations Charter, see J. F. Lalive, "International Organization and Neutrality," 24 *B.Y.I.L.* (1947), pp. 72-89. Cf. Fabela, *Neutralité,* pp. 169 ff.

from giving assistance to any state against which the United Nations is taking preventative or enforcement action.[101]

This is clearly a directive to refrain from that neutrality that is subversive of the principle of collective action,[102] to say nothing of the Soviet aid to North Korea on top of nonparticipation in the collective action taken. As Politis argued in the interwar years, neutrality is incompatible with the idea of *bellum justum.*[103]

Article 2 of the Charter goes even farther in its objection to neutrality when, in its sixth paragraph, it asks the Organization to insure the coöperation of nonmembers in actions in accord with the principles set forth, including those of paragraph 5. However, "insure" need not mean "coerce." To "insure" could hardly mean that the United Nations enjoys legal rights of coercion against nonmembers that may follow a policy of neutrality. Indeed, it is difficult to see how it could coerce even a Member into coöperating in a collective action. "Insure" could mean "coerce" only if a nonmember actively and with prejudice assisted an aggressor.

In so far as Members are concerned, the status of nonparticipation, as contrasted with that of neutrality, is possible in certain circumstances. For reasons of distance, hardship, or lack of need for additional contributions, certain Members might not be called upon to participate in collective action. Or the matter may be left to a free choice; in that case participation, if undertaken at all, might be limited to the sending of medical personnel such as India sent to Korea. Some question might arise concerning just what trade could be carried on between a Member and an aggressor, but perhaps the rules of contraband, either in their old form or as redefined in United Nations directives to coöperating forces, would serve.

The current situation may, perhaps, be summarized in the follow-

---

[101] See also Article 43 on assistance to be given by *all* Members to the Security Council at its request, but in accord with special agreements. Articles 5 (f) and 24 of the Charter of the Organization of American States declare an act of aggression against one to be an act of aggression against all the other American states, a declaration which, if acted upon, would leave no room for neutrality in the circumstances contemplated.

[102] See H. J. Taubenfeld, "International Actions and Neutrality," 47 *A.J.I.L.* (1953), pp. 377-396; Castrén, *The Present Law of War and Neutrality*, pp. 433-435; Stone, *Legal Controls of International Conflict*, p. 382.

[103] N. Politis, *La neutralité et la paix* (Paris, 1935). Cf. Fabela, *op. cit.*, pp. 145-161; Örvik, *The Decline of Neutrality*, pp. 247-278.

ing manner. First, nonmembers of a collective security organization are not bound by decisions of the organization to abandon their neutrality. Second, members are legally bound to participate in collective action directed against violations of international law, including those principles to which they have committed themselves by joining the collective security organization. Such participation must take place in accordance with procedures established in the charter of the organization. Third, members may, in certain circumstances, enjoy with impunity a status of nonparticipation on condition that they do not actively promote the cause of the aggressor. Fourth, in case one of two contending blocs is able to employ the procedures of the organization to promote a struggle for political supremacy in a war in which neither side is opposing a violation of international law (or both are guilty of a violation), members are legally free to follow a policy of neutrality. Fifth, not until statesmen act as if aggression were outlawed, instead of merely making pious declarations, sometimes combined with references to the Nürnberg and Tokyo decisions, can it be said that there is no room in the world for neutral nations.

WAR AND COLLECTIVE SECURITY

26. Is War Inevitable under Collective Security?

HANS J. MORGENTHAU

. . . In the light of this discussion, we must conclude that collective security cannot be made to work in the contemporary world as it

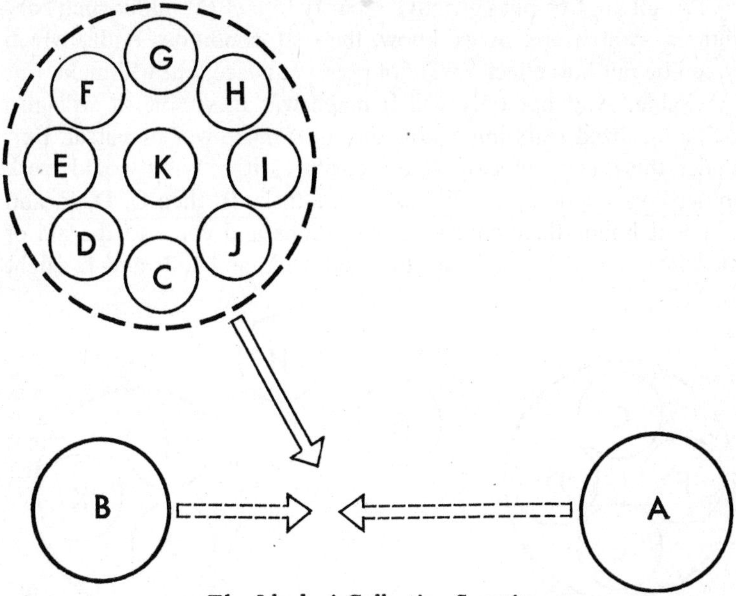

The Ideal of Collective Security

must work according to its ideal assumptions. Yet it is the supreme paradox of collective security that any attempt to make it work with less than ideal perfection will have the opposite effect from what it is supposed to achieve. It is the purpose of collective security to make war impossible by marshaling in defense of the status quo such overwhelming strength that no nation will dare to resort to force in order to change the status quo. But the less ideal are the conditions for making collective security work, the less formidable will be the combined strength of the nations willing to defend the status quo. If an appreciable number of nations are opposed to the status quo and if they are unwilling to give the common good, as defined in terms of collective security, precedence over their opposition, the distribution of power between the status quo and anti-status quo nations will no longer be overwhelmingly in favor of the former. Rather the distribution of power will take on the aspects of a balance of power which may still favor the status quo nations, but no longer to such an extent as to operate as an absolute deterrent upon those opposed to the status quo.

The attempt to put collective security into effect under such conditions—which are, as we know, the only conditions under which it can be put into effect—will not preserve peace, but will make war inevitable. And not only will it make war inevitable, it will also make localized wars impossible and thus make war universal. For, under the regime of collective security as it actually would work under contemporary conditions, if A attacks B, then C, D, E, and F might honor their collective obligations and come to the aid of B, while G and H might try to stand aside and I, J, and K might

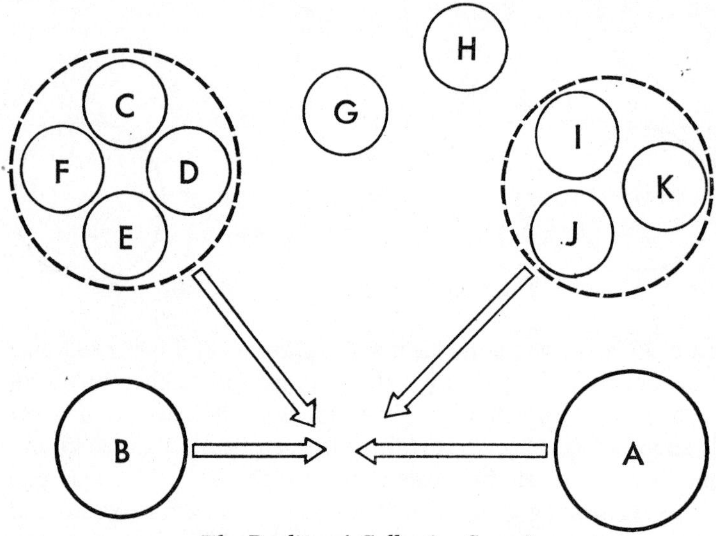

The Reality of Collective Security

support A's aggression. Were there no system of collective security, A might attack B with whatever consequences that might have for A and B, with no other nations being involved in the war. Under a system of collective security operating under less than ideal conditions, war between A and B, or between any other two nations anywhere in the world, of necessity evokes the risk of war among all or at best most nations of the world.

From the beginning of the modern state system to the First World War, it was the main concern of diplomacy to localize an actual or threatened conflict between two nations, in order to prevent it from spreading to other nations. The efforts of British diplomacy in the summer of 1914 to limit the conflict between Austria and Serbia to those two nations are an impressive, however unsuccessful, example. By the very logic of its assumptions, the diplomacy of collective security must aim at transforming all local conflicts into world conflicts. If this cannot be one world of peace, it cannot help being one world of war. Since peace is supposed to be indivisible, it follows that war is indivisible, too. Under the assumptions of collective security, any war anywhere in the world, then, is potentially a world war. Thus a device intent upon making war impossible ends by making war universal. Instead of preserving peace between two nations, collective security, as it must actually operate in the contemporary world, is bound to destroy peace among all nations. . . .

27. What Does the National Interest Require?

WILLARD N. HOGAN

. . . Opposition to reliance upon a collective security system such as that contemplated by the Charter of the United Nations comes from three sources. One of these is found in the various groups which reject the basic validity of the principle of concern. This attitude may be exhibited in isolationism (in the true meaning of the term) or in "neutralism" of one kind or another. It may reflect the belief that a Great Power should "go it alone" or that a small country should avoid the danger of taking sides. These are adaptations of the principle of self-help, relying upon national action or upon alliances in the face of immediate threats, but accepting no commitment in the event of a breach of the peace as such.

Another source of opposition is the "world government" school

Willard N. Hogan, *International Conflict and Collective Security: The Principle of Concern in International Organization* (Lexington, Kentucky: University of Kentucky Press, 1955), pp. 181-184. Reprinted by permission.

of thought, which holds that peace is incompatible with the continuance of national sovereignty. This approach views the nation-state system as productive of wars and holds that dependence cannot be placed in the co-operative action of sovereign states to preserve the peace. Effective supranational government, therefore, is essential in the nature of the case, and it follows that any lesser collective security system is by definition inadequate.

Finally, some scholars criticize the concept of collective security on the ground that it is in principle unworkable. For example, Hans Morgenthau has stated three assumptions which must be fulfilled if collective security is to operate as a device for the prevention of war, yet which, he has concluded, cannot be made to work in the contemporary world. These assumptions are that "(1) the collective system must be able to muster at all times such overwhelming strength against any potential aggressor or coalition of aggressors that the latter would never dare to challenge the order defended by the collective system; (2) at least those nations whose combined strength would meet the requirement under (1) must have the same conception of security which they are supposed to defend; (3) those nations must be willing to subordinate whatever conflicting political interests may still separate them to the common good defined in terms of the collective defense of all member states."[6]

The first two of these assumptions are obvious, if a collective security system is to be completely effective. Morgenthau draws the conclusion, however, that the tendency for a conflict of interests between *status quo* and revisionist nations, such as has existed since 1919, means that "the attempt to freeze the particular status quo by means of collective security is in the long run doomed to failure."[7] This conclusion on the impotence of collective security, however, does not take into consideration the nature of the available alternatives. One might make a plausible case that neither unilateral action by individual Great Powers nor a system of balance-of-power alliances is adequate to provide for orderly and peaceful change of a particular *status quo* and that the prerequisites

---

[6] *Politics among Nations,* 389; cp. also, Frederick L. Schuman, *International Politics,* 127, 235-38, and *The Commonwealth of Man,* 344-420.

[7] P. 390.

and conditions for an effective world government are not presently available. In such a case, no constructive principle of action would remain. Assumptions about the essentials of an effective collective security system and the recognized difficulties in applying this principle do not preclude the possibility that in some cases an attempt to apply this method may be at least as hopeful as any alternative course of action. The "failure" of the League of Nations has not restored traditional neutrality as a dependable basis of international organization, nor has it pointed to reliance on the supranational principle of government.

Morgenthau assumes that the diplomacy of collective security must aim at transforming all local conflicts into world conflicts and that it will result in spreading wars rather than preventing them. He approves, instead, of the type of diplomacy which attempts to localize wars, citing the instance of British efforts in the summer of 1914 to limit the conflict between Austria and Serbia. It is difficult to see how the conclusion drawn from this incident can be prejudicial to the principle of collective security. It seems to indicate that under modern conditions a war once started is likely to spread and that the methods of traditional diplomacy are not adequate to prevent this result. It is the nature of war in modern society, rather than the principle of collective security, which prevents the localization of war.

Morgenthau's third assumption is even more questionable. One of the stated implications is, "Collective security expects the policies of the individual nations to be inspired by the ideal of mutual assistance and a spirit of self-sacrifice which will not shrink even from the supreme sacrifice of war should it be required by that ideal."[8] First of all, this involves the ambiguous concept of "national self-interest." It is axiomatic, of course, that an invasion of a nation, or one of its neighbors, will be viewed with greater concern than some conflict on the other side of the globe. Nevertheless, it is not possible in principle to draw a line around a conception of national interest to exclude the possibility that the start of a war anywhere may be regarded as a violation of national security interest. Under a balance-of-power system, factors which tend to upset the balance

[8] P. 391.

are viewed as threats to national interests, especially by the *status quo* powers. Countries do not wait until an invasion occurs before they begin to form protective alliances, but take their cue from any situation which seems to contain the seeds of a future threat. In view of the nature of modern warfare, is it realistic to say that the American people have less of a "national interest" in preventing *any* act of aggression from sparking a world conflagration than they had in European policy toward South America in 1823, the Oregon boundary in the 1840's, the Spanish treatment of Cubans in 1898, or the terms upon which certain Latin American countries would satisfy their European creditors?

Was it really to the "national interest" of France and Great Britain in 1935 and 1936 to appease Mussolini in the hope of his co-operation against Hitler? It is not necessary to invoke a spirit of self-sacrificing altruism to condemn the policy expressed in the Hoare-Laval agreement and the hesitancy to apply effective sanctions in the Italo-Ethiopian case. Likewise, one may condemn the neutrality legislation of the 1930's on the grounds that it contributed to the spread of Axis aggression and was therefore contrary to the national interest of the United States. The debacle of collective security during the 1930's was not due to a refusal to subordinate national interests to collective security, but to mistaken conceptions of what was required to protect national interests. . . .

28. No One Formula

ROLAND N. STROMBERG

. . . The fourth of the assumptions we have listed is partly dependent upon the prior assumption that war results from the deliberately malevolent action of some state bent on a life of crime, obviously.

Roland N. Stromberg, "The Idea of Collective Security," *Journal of the History of Ideas,* April, 1956, pp. 250-263, at pp. 258-259. Reprinted by permission.

But the maxim "peace is indivisible," which M. Litvinov used to proclaim, or the analogy used by Franklin D. Roosevelt in comparing war to a contagious disease which will spread if not "quarantined," might be taken as a simple statement that war, if not opposed, feeds on itself; regardless of who was to blame for it, all other states have an interest in checking the smallest war, because little wars grow into big ones. Obviously under certain circumstances they may. This is not a new idea, for the old diplomacy with its keen sensitivity to the balance of power always understood that some very small bone might create a very large crisis. Indeed collective security has not been notable for any keen awareness of potential sources of trouble; it has shown a rather lamentable tendency to wait until some breach of peace occurs and then pounce on it with "punitive" action. It has always been known that apparently trivial disputes *may* involve the danger of a big war. But collective security seems to assert dogmatically that this is true of every case. It is certainly true that every threat to peace ought to be a matter of concern to everyone, but it is hardly true that a general intervention is always the most desirable remedy. The latter approach may, of course, succeed not in preventing the growth of a small war but in helping to make a great war of a small one. The comparison of a war with a contagion to be stamped out lest it spread may be compared with the old view that war is an infection which must be localized by neutralizing the areas around it. But all such analogies are misleading. No one formula is likely to cover every case. It is certainly a mistake to think of "sanctions" as a universal panacea, at any rate. Force is not a universal panacea, but a dangerous remedy which ought to be reserved for certain rare and otherwise incurable maladies. Very probably the confusion here would vanish if we banished the illusion, chronic with collective security, that every war is, like a nursery quarrel (to use a phrase from R. G. Collingwood), the work of a wicked child, for whom spanking is the only proper treatment. . . .

[III]

The Assumptions and Conditions of Collective Security

What are the assumptions and conditions which are involved in any attempt to make collective security work? Do they correspond to international reality?

THAT A RATIONAL SOLUTION EXISTS

1. *The assumption that a rational, peaceful solution is always possible or likely to be possible.*

If a collective security system is to work, it cannot rely exclusively or even mainly on the use of force; therefore, it must be based on the assumption that most conflicts between nations will be subject to a reasonable, rational settlement simultaneously satisfactory to all parties concerned (Reading 29). Such a position assumes, furthermore, that nations have in the past resorted to war only because no other alternative was open to them and that, with the existence of collective security instruments and with the increasing education of the masses, it will increasingly be possible to conciliate disputes in a rational way (Reading 30). These assumptions are sharply criticized in Readings 31 and 32.

THAT PEACEFUL CHANGE IS POSSIBLE

2. *The assumption that peaceful change will be possible, provided suitable procedures are established.*

If a collective security system is to work, it must provide an accepted system for peaceful change in vital political situations which nations may regard as intolerable and which they would change by any means available, including force. To make a system of peaceful change meaningful, the dissatisfied must not ask for the moon and the satisfied must be prepared, where necessary, to give up something in the larger interest. In other words, peaceful change of a significant character cannot be accomplished solely by the "other fellow" (Readings 33 and 34).

THAT SANCTIONS ARE POSSIBLE

3. *The assumption that sanctions will be forthcoming when needed, quickly, automatically, forcefully.*

No matter what provisions have been made for mediation, conciliation, and other procedures for the pacific settlement of disputes as well as for peaceful change itself, a collective security system must also promise with a reasonable degree of certainty that, if aggression nevertheless occurs, it will be met with impressive sanctions. Neither the League of Nations nor the United Nations has approached this standard. The provisions of the Covenant (Reading 35) were an ambitious attempt. But efforts to improve on it began very soon after its adoption. In presenting the Geneva Protocol of 1924 to the Assembly, Eduard Beneš, who was later to become the second and last President of the Czechoslovak Republic, both explained the inadequacies of the Covenant and discussed the improvements which could have followed from the adoption of the Protocol (Reading 36).

Although adopted by the Fifth Assembly of the League of Nations, the Geneva Protocol never came into effect. The specific reason for its defeat in practice was its rejection by the newly elected Conservative government of Stanley Baldwin in England, which saw things very differently and perhaps more realistically than had its predecessor. Sir Austen Chamberlain, the new Foreign Minister, argued the case at the Council meeting of March 25, 1925 (Reading 37).

Seeking to learn from League of Nations experience, the drafters of the Charter of the United Nations set down somewhat different sanctions provisions (Readings 38 and 39).

Pursuant to the "Uniting for Peace" Resolution of 1950, a Collective Measures Committee was established, whose purpose was to study and recommend various collective measures which could form at least a framework for collective security. The reactions of a number of United Nations members to the very general suggestions contained in the Collective Measures Report of 1951 are informative (Readings 40, 41, 42, and 43).

THAT WORLD POLITICS PERMITS SANCTIONS

4. *The assumption that all nations will participate in sanctions, and especially those who "count" in a given situation.*

Are all members to enter into collective security actions *even* at the cost of a radical derangement of political relations with other states on issues not directly connected with the conflict?

This classic problem was well illustrated in the dilemma which faced Britain and France in 1935, when their ally, Mussolini, attacked Ethiopia. Themselves weak in Europe, threatened by an aggressive and truculent Nazi Germany, should they have supported League sanctions against Italy in every way, including the possible use of force against their ally? Should they have done so even if such action would have broken up the alignment of Britain, France, and Italy only recently achieved at a meeting in Stresa, and given Hitler an opportunity for expansion in Europe? Or should they have largely ignored the Italian aggression, preserved the Stresa bloc if possible, and sought a compromise solution which would have given Ethiopia "something"?

On December 19, 1935, before a hostile House of Commons, Sir Samuel Hoare explained how he had tried to combine support for a certain degree of sanctions with a policy for the prevention of a European "conflagration." In the process, he had entered into the Hoare-Laval Plan for the division of Ethiopia and called down upon himself and his policy the most violent criticisms (Readings 44 and 45).

Nevertheless, no provisions were made to ease the burdens of nations particularly closely involved with an aggressor, so that they might participate in sanctions without paying an undue price in terms of trade or political ties. It is not surprising therefore that some members of an international organization may be found reluctant to apply sanctions.

THAT OVERWHELMING STRENGTH SUPPORTS SANCTIONS

5. *The assumption that the collective security organization will be able to muster overwhelming strength in any given situation.*

Readings 46 and 47 discuss this assumption.

THAT A RATIONAL SOLUTION EXISTS

29. Everyone Is Satisfied

WALTER SCHIFFER

. . . The basic elements of the concept are to be found in the doctrine of natural law and in the idea of progress. It is easy to understand why the doctrine of natural law was bound to be of decisive importance for the growth of the idea that the world, divided into independent states, was a legal community governed by a global law. Ordinarily, legal rules are created, interpreted, and enforced within a state. The fact that these rules are created by human acts gives them the character of positive law; their existence and binding force depend upon the state organization. Through this organization the legal rules of a state appear as combined in a legal system. As long as the world is divided into independent states, there can be no universal statelike organization. But the idea that, in spite of the absence of such an organization, a global law governs the world can arise if it is assumed that besides positive law there exists another, higher, type of law which is of universal validity and independent of any connection with a state. Such a law is the law of nature. It is supposed to derive directly from the nature of man, to exist and to have binding force without being laid down in statutes, court decisions, or other acts, and to be self-evident to all beings endowed with reason. The natural-law doctrine influenced even those theories which were intended to prove that there existed a global law as positive as the law of the states. This fact is of particular importance with regard to the concept which is the object of the present study, because a global organization

---

Walter Schiffer, *The Legal Community of Mankind* (New York: Columbia University Press, 1954), pp. 8-9. Reprinted by permission.

of the League of Nations type was expected to create conditions that made a universal, positive, legal order possible, although the organization had not the character of a state.

Rules expressing the dictates of nature are supposed to indicate how the individual interests of every member of a community can be reconciled with the interests of all the other members and with those of the community as a whole. From the point of view of a doctrine which assumes the existence of such rules, the harmony of interests—the goal of an orderly and peaceful community—appears as naturally given and ascertainable by reason. The observance of the natural rules seems to guarantee the maintenance of that harmony; their observance seems to depend on the extent to which the human beings endowed with reason actually make use of this capacity. The idea of progress, fully developed during the nineteenth century, gave rise to the belief that the peoples of the world, steadily advancing toward greater reasonableness and toward material and moral perfection, have gradually acquired a better knowledge of their natural interests and have become more and more willing to act in accordance with this knowledge. This belief led to the assumption that mankind was moving toward unity, a unity established by the community of reasonable interests rather than by the existence of a world government. . . .

30. A Problem of Understanding

NORMAN ANGELL

. . . The view taken throughout this book, as the reader may judge for himself, is that war is not due to evil intention; is not made by wicked men knowing themselves to be wrong, but usually by good men passionately convinced—on both sides—that they are

Sir Norman Angell, *The Great Illusion, 1933* (New York: G. P. Putnam's Sons, 1933), pp. 12-13. Reprinted by permission of the author.

right; that the problem is to know why what they believe to be right is in fact unworkable, antisocial, wrong. It is a problem of understanding, the understanding of the kind of international world that has come into being, the nature of the process by which we live, achieve civilization, maintain prosperity; the conditions of economic and political security. Without that understanding the will to peace may be sincere and genuine and yet be defeated by failure to realize the inevitable outcome of the policies which we pursue. . . .

31. A Sharp Criticism

ROBERT STRAUSZ-HUPÉ AND STEFAN T. POSSONY

. . . There is a fallacious assumption underlying much of the heavy thinking on peace: that war is a great evil and that most people recognize it as an extreme misfortune. Granting that war is a negative value, the practical choice rarely lies between a good peace and a bad war. There are many reasons why people go to war, and some of them are foolish. But not infrequently people decide on war because they want to terminate a situation which, rightly or wrongly, they consider to be more disadvantageous than armed conflict. The inmate of a slave-labor camp in Siberia or the member of an ethnical group which suffers oppression views war with sentiments different from those of the owner of a prosperous business in a free country. If a situation is deemed so intolerable that men do not hesitate to sacrifice their own lives in order to remedy it, they rarely put much stock in the argument that war, since it is destructive, must be avoided. People who sacrifice their all in defying a hated conqueror or a despised political police are contemptuous of pacifism which, rightly or wrongly, they equate with cowardice. They hold the conviction—and under many circumstances hold it rightly—that war is the only technique of social change which can bring about the desired improvement. Far from being a clinching argument against war, the atomic bomb might become a powerful argument *for* war; it makes possible a fast and conclusive victory and therefore might transform war from a dull into a sharp and effective instrument.

The point that war is destructive and therefore pointless is more convincing to the skeptic than to the fanatic. A person who thinks that all values are relative will indeed find few reasons to offer his own life for an ideal the validity of which seems doubtful. He whose attitude grants to the hostile ideal as much truth as to his own, or ascribes to it advantages which his own ideal does not display, is forever ready to "talk it over" but always unwilling "to shoot it out." A man who believes strongly in his ideal or political concept and who holds that, in a given conflict, far more is at stake than political or philosophical abstractions usually acknowledges moral obligations toward his convictions. He does not necessarily overlook the high price which must be paid for "standing up and being counted." Undoubtedly, men guided by the teachings of the great moral philosophies, if intellectually competent, will give consideration to the dire implications of extreme violence. But few will be inclined to accept the maintenance of peace as the sole criterion of political decisions. The fact is that pacifists are in a minority, especially during a serious crisis menacing the foundations of a way of life.[34] The second fact is that, at most times, there are situations and conditions which must be changed drastically but which can be changed only through military surgery. Even a government which prefers peace to war often is confronted by the choice of weighing the disadvantages of war against the disadvantages of the continuance of an intolerable situation. . . .

[34] Experience shows that in times of stress "pacifists" easily become proponents of a crusade and reject the idea that a war should be fought for "only" limited objectives. In their opinion, nothing can justify war except the salvation of mankind.

32. Conflict Is Real and Constant

ROLAND N. STROMBERG

. . . Whatever the exact definition of collective security, there can be little doubt that these assumptions are strongly associated with it. They appear to be as follows:

(1) All international disputes are subject to peaceable, just, satisfactory settlement.

(2) Nations are for the most part inclined to peace, not war.

(3) The inclination to war is everything: war results only when at least one side is guilty of a deliberately aggressive action.

(4) Since wars are always caused by a deliberate aggressor, this must be checked in its first stages if it will lead on to ever greater aggression; the incipient criminal will certainly become a hardened one if not caught in time.

(5) As an inference from (3) and (4), all states have an obvious stake in a war no matter where it may occur, and will, if they understand their interests properly, join in helping to suppress it.

In regard to points 1 and 2: such has been the evident, optimistic bias of all the great supporters of collective security, from Wilson to Stimson, and a workable system of this sort seems to require that really troublesome disputes be few in number and susceptible of a "fair" solution. The advocates of collective security have tended to believe that some final and just world order is possible, a stable and reasonable *status quo* where everyone is happy; they have obviously felt that the coercive powers of the international organization would have to be used rarely and, as time goes on, hardly at all. If peace is the rule, and conflict is the exception; if wars are only the occasional deviation from the norm, like madness or chronic criminality in individuals, then the task of a United Nations becomes feasible. But history does not seem to support such a view. Conflict is, unhappily, real and constant in

---

Roland N. Stromberg, "The Idea of Collective Security," *Journal of the History of Ideas,* April, 1956, pp. 250-263, at pp. 255 and 262-263. Reprinted by permission. Footnotes omitted.

the world; it is not, alas, an irrational deviation, but is all too rationally rooted in facts of economics, of ethnology, of the struggle for existence and the clash of cultures. We need go no farther than modern Palestine, or the Istrian peninsula, or the Saar, or the vale of Kashmir, not to speak of larger quarrels, to find clashes too stubborn to yield readily to settlement and too puzzling to allow us to say that one side is "right" and the other "wrong." The problem is not, as the Wilsonians imagined, one of suppressing an infrequent case of diabolism, a clear case of law and decency *versus* the criminal aggressor. . . .

The idea of collective security has managed, through its Wilsonian and Rooseveltian associations, to become closely connected with the liberal tradition. But in conclusion it might be pointed out that a strong case can be made against its liberalism. In Western thought liberalism has held with Locke, and against Hobbes, that law derives not from force but from reason and consent; that a political community must grow, as a result of experience and the working of reason on the not utterly depraved human mind, rather than be imposed by the sword of the strongest. The United Nations as an instrument of education and a place where irrational national prejudices are gradually dissolved is in the liberal tradition; but the appeal to force involved in collective security seems to be Hobbesean: "covenants without the sword are but words and breath." The older approach was surely the more liberal—that which concentrated on the mitigation of war, taking its elimination to be impractical until, by a slow process of education, a sense of international community had time to develop. It is true that the United Nations is not a tyrant-state, far from it; but neither is it, in the collective-security philosophy, a place where habits of compromise are patiently learned. It is a place, rather, where groups of states denounce each other and try to organize coalitions for punishing each other. From time to time well-meaning friends of collective security deplore the fact that the U.N. has degenerated into an arena where the "selfish nationalisms" they had thought to exorcise intrigue and lobby against one another, and convert the halls of international idealism into a place of "power politics." But the very idea of collective security has helped make this inevitable. National interests must continue to exist, and it is not shocking that they should jostle one another and seek adjustments by means of expediency and compromise. But by refusing to adopt a frankly political purpose, by attempting to bring in a rule of law where none can exist, collective security lends to this process of national conflict an air of self-righteousness which is hostile to habits of compromise. The interests of other states appear not natural but criminal, not to be recognized but to be prosecuted. The spirit of liberalism is tolerance; the idea of collective security, as has been noticed from time to time, smacks of a medieval intolerance, the crusade and the "just war." . . .

THAT PEACEFUL CHANGE IS POSSIBLE

33. The Problem Is Wholly Political

CHARLES DE VISSCHER

. . . Often as it has been approached, the problem of changing international situations by peaceful means has never been sounded to its depths. This is to be accounted for largely by a sense of the present fragility of international situations; for there is a natural inclination to regard change not as an inevitable consequence of the evolution of things, but as an event likely to provoke crisis, or at least serious complications.[1] But especially the question has always been looked at from a too exclusively legal point of view.

[1] J. L. Brierly, *The Outlook for International Law,* p. 106.

Confining their effort to the search for procedures (the machinery of peaceful change), authors have neglected the fundamental political obstacle usually thrown up against attempts to effect such change by a will to power determined on altering to its advantage the established ratio of forces.

It is the mark of a consolidated legal system to combine, for the better satisfaction of social needs, suppleness of adaptation with the firmness indispensable to legal ordering. This double requirement is very generally met in the national order by a legally recognized hierarchy of values sustained by appropriate mechanisms of change.[2] There is nothing like this in the international order. Rigid in principle, authoritarian in method, sovereignty is naturally refractory to what Hauriou called "the slow and uniform movement of change in an ordered social system."[3] It asserts itself now in an unbridled dynamism that no legal order could satisfy, now in a shortsighted conservatism that in the end may prove equally dangerous to the stability of law. This being so, the aspiration to change easily takes on the appearance of a threat to the established order and to inviolable rights. Because change is not regarded and dealt with as a normal social need, the aspiration becomes charged with a political potential and results in inarticulate tensions or sharp fluctuations that escape the ordering action of law.

We may leave aside what are called general or impersonal situations, common if not to all States at least to a great number—situations subject to the general rules of international law. These represent balances of interest already largely integrated in law; change in them, proceeding largely by the process of custom, generally occasions no very serious political difficulties. It is different with change in particular or subjective situations, much the most numerous and most important politically, involving interests and rights of which States have in principle the free and exclusive dis-

---

[2] It is well known that at times of crisis municipal law itself often enough bends under political pressures. A rapid succession of laws and their retroactive application are symptoms of this; they introduce instability and fragility into the law. Cf. G. Ripert, *Le déclin du Droit,* 1949; F. Russo, *Réalité Juridique et Réalité Sociale,* 1942.

[3] "Aux sources du Droit," *Cahiers de la Nouvelle Journée,* no. 33, p. 77 (1933).

position. Here the aspiration to change collides head-on with the individualist distribution of power among nations.[4]

This is lost sight of by those who denounce as an essential cause of the insecurity of international relations the excessively static character of international law, its inability to respond to economic and social demands and to redress the imbalances that are incidental to the development of human societies. It is of the essence of law to contain within its regulatory framework the moving and chaotic manifestations of social dynamism. The order that international law seeks to sustain among nations is inseparable from the state of possession that its rules have created. This state of possession, with all the elements of State power that it includes, cannot be submitted to revision except in one of two ways—either by the agreement of those concerned, or by the establishment of a federal organization strong enough to correct disequilibria by a constant redistribution of the elements of power. Meanwhile it is perfectly useless to blame law for the fact that it furnishes no support for demands that have no legal basis.

The jurists, for their part, go astray when, yielding to the fixed idea of the formal completeness of law, they seek to minimize the problem and dispute its dangers to international security and the maintenance of peace. The problem denoted by the vague idea of peaceful change is only too real, but it is wholly political. What it brings into question is not the legality of a state of possession; it is the political expediency of changing it in order to meet the real or pretended needs of dissatisfied collectivities.[5] This is the way the problem was looked at in League of Nations circles in the years before the second world war. There it figured as one element of a system of collective security that sought to eliminate in advance grievances that might provoke war.

[4] On the fundamental nature of this distinction, see Maurice Bourquin, *Stabilité et Mouvement, Rec. A.D.I.*, vol. 64 (1938), pp. 414-415.

[5] D. Schindler, *Rec. A.D.I.*, vol. 46, p. 282: "The legally unassailable finding that each State may do as it will does not end the conflict, for the conflict springs precisely from this liberty. Such conflicts can only be eliminated in the measure that it becomes possible to replace the regime of liberty with a regulatory system of law providing an effective delimitation of interest. . . . The question is not one of applying the existing law, but of creating a new legal situation."

Things are different when the situation is one of those of which the law has already to some extent taken cognizance, especially contractual situations. The imbalances of interests that after a certain time make their appearance here are generally subject to legal regulation. It is for this reason, and not by any means because it exhausts the problem of peaceful change, that treaty revision has always been the focus of discussion.

We must then, first of all, distinguish the change of legal situations from that of situations, not at present legally ordered, which are the subject of political grievances. . . .

34. Security and Justice

JOHN FOSTER DULLES

. . . Our problem is no less than that in its importance. Now, why do I say that? I say that because we all want a world in which force is not used. True, but that is only one side of the coin. If you have a world in which force is not used, you must also have a world in which a just solution of problems of this sort can be achieved. I don't care how many words are written into the charter of the United Nations about not using force. If, in fact, there is not, as a substitute for force, some way to get just resolutions of some of these problems, inevitably the world will fall back again into anarchy and into chaos.

And I would like to point out, fellow delegates, that the United Nations Charter itself does not just say, "There must be peace." What does it say? The very first article of the United Nations Charter says that the purpose of the United Nations is to bring about settlements "by peaceful means, and in conformity with

Extemporaneous Remarks of Secretary of State Dulles at Conclusion of Second Plenary Session, September 19, 1956, Second Suez Canal Conference, London, September 19-21, 1956, *Department of State Bulletin,* October 1, 1956, p. 505.

the principles of justice and international law." And if that latter part is forgotten, the first part of it will inevitably come to be ignored.

We have to realize, when we have to deal with problems of this character, that we are not really in the long run furthering the cause of peace, even peace for those of us who seem remote from the particular problem, if we don't feel that we have just as much a responsibility to try to seek a solution "in conformity with the principles of justice and international law" as we have a responsibility to try to prevent the use of force. If we only put our emphasis upon one side of that problem and forget the other, then our efforts are going to be doomed. And the hopes represented by this charter of the United Nations are equally going to be doomed. . . .

THAT SANCTIONS ARE POSSIBLE

35. Covenant Provisions for Sanctions: Articles 10, 11, 15, 16

COVENANT OF THE LEAGUE OF NATIONS

Article 10. Guaranties against Aggression. The Members of the League undertake to respect and preserve as against external aggression the territorial integrity and existing political independence of all Members of the League. In case of any such aggression or in case of any threat or danger of such aggression the Council

The Treaty of Versailles and After, Annotations of the Text of the Treaty, Department of State Publication 2724, Conference Series 92 (Washington, D.C.: Government Printing Office, 1947), pp. 69-134, at pp. 83-84 and 86-91.

shall advise upon the means by which this obligation shall be fulfilled.

Article 11. Action in Case of War or Threat of War. 1. Any war or threat of war, whether immediately affecting any of the Members of the League or not, is hereby declared a matter of concern to the whole League, and the League shall take any action that may be deemed wise and effectual to safeguard the peace of nations. In case any such emergency should arise the Secretary-General shall on the request of any Member of the League forthwith summon a meeting of the Council.

2. It is also declared to be the friendly right of each Member of the League to bring to the attention of the Assembly or of the Council any circumstance whatever affecting international relations which threatens to disturb international peace or the good understanding between nations upon which peace depends.

Article 15. Disputes Not Submitted to Arbitration or Judicial Settlement. 1. If there should arise between Members of the League any dispute likely to lead to a rupture, which is not submitted to arbitration *or judicial settlement* in accordance with Article 13, the Members of the League agree that they will submit the matter to the Council. Any party to the dispute may effect such submission by giving notice of the existence of the dispute to the Secretary-General, who will make all necessary arrangements for a full investigation and consideration thereof.

2. For this purpose the parties to the dispute will communicate to the Secretary-General, as promptly as possible, statements of their case with all the relevant facts and papers, and the Council may forthwith direct the publication thereof.

3. The Council shall endeavor to effect a settlement of the dispute, and, if such efforts are successful, a statement shall be made public giving such facts and explanations regarding the dispute and the terms of settlement thereof as the Council may deem appropriate.

4. If the dispute is not thus settled, the Council either unanimously or by a majority vote shall make and publish a report containing a statement of the facts of the dispute and the recommendations which are deemed just and proper in regard thereto.

5. Any Member of the League represented on the Council may

make public a statement of the facts of the dispute and of its conclusions regarding the same.

6. If a report by the Council is unanimously agreed to by the Members thereof other than the Representatives of one or more of the parties to the dispute, the Members of the League agree that they will not go to war with any party to the dispute which complies with the recommendations of the report.

7. If the Council fails to reach a report which is unanimously agreed to by the Members thereof, other than the Representatives of one or more of the parties to the dispute, the Members of the League reserve to themselves the right to take such action as they shall consider necessary for the maintenance of right and justice.

8. If the dispute between the parties is claimed by one of them, and is found by the Council, to arise out of a matter which by international law is solely within the domestic jurisdiction of that party, the Council shall so report, and shall make no recommendation as to its settlement.

9. The Council may in any case under this Article refer the dispute to the Assembly. The dispute shall be so referred at the request of either party to the dispute, provided that such request be made within 14 days after the submission of the dispute to the Council.

10. In any case referred to the Assembly, all the provisions of this Article and of Article 12 relating to the action and powers of the Council shall apply to the action and powers of the Assembly, provided that a report made by the Assembly, if concurred in by the Representatives of those Members of the League represented on the Council and of a majority of the other Members of the League, exclusive in each case of the Representatives of the parties to the dispute, shall have the same force as a report by the Council concurred in by all the members thereof other than the Representatives of one or more of the parties to the dispute.

Article 16. Sanctions of Pacific Settlement. 1. Should any Member of the League resort to war in disregard of its covenants under Articles 12, 13 or 15, it shall *ipso facto* be deemed to have committed an act of war against all other Members of the League, which hereby undertake immediately to subject it to the severance of all trade or financial relations, the prohibition of all intercourse between their nationals and the nationals of the covenant-breaking State, and the prevention of all financial, commercial or personal intercourse between the nationals of the covenant-breaking State and the nationals of any other State, whether a Member of the League or not.

2. It shall be the duty of the Council in such case to recommend to the several Governments concerned what effective military, naval or air force the Members of the League shall severally contribute to the armed forces to be used to protect the covenants of the League.

3. The Members of the League agree, further, that they will mutually support one another in the financial and economic measures which are taken under this Article, in order to minimize the loss and inconvenience resulting from the above measures, and that they will mutually support one another in resisting any special measures aimed at one of their number by the covenant-breaking State, and that they will take the necessary steps to afford passage through their territory to the forces of any of the Members of the League which are cooperating to protect the covenants of the League.

4. Any Member of the League which has violated any covenant of the League may be declared to be no longer a Member of the League by a vote of the Council concurred in by the Representatives of all the other Members of the League represented thereon.

36. An Attempt to Strengthen the Covenant of the League of Nations

EDUARD BENEŠ

According to Article 10 of the Covenant, Members of the League undertake to preserve as against external aggression the territorial

League of Nations, *Official Journal,* Record of the Fifth Assembly, Minutes of the Third Committee, Special Supplement No. 26, pp. 208-209.

integrity and existing political independence of all Members of the League. In case of aggression, the Council shall advise upon the means by which this obligation shall be fulfilled.

According to Article 16, should any Member of the League resort to war in disregard of its engagements under Articles 12, 13 or 15, all other Members of the League undertake immediately to apply economic sanctions; furthermore, it shall be the duty of the Council to recommend to the several Governments concerned what effective military, naval or air forces the Members of the League shall severally contribute to the armed forces to be used to protect the engagements of the League.

At the time when they were drafted at the Peace Conference in Paris in 1919, these articles gave rise to keen controversy as to the exact scope of the engagements entered into in these provisions, that is to say, as to the nature and extent of the obligations referred to in Article 10, the exact moment at which such obligations arose, and the legal consequences of the Council recommendations referred to in Article 16, paragraph 2. This controversy continued, as is well known, in the debates here in Geneva, where the question has been discussed in previous years.

Article 11 is intended to settle this controversy. The signatories of the [Geneva] Protocol accept the obligation to apply against the aggressor the various sanctions laid down in the Covenant, as interpreted in Article 11 of the Protocol, when an act of aggression has been established and the Council has called upon the signatory States immediately to apply such sanctions (Article 10, last paragraph). Should they fail so to do, they will not be fulfilling their obligations.

The nature and extent of this obligation is clearly defined in paragraph 2 of Article 11. According to this paragraph, the reply to the question whether a signatory to the Protocol has or has not fulfilled its obligation depends on whether it has loyally and effectively co-operated in resisting the act of aggression to an extent consistent with its geographical position and its particular situation as regards armaments.

The State remains in control of its forces, and itself, and not the Council, directs them, but paragraph 2 of Article 11 gives us positive material upon which to form a judgment as to whether or not the obligation has been carried out in any concrete case. This criterion is supplied by the term: *loyally and effectively.*

In answering the question whether a State has or has not fulfilled its obligations in regard to sanctions, a certain elasticity in the obligations laid down in Article 11 allows of the possibility of *taking into account, from every point of view, the position of each State which is a signatory to the present Protocol.* The signatory States are not all in possession of equal facilities for acting when the time comes to apply the sanctions. This depends upon the geographical position and economic and social condition of the State, the nature of its population, internal institutions, etc.

Indeed, during the discussion as to the system of sanctions, certain delegations declared that their countries were in a special situation by reason of their geographical position or the state of their armaments. These countries desired to co-operate to the fullest extent of their resources in resistance to every act of aggression, but they drew attention to their special conditions. In order to take account of this situation, an addition has been made to paragraph 2 of Article 11 pointing out this state of affairs and laying stress on the particular situation of the countries in question. Moreover, Article 13 of the Protocol allows such countries to inform the Council of these matters beforehand.

I would further add that the obligations I refer to are imperfect obligations in the sense that no sanctions are provided for against any party which shall have failed loyally and effectively to cooperate in protecting the Covenant and resisting every act of aggression. It should, however, be emphasised that such a State would have failed in the fulfillment of its duties and would be guilty of a violation of engagements entered into.

In view of the foregoing, the gist of Article 11, paragraphs 1 and 2, might be expressed as follows: Each State is the judge of the manner in which it shall carry out its obligations but not of the existence of those obligations, that is to say, each State remains the judge of what it will do but no longer remains the judge of what it should do.

Now that the present Protocol has defined more precisely the origin, nature and extent of the obligations arising out of the

Covenant, the *functions of the Council, as provided in Articles* 10 *and* 16, *have become clearer and more definite.*

Directly the Council has called upon the signatories to the Protocol to apply without delay the sanctions provided in Article 11, it becomes a regulating, or rather an advisory, body, but not an executive body. The nature of the acts of aggression may vary considerably; the means for their suppression will also vary. It would frequently be unnecessary to make use of all the means which, according to paragraphs 1 and 2 of Article 11, are, so to speak, available for resisting an act of aggression. It might even be dangerous if, from fear of failing in their duties, States made superfluous efforts. It will devolve upon the Council, which, under Article 13 can be put in possession of the necessary data, to give *its opinion,* should need occur, as to the best means of executing the obligations which arise directly it enjoins the application of sanctions, especially as to the sequence in which the sanctions must be applied.

The practical application of the sanctions would, however, always devolve upon the Governments; the real co-operation would ensue upon their getting into touch, through diplomatic channels—perhaps by conferences—and by direct relations between different General Staffs, as in the last war. The Council would, of course, be aware of all these negotiations, would be consulted and make recommendations.

The difference between the former state of affairs and the new will therefore be as follows:

According to the system laid down by the Covenant:

1. The dispute arises.

2. In cases where neither the arbitral procedure nor the judicial settlement provided for in Article 13 of the Covenant is applied, the Council meets and discusses the dispute, attempts to effect conciliation, mediation, etc.

3. If it be unsuccessful and war breaks out, the Council, if unanimous, has to express an opinion as to which party is guilty. The Members of the League then decide for themselves whether this opinion is justified and whether their obligations to apply economic sanctions become operative.

4. The Council then has, *by a unanimous decision, to recommend* military sanctions.

5. If unanimity cannot be obtained, the Council ceasing to take action, each party is practically free to act as it chooses.

According to the system defined in the Protocol, the situation is as follows:

1. The dispute arises.
2. The system of peaceful settlement provided for by the Protocol comes into play.
3. The Council intervenes, and if, after arbitration has been refused, war is resorted to, if the provisional preventive measures are not observed, etc., the Council decides which party is the aggressor and calls upon the signatory States to apply the sanctions.
4. This decision implies that such sanctions as the case requires—economic, financial, military, naval and air—shall be applied forthwith, and without further recommendations or decisions.

We have therefore the following new elements:

(*a*) The obligation to apply the necessary sanctions of every kind as a direct result of the decision of the Council.

(*b*) The elimination of the case in which all parties would be practically free to abstain from any action. The introduction of a system of arbitration and of provisional measures which permits of the determination in every case of the aggressor.

(*c*) No decision is taken as to the strength of the military, naval and air forces, and no details are given as to the measures which are to be adopted in a particular case. None the less, objective criteria are supplied which define the obligation of each signatory; it is bound, in resistance to an act of aggression, to collaborate *loyally and effectively* in applying the sanctions in accordance with its geographical situation and its particular situation as regards armaments.

That is why I said that *the great omission in the Covenant has been made good.*

It is true that no burden has been imposed on States beyond the sanctions already provided for in the Covenant. But, at present, a State seeking to elude the obligations of the Covenant can reckon on two means of escape:

(1) The Council's recommendations need not be followed.

(2) The Council may fail to obtain unanimity, making impossible any declaration of aggression, so that no obligation to apply military

sanctions will be imposed and everyone will remain free to act as he chooses.

We have abandoned the above system and both these loopholes are now closed.

37. Rejection of the Geneva Protocol

AUSTEN CHAMBERLAIN

. . . As all the world is aware, the League of Nations, in its present shape, is not the League designed by the framers of the Covenant. They no doubt contemplated, and, as far as they could, provided against, the difficulties that might arise from the non-inclusion of a certain number of States, within the circle of League membership. But they never supposed that, among these States, would be found so many of the most powerful nations in the world; least of all did they foresee that one of them would be the United States of America. . . .

. . . But surely it is most unwise to add to the liabilities already incurred without taking stock of the degree to which the machinery of the Covenant has been already weakened by the non-membership of certain great States. For in truth the change, especially as regards the "economic sanctions", amounts to a transformation. The "economic sanction", if simultaneously directed by all the world against a State which is not itself economically self-sufficing, would be a weapon of incalculable power. This, or something not very different from this, was the weapon originally devised by the authors of the Covenant. To them it appeared to be not only bloodless, but cheap, effective and easy to use, in the most improbable event of its use being necessary. But all this is changed by the mere existence of powerful economic communities outside the limits of the League. It might force trade into unaccustomed channels, but it could

League of Nations, *Official Journal,* Records of the Council, April, 1925, pp. 447-450.

hardly stop it; and, though the offending State would no doubt suffer, there is no presumption that it would be crushed or even that it would suffer most. . . .

Articles 7 and 8 of the Protocol are designed for the purpose of preventing a State which has a difference with a neighbour from making any preparations for war between the moment when a dispute arises and the moment when proceedings for a pacific settlement have been concluded. The intentions of these provisions are most laudable. But the framers of the Protocol have not perhaps sufficiently considered that it may embarrass the victim of aggression even more than the aggressor. The aggressor is at liberty to select his own date for picking a quarrel. Until that date arrives he may distribute his armies as he pleases—provided only that he neither mobilises them nor adds to them. When the distribution is as favourable to his designs as he can hope to make them, he starts the dispute. Immediately, the military position becomes temporarily unalterable. His troops, which are more or less in the right position for attack, may (indeed must) be kept there till he wants to use them. The troops, on the other hand, of his prospective victim are (by supposition) in the wrong position for defence. But there they must be kept, or the victim may find himself charged with a breach of the Protocol. Is this a tolerable situation? Is it one that could possibly survive the day of trial?

It may be replied that, if the aggressor attempts to concentrate troops for attack before the dispute arises, means may be found to stop him. Grant that such means exist, which is extremely doubtful, how does the Protocol deal with the case where the peace distribution of the troops belonging to the aggressor is normally more suitable for attack than the peace distribution of the troops belonging to its opponents is suitable for defence? If a dispute were to arise, would the defender be counted as an aggressor solely because he endeavoured to redress this accidental inequality? . . .

. . . The fresh emphasis laid upon sanctions, the new occasions discovered for their employment, the elaboration of military procedure, insensibly suggest the idea that the vital business of the League is not so much to promote friendly co-operation and reasoned harmony in the management of international affairs as to preserve peace by organising war, and (it may be) war on the largest scale. Now, it is unhappily true that circumstances may be easily imagined in which war, conducted by Members of the League, and with its collective assistance and approval, will become a tragic necessity. But such catastrophes belong to the pathology of international life, not to its normal condition. It is not wholesome for the ordinary man to be always brooding over the possibility of some severe surgical operation; nor is it wise for societies to pursue a similar course. It is more likely to hasten the dreaded consummation than to hinder it. And it certainly seems to His Majesty's Government that anything which fosters the idea that the main business of the League is with war rather than with peace is likely to weaken it in its fundamental task of diminishing the causes of war without making it in every respect a satisfactory instrument for organising great military operations should the necessity for them be forced upon the world.

IV.

It may perhaps be urged that these objections to the Protocol, whatever be their value, are far outweighed by the blessings of the disarmament which would immediately follow its acceptance. But why should disarmament immediately follow its acceptance? Why should the new scheme succeed when the old scheme has so lamentably failed? It no doubt claims to have closed some "fissures in the wall of protection erected by the Covenant round the peace of the world." But it is not the possibility of an attack through these (alleged) weak places in the Covenant which haunts the imagination of those who hesitate to disarm. They do not doubt that the Covenant, if kept, would be sufficient to protect them, at least from attack by those who have signed it. What they doubt is whether, when it comes to the point, the Covenant *will* be kept. Either some faithless Member of the League will break its pledges or some predatory nation outside the League will brush Covenant and Protocol ruthlessly aside, defying all the sanction by which they are protected. Brute force is what they fear, and only brute force enlisted in their defence can (as they believe) give them the security of which they feel the need.

His Majesty's Government fail altogether to see how this situation is bettered by the Protocol. Is it to be supposed that the "security" promised by the new system will be so complete that no armaments capable of being used or improvised for offensive purposes will remain in being? If not, is the balance of power between the States which desire peace and those which are plotting war to be adjusted in favour of the former? If so, on what principle? If not, then how are we advanced? How will the unscrupulous aggressors be relatively weakened? How will their potential victims be rendered more capable of defence?

And if the particular case of aggressors who are outside the League be considered, is not the weakness of the Protocol even more manifest? The aggressors within the League are traitors in the sight of all mankind. Their moral position in the face of any opposition within their own borders will be immensely weakened, while in neutral countries they will find none to plead their cause. However low the practical importance of moral considerations such as these may be rated, the eagerness of competing propaganda in times of international crisis may convince the most cynical that a good cause counts at least for something. If so, aggressors outside the League will have a smaller load of infamy to carry than aggressors within it, and will be by so much the more formidable. How does the Protocol deal with them? It requires them to treat the situation as if they were members of the League, to accept its methods and conform to its decisions. If they refuse they are counted as aggressors, they become the common enemy, and every signatory State is bound to go to war with them. They may be in the right and have nothing to fear from impartial judges. Yet national pride, in some cases perhaps the sense of power, dislike of compulsory arbitration, distrust of the League (to which presumably they have already refused to belong)—all these motives, or any of them, may harden their objections to outside interference. If so, the Protocol, designed to ensure universal peace, may only extend the area of war—a possibility which, if realized, will not improve the chances of general disarmament.

V.

It may perhaps be replied that, while every scheme of sanctions is open to criticism, some scheme of sanctions is certainly necessary. Without it a League of Nations would be as insecure as a civilised society without magistrates and police. International engagements which cannot be internationally enforced are little better than a sham. Those, therefore, who object to the plan proposed in the Protocol are bound to suggest a better.

To this challenge His Majesty's Government might be content to reply that, as between the Covenant unamended and the Covenant amended by the Protocol, they have already given reasons for preferring the former. But they are unwilling to conclude their argument on a purely critical note and, though they cannot believe that "security" can be reached by the route so carefully explored by the First and Third Committees of the League in 1924, they are willing to consider whether some approach to it may not be made from the side unsuccessfully attempted in 1923.

They do not agree, indeed, that without "sanctions" the League is powerless and treaties no better than waste paper. Doctrines like these seem to them not only mischievous but self-contradictory. Every "sanction" referred to either in the Covenant or the Protocol depends on treaties; and if no treaties are of value, all sanctions must be worthless. Do what we will, we have no choice but, in the last resort, to depend upon the plighted word.

But this, it must be admitted, does not settle the question whether the sanctions contemplated by the Covenant cannot in certain cases and for certain purposes be supplemented with advantage to the general scheme of the Covenant itself. That scheme may no doubt be trusted in ordinary cases to work smoothly and effectively. The mere threat to employ sanctions will commonly suffice. And if, unfortunately, it does not, their effect, when put into operation, will doubtless be speedy and conclusive. But it is easy to imagine extreme cases, about which we dare not speak with the same assurance; and it is precisely the possibility of these extreme cases, remote though that possibility may be, which fosters international suspicion, makes Governments hesitate to disarm and keeps the world on edge.

His Majesty's Government do not share these alarms, but they recognize their serious effect, and believe them to be the main obstacles to the complete recovery of our shaken civilisation from the disasters of war. How are they to be allayed?

The first expedient that naturally suggests itself is to strengthen the provisions of the Covenant. If the Covenant, as it stands, does not supply an adequate machinery for preserving peace in all conceivable cases, why not alter it till it does?

The futility of this plan is, in the opinion of His Majesty's Government, abundantly proved by the Protocol. For whatever else its proposals give us, they do not give us security. They multiply offences, but do nothing to strengthen remedies. They increase the responsibilities undertaken by individual Members of the League, but do nothing to readjust their burden.

What expedient remains? How is security and, above all, the feeling of security, to be attained? In answering this question it is necessary to keep in mind the characteristics of the "extreme cases," to which reference has already been made. The brooding fears that keep huge armaments in being have little relation to the ordinary misunderstandings inseparable from international (as from social) life—misunderstandings with which the League is so admirably fitted to deal. They spring from deep-lying causes of hostility which, for historic or other reasons, divide great and powerful States. These fears may be groundless; but if they exist they cannot be effectually laid by even the most perfect method of dealing with particular disputes by the machinery of enquiry and arbitration. For what is feared in such cases is not injustice but war—war deliberately undertaken for purposes of conquest or revenge. And, if so, can there be a better way of allaying fears like these than by adopting some scheme which should prove to all the world that such a war would fail?

Since the general provisions of the Covenant cannot be stiffened with advantage, and since the "extreme cases" with which the League may have to deal will probably affect certain nations or groups of nations more nearly than others, His Majesty's Government conclude that the best way of dealing with the situation is, with the co-operation of the League, to supplement the Covenant by making special arrangements in order to meet special needs. That these arrangements should be purely defensive in character, that they should be framed in the spirit of the Covenant, working in close harmony with the League and under its guidance, is manifest. And, in the opinion of His Majesty's Government, these objects can best be attained by knitting together the nations most immediately concerned, and whose differences might lead to a renewal of strife, by means of treaties framed with the sole object of maintaining, as between themselves, an unbroken peace. Within its limits no quicker remedy for our present ills can easily be found or any surer safeguard against future calamities.

That, gentlemen, is the declaration which His Majesty's Government have instructed me to make. . . .

38. Charter Provisions for Sanctions: Articles 25, 39, 41, 42, 43

CHARTER OF THE UNITED NATIONS

Article 25. The Members of the United Nations agree to accept and carry out the decisions of the Security Council in accordance with the present Charter.

CHAPTER VII. ACTION WITH RESPECT TO THREATS TO THE PEACE, BREACHES OF THE PEACE, AND ACTS OF AGGRESSION

Article 39. The Security Council shall determine the existence of any threat to the peace, breach of the peace, or act of aggression and shall make recommendations, or decide what measures shall be taken in accordance with Articles 41 and 42, to maintain or restore international peace and security.

Article 41. The Security Council may decide what measures not involving the use of armed force are to be employed to give effect to its decisions, and it may call upon the Members of the United Nations to apply such measures. These may include complete or partial interruption of economic relations and of rail, sea, air, postal, telegraphic, radio, and other means of communication, and the severance of diplomatic relations.

Charter of the United Nations together with the Statute of the International Court of Justice, signed at the United Nations Conference on International Organization, San Francisco, California, June 26, 1945, Department of State Publication 2353, Conference Series 74 (Washington, D.C.: Government Printing Office, 1945).

Article 42. Should the Security Council consider that measures provided for in Article 41 would be inadequate or have proved to be inadequate, it may take such action by air, sea, or land forces as may be necessary to maintain or restore international peace and security. Such action may include demonstrations, blockade, and other operations by air, sea, or land forces of Members of the United Nations.

Article 43. 1. All Members of the United Nations, in order to contribute to the maintenance of international peace and security, undertake to make available to the Security Council, on its call and in accordance with a special agreement or agreements, armed forces, assistance, and facilities, including rights of passage, necessary for the purpose of maintaining international peace and security.

2. Such agreement or agreements shall govern the numbers and types of forces, their degree of readiness and general location, and the nature of the facilities and assistance to be provided.

3. The agreement or agreements shall be negotiated as soon as possible on the initiative of the Security Council. They shall be concluded between the Security Council and Members or between the Security Council and groups of Members and shall be subject to ratification by the signatory states in accordance with their respective constitutional processes.

39. Why Article 43 Has Remained a Dead Letter

INIS L. CLAUDE, JR.

. . . It is not necessary to undertake the difficult task of determining whether the Soviet appraisal of Western motives was justified. What is more relevant is the suggestion that the Western powers reciprocated the Soviet mistrust. The evidence is less clear on the Western side, but it is plausible to interpret the proceedings as indicating that the United States and its friends were concerned to

Inis L. Claude, Jr., "The UN and the Use of Force," *International Conciliation,* No. 532, March, 1961, pp. 325-384, at pp. 353-355.

develop an arrangement under Article 43 which would minimize the danger that the Soviet Union could manipulate the projected enforcement system to extend its influence over other countries. According to this view, the Western powers were not so much conspiring to dominate United Nations enforcement actions as attempting to forestall the possibility that Soviet ground forces might be brought into troubled areas under United Nations auspices and used by their government to promote Soviet interests.[33] In these terms, each side regarded itself as reacting defensively to the other's ambition to dominate. From one perspective, the West was trying to "squeeze out" the Soviet Union, so as to use the United Nations mechanism for Western purposes; from the other, the Soviet Union was trying to "muscle in," so as to achieve control for itself. Each side appeared to the other to be jockeying for a position which would enable it to exploit the possibility of moving its armed forces abroad under United Nations auspices, but not for the ideal purposes of the United Nations.

In the final analysis, it would appear that the failure to create the mechanism for enforcement action envisaged in the United Nations Charter is attributable not to the unilateral opposition of the Soviet Union, but to the bilateral mistrust of the Soviet Union and of the Western bloc, led by the United States. It should be stressed that the difficulty in implementing Article 43 has *not* been a reluctance on the part of the United States or the Soviet Union to bear the "burden" of supporting United Nations military effort. Neither has been worried that the other would "shirk its duty"; on the contrary, each has been afraid that the other would insist upon participating in United Nations actions—and treat such participation as a privilege to be abused. The rival great powers have viewed the obligation of giving military support to the Security Council as an opportunity for their competitors to put their fingers into pies which ought to remain untouched—at least by their competitors.

This record suggests that the framers of the Charter were not excessively, but inadequately, cautious in estimating the possibilities of collective security in the postwar world. They acknowledged the

---

[33] See the analysis of the Soviet and American apprehensions in William Reitzel, Morton A. Kaplan, and Constance G. Coblenz, *United States Foreign Policy, 1945-1955* (Washington, The Brookings Institution, 1956), pp. 239-240.

reality that no collective enforcement scheme could operate safely and effectively against any of the great powers, and confined their ambition to the project of designing a scheme which would be operated jointly by the great powers. What they failed to anticipate was the development of a power struggle so bitter that it would render an enforcement scheme requiring the major powers to fight *with* each other as difficult to put into effect as one that might involve those powers in fighting *against* each other. The plan for a collective enforcement system of limited applicability has been aborted by precisely those difficulties; the United States and the Soviet Union have felt impelled to deny each other the chance to establish a foothold in troubled zones which might be provided by participation in collective action. Hence, the United Nations is equipped neither to suppress the aggression that might arise from a great-power split nor to utilize great-power solidarity for coping with other breaches of the peace.

40. The Particular Circumstances Prevailing

AUSTRALIAN REPRESENTATIVE

. . . 9. The Australian Government recognized the desirability of advance consideration of the problems involved in providing assistance and facilities to United Nations armed forces engaged in collective security measures, but held that any action taken under paragraphs of the joint draft resolution would have to be determined by governments in the light of particular circumstances prevailing.

10. His Government had also had under review for some time the matter of removing any obstacles to prompt action in support of collective measures. It believed, in the light of the immediate response which Australia had been able to make to the United Nations action in Korea, that no further action was required of

Statement of the Australian Representative, *General Assembly Official Records,* Sixth Session, First Committee, 476th Mtg., January 4, 1952, p. 122.

Australia at present, though it was intended to keep the matter under review.

11. He agreed generally with the principle of equitable sharing of economic burdens in relation to collective measures, dealt with in paragraph 5 of the joint draft resolution, but believed that the extent to which such sharing was in fact practicable and equitable should be determined in each case, as had been recognized in the Collective Measures Committee. . . .

41. The Special Position

VENEZUELAN REPRESENTATIVE

. . . 8. The special position of countries far removed from the theatre of operations and the need to develop their production of strategic materials, when circumstances so required, should likewise be considered.

9. The representative of Venezuela also stressed the importance of certain raw materials produced in Venezuela, such as petroleum and iron ore. The special position of countries producing such commodities would require further study, since the importance of their contribution to any international effort had not yet been exactly assessed. Mr. Gonzalez recalled the statement made in Washington in April 1951 by the Venezuelan Minister for Foreign Affairs who had said that in the event of international conflict Venezuela would spare no effort to defend its sources of production against any attempts at sabotage as well as against external attack. Although the report of the Collective Measures Committee dealt with the imposition of an embargo on exports of strategic materials, it dealt nowhere with the production of such materials for supply to a victim of aggression. Such production was, however, of undeniable military importance and the problems it raised should be further studied.

Statement of the Venezuelan Representative, *General Assembly Official Records,* Sixth Session, First Committee, 478th Mtg., January 3, 1952, p. 130.

10. In those circumstances, the Government of Venezuela wished to state that Venezuela would be obliged to pay very special attention to the defence of its own territory and that it could only despatch forces to neighbouring territories in specific cases and subject to agreement.

11. In conclusion, the representative of Venezuela said that the members of the Collective Measures Committee had been guided by the view that aggression should be discouraged before it took place. Nevertheless, the United Nations must be in a position to assist, where necessary, the victim of aggression and to repel the aggressor. Mr. Gonzalez expressed the hope that the eleven-Power draft resolution (A/C.1/676) would receive the support of a majority of the members of the First Committee. . . .

42. Mediation and Sanctions

INDONESIAN REPRESENTATIVE

. . . 18. The Indonesian delegation believed that situations might arise wherein it would feel quite justified in opposing the application of collective measures and in adopting a mediator's role, preferably in co-operation, so far as possible, with other countries. Indonesia would of course always seize the opportunity to abide by any resolution adopted by the General Assembly, as it had shown by its compliance with the embargo imposed by the General Assembly on trade with China, although it had abstained from voting on that question.

19. The Indonesian delegation supported the purposes and principles set out in the preamble of the eleven-Power draft resolution. With regard to the sixth paragraph of the preamble, Indonesia had no constitutional machinery enabling it to maintain elements within its national armed forces which could be made available for United Nations service. Furthermore, its armed forces were for the moment essential for maintaining order within the country. Again, Indonesia

Statement of the Indonesian Representative, *General Assembly Official Records,* Sixth Session, First Committee, 478th Mtg., January 3, 1952, p. 130.

would not be able to comply with the recommendations in paragraphs 2, 3, 4, and 5 of the operative part until it had the necessary constitutional machinery. . . .

43. Sanctions and Domestic Law

MEXICAN REPRESENTATIVE

. . . The present text had the very serious drawback that it claimed to impose on Member States at least a moral obligation to review their legislation, both constitutional and ordinary, so as to ensure the prompt and effective implementation of the collective measures of the United Nations. The intention appeared to be that Member States should make ready to amend their laws with that object in view. Such an obligation could not be accepted by the Mexican Government which regarded the amendment of its laws as a sovereign right not liable to subordination or compromise of any sort. . . .

Statement of the Mexican Representative, *General Assembly Official Records,* Sixth Session, First Committee, 480th Mtg., January 4, 1952, p. 141.

THAT WORLD POLITICS PERMITS SANCTIONS

44. The Problem Stated

SAMUEL HOARE

Ever since I have been at the Foreign Office I have been obsessed with the urgency of two grave issues. Day in and day out I have

Sir Samuel Hoare, House of Commons, *Hansard,* Vol. 307, December 19, 1935, coll. 2003-2012, at coll. 2007-2010.

been obsessed with the urgent necessity of doing everything in my power to prevent a European conflagration. Secondly, I have been no less obsessed with the urgent duty of doing everything in my power to avoid an isolated war between Great Britain and Italy. I believe that those two grave issues were two of the issues that were mainly in the minds of the electors at the last Election, the fear, on the one hand, of a general European conflagration; the fear, on the other hand, of isolated war between Great Britain and Italy. When the Election came to an end, war had already been in progress for some weeks. We had done our best to stop its outbreak. I, myself, had done everything within my power to mobilise world opinion against it at the Assembly at Geneva. In spite of our efforts the war broke out, and every day that it continued it involved the world in greater and more dangerous problems. There was trouble in the East; there was trouble in Egypt; there was trouble brewing in more than one quarter of Europe; and, not least, there was the depressing fact that the war seemed to be compromising British relations with a large body of public opinion in France.

It must have been clear to every hon. Member that the threat of war and the outbreak of war had raised very difficult questions between ourselves and France. It must have been obvious to every hon. Member that a great body of opinion in France was intensely nervous of a breach with Italy, and intensely nervous of anything that was likely to weaken French defence. In view of those facts, I did everything in my power to make a settlement possible, and while loyally continuing a policy of sanctions and coercive action—I do not think anyone can charge me with any hesitation in pushing that policy both here and at Geneva—I never allowed a day to pass without attempting by some means or another to find a peaceful settlement to this hateful controversy. That was the position after the Election. We were engaged upon our double task of taking our full share in collective action and also with that other task imposed upon us by the League itself of trying to find a basis of settlement of this unfortunate dispute. Particularly was I concentrating upon the second of those two tasks in view of the situation that I saw inevitably developing before me in the immediate future.

In both these fields, in both the field of collective action and also in the field of peaceful negotiations, we reached a turning point about a fortnight ago. The turning point came sooner than many of us expected. Perhaps it came as a result of the success of the sanctions that had already been imposed and the collective front that, I am glad to say, had been created at Geneva. In any case, about a fortnight ago it was clear that a new situation was about to be created by the question of the oil embargo. It seemed clear that, supposing an oil embargo were to be imposed and that the non-member States took an effective part in it, the oil embargo might have such an effect upon the hostilities as to force their termination. Just because of the effectiveness of the oil sanction, provided that the non-member States had a full part in it, the situation immediately became more dangerous from the point of view of Italian resistance. From all sides we received reports that no responsible Government could disregard that Italy would regard the oil embargo as a military sanction or an act involving war against her. Let me make our position quite clear. We had no fear as a nation whatever of any Italian threats. If the Italians attacked us we should retaliate, and, judging from our past history, we should retaliate with full success. What was in our mind was something very different, that an isolated attack of this kind launched upon one Power without it may be—and I shall refer to this subject again in a minute—without it may be the full support of the other Powers, would, it seemed to me, almost inevitably lead to the dissolution of the League.

It was in these circumstances 10 days ago that I went to Paris. I did not want to go to Paris. I was in urgent need of a period of rest, but, apart from that fact, I dislike intensely the practice of the Foreign Minister leaving this country and conducting negotiations in a foreign capital. None the less, I was pressed on all sides to go, and I was pressed in such a way as to make refusal impossible. It was in an atmosphere of threatened war that the conversations began, and it was in an atmosphere in which the majority of the member States—indeed, I would say the totality of the member States—appeared to be opposed to military action. It was a moment of great urgency. Within five days the question of the oil embargo was to come up at Geneva, and I did not feel myself justified in proposing any postponement of the embargo, unless it could be shown to the League that negotiations had actually started.

It was a moment when, while most member States had taken a part in the economic sanctions, no member State except ourselves had taken any military precautions.

Lastly, it was a moment when it seemed to me that Anglo-French co-operation was essential if there was to be no breach at Geneva and if the sanctions when functioning were not to be destroyed. For two days M. Laval and I discussed the basis of a possible negotiation. We were not discussing terms to be imposed upon the belligerents. We were discussing proposals that might bring the two parties into the same room and that might make subsequent negotiation possible. The proposals that emerged from those discussions were not French proposals or British proposals in the sense that we liked them. Neither M. Laval nor I liked many features of them. But that basis did seem to us to be the only basis upon which it was even remotely likely that we could at least start a peace discussion. It was certainly the minimum basis upon which the French Government were prepared to proceed, and this minimum was only reached after two days of strenuous discussion. So far as I myself was concerned it seemed to me to be so important to start a negotiation, even if it had to be on this basis that, much as I disliked some features of the scheme, I could not withhold my provisional assent. I felt that the issues were so grave and the dangers of the continuance of the war were so serious that it was worth making an attempt, and that it was essential to maintain Anglo-French solidarity. . . .

45. The Setting at Geneva

WILLIAM E. RAPPARD

. . . Such then was the moral climate in Geneva on the morrow of Italy's premeditated attack upon a helpless African State which,

William E. Rappard, *The Quest for Peace* (Cambridge: Harvard University Press, 1940), pp. 297-298. Reprinted by permission.

with her support, had become her fellow-member in the League of Nations twelve years before. The violation of the Covenant was so flagrant that the question, once frankly put to the Council and to the Assembly by the aggrieved party, could only be answered in the affirmative. Moreover, in contrast to the previous case of the almost equally flagrant breach of the Covenant by Japan, it was one which, on purely geographical and strategic grounds, was clearly susceptible of a successful solution by concerted action on the part of the law-abiding Members of the League. Had they been unanimously and unqualifiedly determined to carry out their full obligations under Article 16, Italy's capitulation would have been certain. A complete economic blockade and the severance by naval means, if necessary, of Italy's communications with her troops in the far-off theater of operations beyond the Suez Canal could have had no other result. This was especially so as the United States had made it clear to all within and without Italy that, from that quarter, the League would not have been exposed to any interference and might indeed have enjoyed some measure of support in any legal action it might have undertaken in favor of Ethiopia.

On the other hand Japan and Germany were no longer Members of the League and would doubtless have looked upon its success with more displeasure than satisfaction. Furthermore France was most reluctant to forfeit the good will of Italy, to whom she had recently made important and ill-defined concessions in Africa. This good will seemed all the more precious to France as Germany, under Herr Hitler's aggressive leadership, was fast becoming a menace to her security. Great Britain, in spite of the relatively weak position to which her policies of disarmament had reduced her navy, was still supreme in the Mediterranean. This supremacy, however, was no longer unchallenged and she was unwilling to assert it unless assured of complete French support. As this support was not forthcoming, Great Britain, and with her all the other loyal Members of the League, felt, if not unable, at least unwilling to do more than to bring a certain measure of pressure to bear on Italy. Had Italy been completely isolated or had she been governed by a weak or by a truly pacific government, this would doubtless have sufficed to bring about a negotiated settlement with Ethiopia. As it was, the action of the League, sufficiently unfriendly to arouse the national pride of the Fascist Kingdom, yet insufficiently drastic and determined to deter her daring but realistic leader from the undertaking on which he had set his heart, hastened rather than impeded the conquest of Ethiopia. . . .

THAT OVERWHELMING STRENGTH SUPPORTS SANCTIONS

46. It Is Very Difficult

ANTHONY EDEN

. . . So I come to the present-day situation in the Far East. I am really not trying to make debating points, but to discover what it is we are supposed to be failing to do which is going to have this remarkable result for the world. We were told that in the Far East to-day we ought to be upholding the rule of law. Both the Leader of the Opposition and the right hon. Gentleman who has just spoken asked what we were doing to uphold the rule of law. Here I want to say something frankly in the same terms as the right hon. Gentleman the Member for Caithness (Sir A. Sinclair). If hon. Members opposite are advocating sanctions by the League—they have not said so, but I am supposing that is what they meant—if they think the League ought to impose sanctions in the present dispute in the Far East, I would remind them that there are two possible forms of sanctions—the ineffective, which are not worth putting on, and the effective, which means the risk, if not the

Statement of the Secretary for Foreign Affairs, Anthony Eden, *Hansard,* December 21, 1937, coll. 1882-1883.

certainty, of war. I say deliberately that nobody could contemplate any action of that kind in the Far East unless they are convinced that they have overwhelming force to back their policy.

Do right hon. Gentlemen opposite really think that the League of Nations to-day, with only two great naval Powers in it, ourselves and France, have got that overwhelming force? It must be perfectly clear to everyone that that overwhelming force does not exist. [*Interruption.*] Will the hon. Member allow me to develop my argument? Every nation at Geneva from the beginning of this dispute knows perfectly well that the very thought of action of any kind in the Far East must depend on the co-operation of other nations besides those who are actually members of the League at this time. . . .

47. Under Conditions of Bipolarity?

INIS L. CLAUDE, JR.

. . . Closely related to the revolution in military technology is the phenomenon of bipolarization. While it is by no means the case that the Soviet Union and the United States have emerged as the only significant states in world politics, or that the clustering of the world's states around these two centers has been either completely or definitively accomplished, or that a dualistic pattern of international politics can be confidently predicted for the future, it is evident that the period since World War II has been marked by the military predominance of these two giants. The diffusion of power among a number of major states, along with a congeries of minor states, a condition which is requisite to the effective operation of a collective security system, has at least temporarily disappeared. Given such a pattern of power distribution as existed a generation ago, it was possible to conceive that any member of the state system might be so overwhelmingly outclassed by the combined power of all or most of the other members that it could not expect to carry off an aggressive enterprise against their collective opposition. Collective security assumes a world in which every state is so vulnerable to collective sanctions that no state is free to commit aggression. This is certainly not the situation which has prevailed in the post-World War II period. In this era, neither the Soviet Union nor the United States exhibits such vulnerability. Each possesses such a great percentage of the world's military power as to make the mobilization of an overwhelming preponderance of power against either inherently impossible; either might be defeated, but neither could be decisively outclassed by the power which might be assembled by a collective security organization. A collective security operation directed against the Soviet Union or the United States would be a major war, not a device for preventing such a war. Collective security promised a system in which states could prevent the outbreak of all-out war by the collective intimidation of any violator of the peace; the day in which that promise could be fulfilled has passed. . . .

[IV]

The Justification of International Concern and Response to Aggression

At what point does a situation become of international concern as a threat to the peace or as an act of aggression justifying international concern and response, including collective security measures?

This problem breaks down into two broad sections: *the identification of a situation* calling for international concern, discussion, and action; and *the identification of the peacebreaker* against whom action may justifiably be taken.

IDENTIFICATION OF A SITUATION

Justifiable international concern and international action by a collective security organization hinge on whether a particular situation has international results of a certain nature. In other words, a domestic situation is excluded from the reach of international organizations, unless it presents a threat to the peace. In some instances, the distinction between "domestic" and "international" is easy enough to make, as in the case of the Nazi attack on Poland in 1939, in instances of complaints by a government against outside threats to its security, or the like.

In modern times the line between domestic and international is being shifted by new developments toward an increasingly broader interpretation of the international at the expense of the domestic. Thus, for example, the placement of Soviet missiles in Cuba in 1962 drew the most urgent international response from the United

States, which felt that the nature of the missiles made the arming of Cuba a threat to United States security and therefore not solely a matter for Cuban domestic concern. In another field, the majority of the United Nations has decided on an ever-broadening concept of a common concern in the field of human rights. It is probable that no final solution or demarcation can ever be expected, as each period will find its own answers to this question.

1. *Is internal subversion directed from the outside a proper subject for international concern?*

This question is discussed in Reading 48.

2. *Is suppression of human rights a proper subject for international concern and, if so, for what kind of international action?*

This question has been much debated in the past. At the San Francisco Conference in 1945, for example, with the memories of Nazi outrages still vividly fresh, the French Delegation introduced an amendment to the Dumbarton Oaks proposals designed to except from domestic jurisdiction certain human rights matters. The amendment, which was not accepted, ran as follows:

> . . . the international jurisdiction should not apply to situations or disputes arising out of matters which by international law are solely within the domestic jurisdiction of the state concerned, *unless the clear violation of essential liberties and of human rights constitutes in itself a threat capable of compromising peace.*[1]

The question has remained one of interest, rising to a new crescendo in connection with United Nations consideration of problems raised by the *apartheid* policy followed by the Union of South Africa. Readings 49, 50, and 51 deal with various reactions to the question here posed.

Secretary-General U Thant expressed the view of the majority of the United Nations in Reading 49, in which he adopted a broad view of international jurisdiction in human rights matters.

---

[1] Amendments proposed by the French Government to the Proposals Relative to the Establishment of a General International Organization, *Documents of the United Nations Conference on International Organization,* San Francisco, 1945, Vol. III, Dumbarton Oaks Proposals, Comments and Proposed Amendments, 1945, p. 386.

The view discussed in Reading 50 by the French representative to the United Nations is no longer held by the French government but states a position of continuing interest.

If international concern is justified in the *apartheid* situation, the further question arises of what concrete steps are justified under the provisions of the Charter of the United Nations. The mood of the majority is toward the application of ever-broadening sanctions. Ambassador Adlai Stevenson of the United States discusses in Reading 51 whether it was the intent of the Charter to apply Chapter VII to such a situation.

How does the Charter of the United Nations attempt to set the boundaries in this question? The pertinent Articles are set forth in Reading 52.

How has the distinction between the authority of states and the authority of the United Nations with respect to the maintenance of international peace and security been drawn in practice? A United States representative to the General Assembly, Francis T. P. Plimpton, in Reading 53, discusses the intent of the Charter and its interpretation through practice.

IDENTIFICATION OF THE PEACEBREAKER

In addition to identifying the specific instances which justify international concern and response, international organizations charged with keeping the peace also have to determine against whom collective security measures should be taken. Since there are very few clear-cut examples of aggression, such as Hitler's attack on Poland in 1939 or the North Korean attack on South Korea in 1950, the answer to this question only *seems* obvious. Given the nature of international conflict, the way in which it may build up through provocation and response on both sides, and the often unequal power relationship between the contenders, it may actually be extremely difficult to determine which state is the aggressor and which acting in self-defense and it may even be irrelevant to seek to determine which state was in the right and which in the wrong.

Nevertheless, an international collective security or peace-keeping organization must be able to make some determinations as to the nature of a conflict in order to be able to act. In the League of Nations period, emphasis was placed on seeking to define aggression and the aggressor state; this search, which was not crowned with striking success, has continued to some extent under the United Nations. However, impressed by the League's lack of success, the drafters of the Charter deliberately fashioned a broad formula for United Nations action, putting it in the framework of a "breach of the peace, threat to the peace, or act of aggression."

Under the League, then, the search was for a neat definition, ahead of time, of the aggressor; under the United Nations, the Security Council is given the different mandate of determining whether a certain type of situation exists, within which a definition of aggression may or may not be relevant.

1. *Identifying the aggressor by procedural test.*

Under this test, the aggressor is that state which first violates a set procedure for peaceful settlement. Tending to avoid the thorny question of the right and the wrong of a particular dispute, the test was seen as a reliable, clear, diagnostic tool. The major efforts to translate this test into a general international obligation came in the 1920's, especially in the Geneva Protocol of 1924, and in the Convention to Improve the Means of Preventing War of 1931, both unratified. Professor Quincy Wright, in Reading 54, discusses this attempt.

2. *Identifying the aggressor by the "first use of force" test.*

This test identified the aggressor as that state which first uses physical force against another state. This misleadingly simple definition of aggression has been most prominently though not entirely consistently sponsored by the Soviet Union. Thus, the definition advanced by Soviet representative P. D. Morozov before the Legal Committee of the General Assembly in 1952 (Reading 55) reminds one of Maxim Litvinov's famous definition before the Disarmament Conference in 1933 and of later Soviet proposals as well. In such a definition, the attempt is made to list ahead of time certain acts which would identify as an aggressor the state which first performed them. It is important to try to think through just how such a definition could be applied in the case of an actual developing conflict between two states, one of them perhaps much weaker than the other.

The effort to define aggression ahead of time and to provide more or less automatic identification of the aggressor raises certain basic doubts: Can such identification work and be fair, in the absence of obligatory international law, of an international police force, and of significant provisions for peaceful change? Under existing conditions, how can the line be drawn ahead of time between aggression and legitimate self-defense? If it fears for its national existence, especially in the age of nuclear weapons, can a state afford to wait for the first overt act of aggression on the part of a hostile power or neighbor?

A criticism in general terms of efforts to define aggression ahead of time was made by Jean Spiropoulos, a Greek international lawyer, speaking as a member of the Sixth Committee of the General Assembly (Reading 56).

The difficulty of identifying any one act as the act of aggression was clearly illustrated in the debates on the Middle Eastern crisis of 1956, in which the General Assembly avoided any determination of aggression, or breach of the Charter for that matter. In presenting his government's case before the General Assembly, Mr. Abba Eban of Israel illustrated this point in the practical terms of national security and even survival (Reading 57).

3. *In the age of nuclear weapons, is the attempt to define an aggressor ahead of time relevant?*

Inis L. Claude, Jr., discusses the question in Reading 58.

PRIOR DEFINITION OF THE PEACEBREAKER

4. *Is a definition of aggression an essential prerequisite for collective security measures?*

In his report to the President on the results of the San Francisco Conference in 1945, Secretary of State Edward R. Stettinius explained the decision of the Conference not to define acts of aggression and to leave the Security Council the freedom to make its own decision (Reading 59).

IDENTIFICATION OF A SITUATION

48. An Inter-American Conclusion

OAS COMMITTEE

A

In formulating its conclusions, the committee considers it pertinent to make some general observations on the policy of intervention in the hemisphere of the present Government of Cuba, which has been substantiated in the investigation of the charges made by Venezuela:

1. The present Government of Cuba since its institution in 1959 has carried on, supported, and directed in various ways a policy of intervention in the hemisphere through propaganda methods, provision of funds, training in sabotage and guerrilla operations, and the supply of arms to support those movements that seek to subvert national institutions through force in order to install communist regimes.

2. This support of subversion, which generally takes the form of political aggression, has had positive application in the Republic of Venezuela, the primary objective in Cuba's policy of expansion and ideological penetration in the hemisphere. The vast natural resources of Venezuela, its strategic importance in the hemisphere, and its status as a democratic country were factors that motivated the present Government of Cuba to make use of the subversive action of organizations that employ force and violence to overthrow that democratic government.

B

1. The Republic of Venezuela has been the target of a series of actions sponsored and directed by the Government of Cuba, openly

Report of the Investigating Committee Appointed by the Council of the Organization of American States, Acting Provisionally as an Organ of Consultation, OEA/Ser.G/IV,C-i-658, February 18, 1964, Council of the OAS, Pan American Union, Washington, D.C., pp. 35-37.

intended to subvert Venezuelan institutions and to overthrow the democratic Government of Venezuela through terrorism, sabotage, assault, and guerrilla warfare.

2. A characteristic manifestation of this policy of aggression has been the systematic and hostile propaganda campaign carried out through information organs that are under the control of the Government of Cuba and that are directed against Venezuelan institutions, the President of the Republic, and other high government officials, inciting the people of Venezuela to rebellion and, in addition, giving direct support to subversive movements.

3. Other manifestations of this policy of aggression are found in the supply of funds and the indoctrination and training in Cuba of numerous Venezuelans who later returned to their country to participate in subversive movements.

4. An important element in this intervention in Venezuela, directed by the Government of Cuba, was the shipment of arms that was found on the Peninsula of Paraguaná in the State of Falcón on November 1, 1963, close to the date of the general elections. The shipment was made up of arms originating in Cuba that were surreptitiously landed at a solitary spot on the coast, for the purpose of being used in subversive operations to overthrow the constitutional Government of Venezuela. . . .

5. The policy of aggression on the part of the Government of Cuba was confirmed by the discovery on November 4, 1963, by Venezuelan authorities, of a plan of operations, the "Caracas Plan," prepared for the subversive action of the so-called "Armed Forces of National Liberation." This plan anticipated the use of arms similar in type and numerical proportion to the shipment of arms mentioned in the preceding paragraph. The objective of the plan was to capture the city of Caracas, to prevent the holding of elections on December 1, 1963, and to seize control of the country.

6. Consequently, the acts of intervention that have been outlined, and, in particular, the shipment of arms, constitute a policy of aggression on the part of the present Government of Cuba against the territorial integrity, the political sovereignty, and the stability of the democratic institutions of Venezuela.

49. A Source of Conflict

U THANT

. . . There is clear prospect that racial conflict, if we cannot curb and finally eliminate it, will grow into a destructive monster compared to which the religious or ideological conflicts of the past will seem like small family quarrels. Such a conflict will eat away the possibilities for good of all that mankind has hitherto achieved and reduce men to the lowest and most bestial level of intolerance and hatred. This . . . must not be permitted to happen. . . .

The disease [of racial discrimination], however, must be treated as a most dangerous form of sickness rather than as a reason for retaliation and violence—that is, with restraint, with the greatest care and with the firm belief that racists are human beings, albeit mentally ill, who must be rescued and cured from the affliction that they sometimes do not even recognize. The ailment must be diagnosed, its course noted, its virulence isolated, prescribed for and all possible cures tried. Otherwise hate will breed hate and violence will breed violence in a disastrous and vicious circle. . . .

Address before the Algerian National Assembly, February 4, 1964, UN Press Rel. SG/SN/3/Rev/1, as quoted in Amelia C. Leiss, editor, *Apartheid and United Nations Collective Measures* (New York: Carnegie Endowment for International Peace, 1965), p. 162.

50. A Minority View of Interest

FRENCH REPRESENTATIVE

. . . 117. The policy practised by the government of any Member State towards its own nationals, within its own frontiers, is an intrinsic part of the sovereign rights reserved for the jurisdiction of

Statement of the French Representative, *General Assembly Official Records,* Seventh Session, 401st Pl. Mtg., December 5, 1952, p. 335.

each State and jealously safeguarded against even the best intentioned incursions by the organized collectivity of the other members of the international community. By committing one violation of those rights, no matter how important the particular case may be, the United Nations collectively commits a breach of the Charter and at the same time endangers the security of each Member.

118. None of us can disregard that inescapable consequence nor pretend momentarily to forget it to satisfy a particular concern. No matter how essential the isolated stake in a given question may appear to some of us, our Assembly cannot allow itself to lose sight of the more general and higher stake involved in the final paragraph of Chapter I of the Charter. . . .

51. The Intent of the Charter

ADLAI E. STEVENSON

. . . First, we have affirmed and reaffirmed that *apartheid* is abhorrent. Our belief in the self-evident truths about human equality is enshrined in the Charter. *Apartheid* and racism, despite all of the tortured rationalizations that we have heard from the apologists, are incompatible with the moral, social, and constitutional foundations of our societies.

A second basic principle on which we are agreed is that all Members of the Organization have pledged themselves to take action, in co-operation with the Organization, to promote observance of human rights, without distinction as to race.

Thirdly, we continue to believe that this matter is of proper and legitimate concern to the United Nations. We have often stated, in the General Assembly, our belief that the Assembly can properly consider questions of racial discrimination and other violations of human rights where they are a Member's official policy and are inconsistent with the obligations of that Member, under Articles

Security Council, 1052nd Mtg., August 2, 1963, S/PV/1052, pp. 33-38.

55 and 56 of the Charter, to promote observance of human rights, without distinction as to race.

Moreover, the *apartheid* policy of South Africa has clearly led to a situation the continuance of which is likely to endanger international peace and security. We also believe that all Members, in the words of the resolution passed almost unanimously by the sixteenth General Assembly, should take such separate and collective action to bring about an abandonment of *apartheid* as is open to them in conformity with the Charter.

The United States supported that resolution and has complied with it.

I should like to take this occasion to bring up to date the record of the measures the United States has taken to carry out this purpose. First, we have continued and indeed have accelerated our official representations to the Government of South Africa on all aspects of *apartheid* in that country. We have done this through public words and private diplomacy, expressing our earnest hope that the South African Government would take steps to reconsider and to revise its racial policies and to extend the full range of civic rights and opportunities to non-whites in the life of their country. And we have observed to the South African Government that in the absence of an indication of change, the United States would not co-operate in matters that would lend support to South Africa's present racial policies.

We have utilized our diplomatic and our consular establishments in South Africa to demonstrate by words and by deeds our official disapproval of *apartheid* and, as the United States representative informed the Special Political Committee of the General Assembly on 19 October last, the United States has adopted and is enforcing the policy of forbidding the sale to the South African Government of arms and military equipment whether from government or commercial sources, which could be used by that Government to enforce *apartheid* either in South Africa or in the Administration of South West Africa. We have carefully screened both government and commercial shipments of military equipment to make sure that this policy is rigorously enforced.

But I am now authorized to inform the Security Council of still another important step which my Government is prepared to take.

We expect to bring to an end the sale of all military equipment to the Government of South Africa by the end of this calendar year, in order further to contribute to a peaceful solution and to avoid any steps which might at this point directly contribute to international friction in the area. There are existing contracts which provide for limited quantities of strategic equipment for defence against external threats, such as air-to-air missiles and torpedoes for submarines. We must honour these contracts. The Council should be aware that in announcing this policy the United States, as a nation with many responsibilities in many parts of the world, naturally reserves the right in the future to interpret this policy in the light of requirements for assuring the maintenance of international peace and security.

If the interests of the world community require the provision of equipment for use in the common defence effort, we would naturally feel able to do so without violating the spirit and the intent of this resolution. We are taking this further step to indicate the deep concern which the Government of the United States feels at the failure of the Republic of South Africa to abandon its policy of *apartheid*. In pursuing this policy the Republic of South Africa, as we have so often said, is failing to discharge its obligations under Articles 55 and 56 of the Charter whereby Members pledge themselves "to take joint and separate action in co-operation" with our Organization for the achievement, among other things, of:

> universal respect for, and observance of, human rights and fundamental freedoms for all without distinction as to race, sex, language, or religion.

Stopping the sale of arms to South Africa emphasizes our hope that the Republic will now reassess its attitude towards *apartheid* in the light of the constantly growing international concern at its failure to heed the numerous appeals made to it by various organs of the United Nations, as well as appeals of Member States such as my Government.

As to the action of this Council in this proceeding, we are prepared to consult with other members and with the African Foreign Ministers present at the table and we will have some suggestions to make. It is clear to my delegation that the application of sanctions under Chapter VII in the situation now before us would be both bad law and bad policy. It would be bad law because the extreme measures provided in Chapter VII were never intended and cannot reasonably be interpreted to apply to situations of this kind. The founders of the United Nations were very careful to reserve the right of the Organization to employ mandatory coercive measures in situations where there was an actuality of international violence or such a clear and present threat to the peace as to leave no reasonable alternative but resort to coercion.

We do not have that kind of a situation here. Fortunately for all of us, there is still some time to work out a solution through measures of pacific settlement, and any solution adopted by this Council must be reasonably calculated to promote such settlement. It is bad policy because the application of sanctions in this situation is not likely to bring about the practical result that we seek, that is, the abandonment of *apartheid*. Far from encouraging the beginning of a dialogue between the Government of South Africa and its African population, punitive measures would only provoke intransigence and harden the existing situation. Furthermore, the result of the adoption of such measures, particularly if compliance is not widespread and sincere, would create doubts about the validity of and diminish respect for the authority of the United Nations and the efficacy of the sanction process envisioned in the Charter. . . .

52. Boundaries Defined by the Charter: Articles 2, 11, 24, 34, 39

CHARTER OF THE UNITED NATIONS

Article 2. Domestic Jurisdiction. 7. Nothing contained in the present Charter shall authorize the United Nations to intervene

Charter of the United Nations together with the Statute of the International Court of Justice, signed at the United Nations Conference on International Organization, San Francisco, California, June 26, 1945, Department of State Publication 2353, Conference Series 74 (Washington, D.C.: Government Printing Office, 1945).

in matters which are essentially within the domestic jurisdiction of any state or shall require the Members to submit such matters to settlement under the present Charter; but this principle shall not prejudice the application of enforcement measures under Chapter VII.

GENERAL ASSEMBLY.

Article 11. 1. The General Assembly may consider the general principles of cooperation in the maintenance of international peace and security, including the principles governing disarmament and the regulation of armaments, and may make recommendations with regard to such principles to the Members or to the Security Council or to both.

2. The General Assembly may discuss any questions relating to the maintenance of international peace and security brought before it by any Member of the United Nations, or by the Security Council, or by a state which is not a Member of the United Nations in accordance with Article 35, paragraph 2, and, except as provided in Article 12, may make recommendations with regard to any such questions to the state or states concerned or to the Security Council or to both. Any such question on which action is necessary shall be referred to the Security Council by the General Assembly either before or after discussion.

3. The General Assembly may call the attention of the Security Council to situations which are likely to endanger international peace and security.

4. The powers of the General Assembly set forth in this Article shall not limit the general scope of Article 10.

SECURITY COUNCIL.

Article 24. 1. In order to ensure prompt and effective action by the United Nations, its Members confer on the Security Council primary responsibility for the maintenance of international peace and security, and agree that in carrying out its duties under this responsibility the Security Council acts on their behalf.

2. In discharging these duties the Security Council shall act in accordance with the Purposes and Principles of the United Nations. The specific powers granted to the Security Council for the dis-

charge of these duties are laid down in Chapters VI, VII, VIII, and XII.

3. The Security Council shall submit annual and, when necessary, special reports to the General Assembly for its consideration.

CHAPTER VI.

Article 34. The Security Council may investigate any dispute, or any situation which might lead to international friction or give rise to a dispute, in order to determine whether the continuance of the dispute or situation is likely to endanger the maintenance of international peace and security.

CHAPTER VII.

Article 39. The Security Council shall determine the existence of any threat to the peace, breach of the peace, or act of aggression and shall make recommendations, or decide what measures shall be taken, in accordance with Articles 41 and 42, to maintain or restore international peace and security.

53. The Intent of the Charter: Interpretation through Practice

FRANCIS T. P. PLIMPTON

. . . In any event, in the area of most immediate concern, namely, the maintenance of international peace and security, it is clear that the provisions of the charter have placed within the international sphere the full competence necessary for effective action by United Nations organs. In becoming parties to the charter, the members of the organization have assumed the obligations contemplated in

Francis T. P. Plimpton, "Principles of International Law Concerning Friendly Relations and Cooperation Among States: International Law and Non-intervention," *Department of State Bulletin,* January 27, 1964, pp. 133-143, at p. 140.

paragraphs 3, 4, and 5 of article 2. Matters relating to those provisions could, accordingly, not lie essentially within the domestic jurisdiction of states.

Thus the Security Council acts with regard to disputes or situations whose continuance is likely to endanger the maintenance of international peace and security, under chapter VI. It also acts with regard to threats to the peace, breaches of the peace, and acts of aggression, under chapter VII. The General Assembly may discuss and make recommendations as to any questions or matters within the scope of the charter, as stated in article 10, except that, while the Security Council is exercising its functions in respect of a dispute or situation, the General Assembly, as provided in article 12, may not make any recommendations as to that dispute or situation unless the Council requests. Neither organ, acting within the scope of its assigned competence under the charter, may intervene in matters essentially within the domestic jurisdiction of states. The authors of the charter recognized this rule. The *rapporteur* of Committee 1 of Commission I at San Francisco observed that "Both the rule and the exception can be looked upon as being really implicit in any organization which is genuinely *international* in character."[9]

Recognition of the fact that a matter cannot lie essentially within the domestic jurisdiction of a state if it, or its continuation, would be likely, in the words of chapter VI, article 33, to endanger the maintenance of international peace and security has received repeated reaffirmation in the practice of the United Nations from its earliest years. The organization has, on a number of occasions, dealt with questions which might, under other circumstances, have been considered essentially within the domestic jurisdiction of the state concerned. Objections to competence have been rejected, the organ concerned basing its actions on its responsibility for keeping the peace. It need not be added that the determination of whether a matter is likely to endanger the maintenance of international peace and security is an important question, which must be answered, in good faith, with a regard for the facts. Merely saying

[9] United Nations Conference on International Organization, *Documents,* vol. 6, p. 487.

that a matter is likely to endanger the maintenance of international peace and security, or in the words of chapter VII, article 39, is a threat to the peace does not in fact make it so. Here, too, loose and emotional usage could weaken the credit and creditability of the organization's holdings—could debase the currency of international confidence which the organization must maintain. . . .

IDENTIFICATION OF THE PEACEBREAKER

54. Aggressor Identification by Procedural Test

QUINCY WRIGHT

. . . The determination of aggression, or resort to violence contrary to international obligations, seems at first sight to present difficulties because of the possibility that a government may provoke its intended victim to strike the first blow or may compel such a victim to first cross a frontier as a defensive necessity, and because of the difficulty of assembling evidence at the place where hostilities begin and of weighing such evidence in the highly charged atmosphere of war. The problem cannot be solved unless it is divorced from the problem of determining the merits of the dispute. The problem of aggression does not concern the nature of grievances but the method of dealing with them. There are, however, a wide variety of methods for settling disputes and every dispute has many aspects. Only one of these methods, resort to armed force, constitutes aggression, but it does so if utilized in connection with any aspect of the dispute or at any stage of the procedure. Thus, neither determination

Quincy Wright, "Peace and Political Organization," in *Preliminary Report and Monographs,* Commission to Study the Organization of Peace, *International Conciliation,* No. 369, April, 1941, pp. 454-467, at p. 459.

of the merits, nor determination of the party willing to submit certain aspects of the controversy to some form of pacific settlement, bears directly on the problem of determining which government resorted to force contrary to its obligation. The experience of the League of Nations has indicated that the aggressor can usually be determined if, as soon as the crisis becomes dangerous, an international body, vested with adequate legal powers, such as were to be conferred on the League by the unratified convention to improve the means of preventing war signed in 1931, invite the disputing governments to observe interim or conservatory measures, such as armistice and troop withdrawals from stated areas. The government which rejects such measures or fails to observe them can ordinarily be ascertained by international observers on the spot and can properly be considered the aggressor. . . .

55. Aggressor Identification by "First Use of Force" Test

P. D. MOROZOV

. . . In an international conflict that State should be declared the attacker which first committed one of the following acts:

(*a*) Declaration of war against another State;

(*b*) Invasion by its armed forces, even without a declaration of war, of the territory of another State;

(*c*) Bombardment by its land, sea or air forces of the territory, or deliberately attacking the ships or aircraft, of another State;

(*d*) The landing or penetration of its land, sea or air forces inside the boundaries of another State without the permission of the Government of the latter, or the violation of the conditions of such permission, particularly as regards the length of their stay or the extent of the area in which they might stay;

General Assembly Official Records, Sixth Session, Sixth Committee, 278th Mtg., January 5, 1952, p. 150.

(*e*) Naval blockade of the coasts or ports of another State;

(*f*) Support of armed bands organized in its own territory which invaded the territory of another State, or refusal, on being requested by the invaded State, to take in its own territory any action within its power to deny such bands any aid or protection.

34. Those proposals stated expressly that aggression could not be justified by any arguments of a political, strategic or economic nature, or by the desire to exploit natural resources in the territory of the State attacked or to derive any other advantage or privilege, or by reference to the amount of capital invested in the State attacked or to any other particular interests in its territory, or by the affirmation that the State attacked lacked the distinguishing marks of statehood.

35. Those arguments had invariably been relied on by aggressors for the purpose of deceiving public opinion and escaping responsibility. Accordingly the Soviet Union draft resolution provided that, in particular, the following could not be used as justifications for attack:

A. The internal position of any State; as, for example:

(*a*) The backwardness of any nation politically, economically or culturally;

(*b*) Alleged shortcomings of its administration;

(*c*) Any danger which might threaten the life or property of aliens;

(*d*) Any revolutionary or counter-revolutionary movement, civil war, disorders or strikes;

(*e*) The establishment or maintenance in any State of any political, economic or social system;

B. Any acts, legislation or orders of any State, as for example:

(*a*) The violation of international treaties;

(*b*) The violation of rights and interests in the sphere of trade, concessions or any other kind of economic activity acquired by another State or its citizens;

(*c*) The rupture of diplomatic or economic relations;

(*d*) Measures in connexion with an economic or financial boycott;

(*e*) Repudiation of debts;

(*f*) Prohibition or restriction of immigration or modification of the status of foreigners;

(*g*) The violation of privileges granted to the official representatives of another State;

(*h*) Refusal to allow the passage of armed forces proceeding to the territory of a third State;

(*i*) Measures of a religious or anti-religious nature;

(*j*) Frontier incidents. . . .

56. A Criticism of Defining Aggression Ahead of Time

JEAN SPIROPOULOS

. . . 8. The natural notion of aggression contained two elements, one objective and the other subjective. The objective criterion of aggression was violence, direct, indirect or concealed, committed by a State before any similar act was committed by the other party. It was impossible to enumerate all imaginable cases of such acts because they were in a constant process of evolution. . . .

9. It was impossible to forecast what further classes of acts would be recognized in the future by the international community as constituting aggression. According to the law in force, no State was obliged to prevent its nationals from fighting in foreign armies as volunteers, provided they had not been trained for the purpose in their own country. Greeks had fought in the French army in the First and Second World Wars. But volunteers were legitimate only when their numbers was small. If half the adult male population of a State was allowed to fight in a foreign army as private individuals, the State of which they were nationals would undoubtedly be guilty of aggression. That was a very unlikely case but all possible cases would have to be included in an exhaustive definition. At the pre-

General Assembly Official Records, Sixth Session, Sixth Committee, 279th Mtg., January 7, 1952, pp. 154-155.

vious session the General Assembly had added to the list of acts of aggression incitement to civil war in another State (resolution 380 (V)). Further additions might be made *ad infinitum.* His provisional conclusion was that it was impossible to give an *a priori* definition which included all types of aggression.

10. Beside the objective criterion there was the subjective criterion of aggression. The act as such did not always constitute aggression. There must also be aggressive intention. . . . The right to shoot first in self-defence was recognized in all criminal codes. When there was impending aggression a State had the right to attack first in self-defence, although no actual act of aggression had taken place to counter the aggressive intention of the other State. The League of Nations Permanent Advisory Commission (opinion of the Belgian, Brazilian, French and Swedish delegations) had expressed a similar idea.[7] Moreover, conflicts were possible in which there was no aggressor. In a case in which two States, through a series of misunderstandings, were finally driven to armed conflict there would be no aggressor, unless one of the States had aggressive intention and the other was acting in self-defence; if they both desired to settle their differences by war neither State would be a victim acting in legitimate self-defence and there could consequently be no aggression.

11. The objective and subjective criteria of aggression together constituted a single whole. The total circumstances had to be taken into account. The idea of aggression was a thing in itself, and as such could not be defined by the enumerative method. In the words of the League of Nations Permanent Advisory Commission, "under the conditions of modern warfare, it would seem impossible to decide even in theory what constitutes a case of aggression".[8] The same conclusion had been arrived at by various practical men and men of science. For example when the United States had tried to win acceptance for the Politis definition at the International Conference on Military Trials, held in London in 1945, which drew up the Charter of the Nürnberg Tribunal, General Nikitchenko, representing the USSR, had said that though aggression could be identi-

[7] See *League of Nations, Official Journal, Special Supplement No. 16,* pages 114-118.

[8] *Ibid.*, page 116.

fied in particular cases it was not yet possible to draft a definition of it.[9] So much for the idea of an exhaustive definition, enumerating all the elements of aggression.

12. Another possibility was to adopt a general abstract definition of aggression rather than a complete enumerative definition. The International Law Commission had decided to consider an abstract definition and, although only twelve members had been present during the discussions, six consecutive drafts had been submitted by as many members, because in each case the author of the new draft had felt that the former draft was not quite satisfactory. If a similar pattern were followed in the Sixth Committee it would have to deal with about thirty different drafts. . . .

13. It would of course always be possible to define the term "aggression" just as it was possible to define any other word, but a definition of aggression would always be artificial because it would inevitably leave out some possible cases of aggression and at the same time include certain acts which, if considered in their proper context, would not be felt by the conscience of the international community as being acts of aggression at all. It depended on the circumstances of each act whether or not it really constituted aggression. For example, no one would ever dream of denying that the incident at Pearl Harbor had constituted aggression, but, on the other hand, if a small group of soldiers fired across a frontier and wounded some soldiers on the other side, that could hardly be termed aggression even if the soldiers had been acting on the instructions of their Government. Both cases would, however, be regarded as aggression under sub-paragraph 1(b) of the USSR draft resolution (A/C.6/L/208). Obviously, a rigid definition could never apply to all cases; each case had to be considered on its merits. Consequently, although it would be possible to adopt a definition of aggression in theory, the definition could never be complete and perfect in every respect and would be extremely difficult to apply in practice.

Having dealt with the question of the possibility of defining aggression, he turned next to the question of the desirability of

---

[9] See *Report of Robert H. Jackson, United States Representative to the International Conference on Military Trials,* Department of State Publication 3080, Washington, 1949.

adopting such a definition. He doubted whether a theoretical definition of aggression, although it might be possible to achieve one, would be of any real value in practice. In complicated cases—and it was only in such cases that a definition of aggression would have any practical value at all—the difficulties of determining the aggressor would be so great that the existence of a definition of aggression would appear a rather unimportant, in some cases even a disturbing, factor. Thus, for instance, in the case of an armed conflict between States or among a group of States, preceded by a period of misunderstandings, political tension, general armament, mobilization, etc., the fact that there was a definition of aggression enumerating acts to be considered as a test of aggression, would scarcely have any practical importance. Moreover, the existence of an imperfect and incomplete definition of aggression might even be extremely dangerous. Mr. Spiropoulos quoted from the report of the Rapporteur of Committee III/3 to Commission III of the San Francisco Conference to illustrate that point:

"Although this proposition (to insert a definition of aggression in the Charter) evoked considerable support, it nevertheless became clear to a majority of the Committee that a preliminary definition of aggression went beyond the possibilities of this Conference and the purpose of the Charter. The progress of the technique of modern warfare renders very difficult the definition of all cases of aggression. It may be noted that, the list of such cases being necessarily incomplete, the Council would have a tendency to consider of less importance the acts not mentioned therein; these omissions would encourage the aggressor to distort the definition or might delay action by the Council. Furthermore, in the other cases listed, automatic action by the Council might bring about a premature application of enforcement measures".[10]

The Committee had therefore decided to adhere to the text of the draft charter drawn up at Dumbarton Oaks and to leave to the Security Council the entire decision as to what constituted a threat to peace, a breach of the peace, or an act of aggression.

15. Without being unduly cynical, he felt that a realistic approach was needed. There could never be a perfect definition of

[10] See *Documents of the United Nations Conference on International Organization, San Francisco,* 1945, Vol. XII, Commission III, page 519.

aggression and, even if a somewhat imperfect and incomplete definition were adopted, it would not be a legal organ but a political one which would be called upon to apply it. He had no wish to enter into a political discussion and he was not looking for any reply to his remarks, but he thought it would be useful to mention two examples in order to show how the matter had been dealt with by the political organs of the United Nations in the past. Firstly, there was the case of Korea, where the existence of an act of aggression had been recognized immediately after the first invasion. Secondly, there was the case of Greece, where the General Assembly had recognized all the facts but had never called them by their proper name. . . .

57. Aggressor Identification and National Security

ABBA EBAN

. . . 141. In an address to the Security Council on 30 October [*749th meeting*], I submitted a detailed chronicle of acts of violence carried out by penetrating *fedayeen* units, day by day and night by night, in the period between April of this year and a few days ago. Throughout the whole of that period, United Nations officials concerned with security on our frontier were devoting great attention to this problem. On 8 April 1956, the United Nations Chief of Staff addressed a letter to the Foreign Minister of Israel. In that letter, General Burns includes the following passages:

"I am dispatching to the Foreign Minister of Egypt a protest against the action of the *fedayeen,* assuming it to have been authorized or tolerated by the Egyptian authorities, and requesting the immediate withdrawal of any persons under Egyptian control from the territory of Israel . . .

General Assembly Official Records, First Emergency Session, 562nd Pl. Mtg., November 1, 1956, p. 23.

"I consider that if Egypt has ordered these *fedayeen* raids, it has now put itself in the position of the aggressor."

142. I will not weary the General Assembly with this sordid chronicle in all its details. Suffice it to say that, during this period of Egyptian belligerency, there had taken place against Israel 435 cases of armed incursion, nearly 2,000 cases of armed robbery and theft, 1,300 cases of armed clashes with Egyptian armed forces, 172 cases of sabotage perpetrated by Egyptian military units and *fedayeen* in Israel. As a result of these activities, 465 of our people have been killed or wounded. In 1956 alone, so far, as a result of this one aspect of Egyptian belligerency, 28 of our people have been killed and 127 have been wounded.

143. I have said that this activity is merely the spearhead of Egyptian belligerency. It is a new device for making war and for making it with safety. The doctrine is one of unilateral belligerency. The Egyptian-Israel frontier is to be a one-way street. It is to be wide open for these armed Egyptian units to penetrate deeply into Israel to accomplish their mission and to return. It is to be closed in their favour against any offensive response.

144. It was in these circumstances that the Government of Israel faced the tormenting problems of its duties and obligations under the Charter of the United Nations. We are not satisfied with a justification of our actions in pure terms of national expediency. There is perhaps no Member of this Organization more sensitive to all the currents of international opinion, more vulnerable to the disfavour and the dissent of friendly world opinion, broader in the scope and extent of its universal associations, less able to maintain its life and its existence on any principle of self-sufficiency and of autarchy.

145. It was with full knowledge of this fact that we have been forced to interpret Article 51 of the Charter as furnishing both a legal and a moral basis for such defensive action as is literally and specifically applicable to the dangers which we face. Under Article 51 of the Charter, the right of self-defence is described as "inherent"; in the French translation it is *"naturel"*. It is something which emerges from the very nature of a State and of humanity.

This inherent right of self-defence is conditioned in the Charter by the existence of armed attacks against a Member State.

146. Can anyone say that this long and uninterrupted series of encroachments did not constitute in its totality the essence and the reality of an armed attack? Can it seriously be suggested that we made no attempt to exhaust peaceful remedies. Time after time at the table of the Security Council and in meetings of the Mixed Armistice Commission efforts were made to bring about tranquillity on this frontier. Yet all of this well-intentioned, enlightened, and, at certain times, hopeful effort ended without making the life or the security of a single citizen of Israel greater than it was before. . . .

58. Aggressor Identification and the Nuclear Age

INIS L. CLAUDE, JR.

. . . In certain basic respects the doctrine of collective security is obsolete—it envisages a system which might have been feasible in an earlier period of international relations, but can hardly be expected to operate effectively in the setting which has been produced by the transformations of recent years.

Collective security was originally conceived with reference to a kind of war which must now be designated old-fashioned. In the days of mass armies, equipped with conventional weapons, brought into mutual confrontation by rather ponderous and quite visible mobilization and supported in action by economic machines which moved slowly to peak production during the early stages of hostilities, one could conceive of effective collective security action under the auspices of an international agency. Once a potential aggressor showed his hand or began actual movement, states committed to the defense of international order could quickly develop a coordinated economic boycott and, if necessary, contrive an emergency

From *Power and International Relations*, by Inis L. Claude, Jr.

plan for combined military operations. The technical ease of meeting an act of deliberate aggression with hastily assembled collective forces in this era should not be exaggerated. The attacker, who could develop his plans and preparations with care and at leisure, and determine at will the time and place of his assault, always enjoyed a considerable advantage over a hypothetical assemblage of contributors to collective security whose reactions, in the nature of the case, would have to be improvised on the spur of the moment. In these terms, the power of a collective security grouping would always be less than that of the sum of its parts; the hypothetical preponderance of the defenders of the system over any aggressor would always be somewhat reduced by lack of clear foreknowledge as to where, when, against whom, and in collaboration with whom, military action might be necessary, and by the inherent difficulties of *ad hoc* coalition warfare. Nevertheless, it was possible in the era of old-fashioned war for a reasonable man to believe that any aggressor might be deterred by the prospect, or defeated in short order by the actuality, of massive power sent against him by a large collection of states, acting perforce with little or no advance preparation for this specific undertaking.

Such warfare as that described above has not been altogether outmoded by recent developments. The Korean War, for instance, was of that general variety. The anti-aggression campaign waged in Korea by a number of states was in important respects similar to the collective military sanctions which might have been launched under the auspices of a collective security system, and its results tended to confirm the proposition that collective security might be militarily feasible in cases of conventional warfare. South Korea was, after all, successfully defended.

The critical security problem of our time, however, has been defined by the radical transformations in military technology which have occurred since 1945. The threat of thermonuclear war—a war of missiles, rockets, atomic and hydrogen warheads, and whatever additional varieties of engines of destruction may appear on the military scene—poses new problems which make collective security appear as irrelevant to the management of power relations as machine guns have become to the frustration of great-power aggression. Who can imagine that a contemporary superpower, brandishing his fiendishly powerful modern weapons, could be deterred from aggression by the threat of the United Nations to improvise a collective military venture? The complexities of warfare in the mid-twentieth century are such that an effective military enterprise cannot be hurriedly contrived by an *ad hoc* grouping of states, acting without advance knowledge of the identity of aggressor or aggressee but committed simply to rally to the defense of any state assaulted by any enemy. The speed of ultra-modern warfare is likely to be such that a victim of aggression may be utterly destroyed before a collective security organ can so much as meet to consider the situation; the war may be over before an aggressor can be designated. The destructiveness of war has been so enhanced that any inclination states might have to participate in a collective security system is likely to be dispelled by the sense that the ultimate issue of national life or death cannot be left to the decision of any international organ. In short, the theory of collective security, developed with primary reference to the military realities of World War I, can hardly have substantial relevance to the military realities of a possible World War III. . . .

PRIOR DEFINITION OF THE PEACEBREAKER

59. The Decision of the San Francisco Conference

EDWARD R. STETTINIUS

. . . One of the most significant lines upon which debate concerning the liberty of action of the Council proceeded, was that which con-

Report to the President on the Results of the San Francisco Conference, by the Chairman of the United States Delegation, the secretary of State, June 26, 1945, Department of State Publication 2349, Conference Series 71 (Washington, D.C.: Government Printing Office, 1945), pp. 91-92.

cerned the proposed inclusion in the Charter of provisions with respect to determination of acts of aggression. Various amendments proposed on the subject, including those of Bolivia and the Philippine Commonwealth, offered a list of sharply-defined eventualities (such as invasion of, or attack on, another state, interfering with its internal affairs, etc.) in which the Council would be bound to determine by formula not only the existence of aggression but also the identity of the aggressor. These proposals also implied that in such cases the action of the Council would be automatic. The United States Delegation, believing that the acceptance of such a concept was most undesirable, played an active part in opposing the amendments. The Conference finally agreed that even the most simple and obvious cases of aggression might fall outside any of the formulae suggested, and, conversely, that a nation which according to a formula strictly interpreted could be deemed the offender in any particular instance might actually—when all circumstances were considered—be found to be the victim of intolerable provocation. Since it was admittedly impossible to provide a complete list, the Security Council might have a tendency to consider of less importance acts of aggression not specifically covered therein. The problem was especially complicated by the progress in modern techniques of warfare and the development of novel methods of propaganda and provocation.

Finally, it was recognized that if the Council were bound to automatic action, the result might be that enforcement measures would be applied prematurely. The Technical Committee dealing with this question therefore decided to hold to the provision quoted above which gives the Council ample authority to decide what constitutes a threat to the peace, a breach of the peace, or an act of aggression, and to decide also which of the disputing parties has been mainly at fault. . . .

[V]

Implementation of the Common Concern

Against whom and for what purpose is the common concern to be implemented?

IMPLEMENTATION AGAINST WHOM?

1. *Is it to be implemented against any and all members?*

Under Article 5(1) of the Covenant of the League of Nations it was provided that, with certain exceptions, substantive decisions in both the Council and the Assembly were to be taken by unanimous vote. Thus all members had the protection of a veto power. Furthermore, the decision to submit a dispute to the procedures provided in the Covenant was left to the disputants, and the decision to apply sanctions came to be left to individual decision as well.

In the United Nations system, as is well known, the five permanent members of the Security Council have a special position in that they are protected by the "veto" power in Article 27 against Security Council decisions with which they disagree, except in the event that they should be parties to a dispute under Chapter VI and under paragraph 3 of Article 52, in which cases they must abstain from voting. They are, however, protected by the veto in Chapter VII proceedings. An explanation of the veto power is given in Reading 60 by Grayson Kirk, President of Columbia University, New York City, who was Executive Officer of Commission III (Security Council) at the San Francisco Conference of 1945.

Contrary to popular impression and indeed to the statements at San Francisco of a number of small-nation representatives, it should not be assumed that the small powers are necessarily against the veto power of the permanent Security Council members. Indeed, smaller nations may regard it as a protection (Readings 61 and 62).

2. *Keeping these views in mind, can the United Nations properly be called a collective security organization?*

An argument that the Charter endorsed the ideal of collective security but envisaged its application in severely limited terms is set forth in Reading 63 and rebutted in Reading 64.

3. *If the Security Council is not operating, can the General Assembly serve as the collective security body of the United Nations?*

Numerous difficulties, both theoretical and practical, stand in the way of such a role for the General Assembly (Reading 65). Nevertheless, the United States, Britain, France, and four other members of the Security Council, acknowledging in 1950 that the Security Council was prevented from fulfilling its task through the Soviet use of the veto power, submitted what came to be known as the "Uniting for Peace" Resolution to the General Assembly (Reading 66). It was passed by a vote of 52 to 5.

The opposing views on this move which are stated in Readings 67 and 68 reflect a deep and continuing political and constitutional controversy as to the proper role of United Nations bodies, a controversy which in 1964-1965 reached an acute point in the matter of payment for peace-keeping operations not authorized by the Security Council.

IMPLEMENTATION FOR WHAT PURPOSE?

1. *Is collective security intended primarily to deter aggression?*

In present circumstances, whom is a collective security arrangement likely to deter? See Readings 12 and 58.

2. *If collective security is to deter aggression, are there any "signals" which would warn ahead of time that aggression is to take place?*

An early example is cited in Reading 69. Reading 70 discusses whether it is possible under present conditions to establish helpful warning devices against preparation for conventional attack.

3. *Assuming that disturbance of the peace has occurred and the organization has decided to apply collective security measures, what should be the primary purpose of such actions?*

Was the United Nations intended to be a "punishing" organization (Reading 71)? Should it place a primary emphasis on repelling aggression, as was argued in 1951 by American Ambassador Warren R. Austin (Reading 72), or on the process of peaceful persuasion, as was argued by British representative Sir Gladwyn Jebb (Reading 73).

In surveying United Nations experience in the political field, Secretary-General Dag Hammarskjöld underlined the evolution of a concept of preventive diplomacy (Reading 74), while his successor, U Thant, explained how the concept of collective security had yielded to that of "peace-keeping" (Reading 75).

In actual practice, the objectives sought may be, and most probably will be, a combination of a number of goals (Reading 76).

THE PROTECTION OF VITAL NATIONAL INTERESTS

4. *Does experience indicate that responsible national leaders can safely put their trust in a collective action for the protection of vital national interests?*

The existence of Article 51 would seem to indicate that they cannot (Reading 77). This issue came up in concrete form in the Suez crisis of 1956, when Britain and France decided to act independently of the United Nations in trying to deal with the situation which had followed on Egyptian nationalization of the important waterway (Reading 78).

Furthermore, no nation can be certain that (1) an international organization will succeed in reaching a decision, (2) that the decision will be acceptable to it, or (3) that it will be reached in time to make any difference. A classic account of the French government's attempt to deal with such difficulties during the interwar period illustrates this basic problem of collective security (Reading 79).

ARE THE CONDITIONS ANOMALOUS?

5. *Is the concept of collective security based on a "circular argument"?*

Readings 80 and 81 discuss this question.

IMPLEMENTATION AGAINST WHOM?

60. The Veto Power

GRAYSON KIRK

. . . Open as it is, on theoretical democratic grounds, to serious objection, this Council voting arrangement rests upon two basic assumptions to which the sponsoring powers attached great importance. The first was that in any enforcement action the permanent members of the Council would be those whose forces must necessarily bear the predominant burden. In consequence, it would be unrealistic to expect these Council members to allow their own forces to be committed to an action which they, or any one of them, opposed. The other argument was that the organization must depend for its strength upon the essential solidarity of the great powers. If this solidarity fails, then the security enforcement arrangements will as surely fail. Therefore, all measures which will further and which will rest upon such a presumption of solidarity are of such a vital necessity that they override all other considerations.

These views were accepted by the Third Commission, although with reluctance on the part of many members who objected to the enshrinement of such special privileges in a great international constitutional document. There was general agreement, however, that this concession to the views of the sponsoring powers was, in itself, not too large a price to pay if it would genuinely contribute toward the establishment of an organization which would be effective and enduring.

In retrospect, the work of the Committees of the Third Commission was accomplished in a spirit of determination to do all that was humanly possible to create an instrument which would

---

Grayson Kirk, "Third Commission: The Security Council," *International Conciliation,* September, 1945, No. 413, Part I, pp. 461-468, at p. 468.

not fail, through organic or procedural defects, to meet a future challenge. If there was little starry-eyed optimism, there was also little of the cynicism which comes so easily to men who deal professionally with matters of diplomacy. The matter is now in the hands of the future. . . .

61. The Mexican Position

JORGE CASTAÑEDA

. . . The elimination of the veto in cases of serious threats to the peace or breaches of the peace or acts of aggression would not benefit the small and medium-sized powers. The veto serves as a check against dragging small countries, often against their will, into undertakings which fundamentally serve the interest of the great powers. Paradoxically, the veto is more a defense of the small than of the great countries. The fact that the small countries dispose of a large number of votes in the United Nations, with which theoretically they could prevent the adoption of dangerous decisions which they do not want, does not signify a "real" defense for them. The close political dependence of all the small countries on some great powers and the fear of reprisals has obliged the former more frequently than is generally believed to support positions contrary to their best interests, or, in any case, they have been led to act irresponsibly, voting for the application of measures that they are not willing to fulfil or that they are not capable of effectively sustaining.

A good example of this phenomenon was the reaction of the Latin American countries to the request for troops to be sent to Korea. Despite their having appeared to be the most enthusiastic supporters of collective action in Korea and despite their close political and economic connection with the United States, only one country (Colombia) of the twenty sent troops to Korea. The

Jorge Castañeda, *Mexico and the United Nations,* National Studies on International Organization, prepared for El Colegio de Mexico and the Carnegie Endowment for International Peace (New York: Manhattan Publishing Co., 1958), pp. 139-140.

true reason for this paradoxical situation was not the total impossibility of sending them—since, for this purpose, a tiny symbolic force like that of Luxembourg would have been enough—but probably the authorities' fear of an unfavorable reaction of public opinion. At any rate, the recommendation to give military support to the collective action in Korea was a sufficiently unpopular measure in Latin America to go practically unheeded. This fact cannot lead logically to any other conclusion than that such a recommendation represented a burdensome and difficult political commitment which was actually not desired in Latin America nor did it serve Latin American interest. A Soviet veto which would have prevented its adoption—although leaving those who voluntarily wished to aid the victim through the exercise of collective self-defense free to do so—would not necessarily have been detrimental to Latin America.

Even though the small countries—Mexico among them—in San Francisco were supporters in principle of broadening as much as possible the functions of the Assembly, where they have a majority, the experience of these last years should make them see the dangers of the Assembly being able to take enforcement action, urged on by political pressures difficult to resist and free of legal checks, in case of serious threats to the peace, breaches of the peace, and acts of aggression. The small and medium-sized powers would be benefited by the strict application of those fundamental provisions of the Charter which establish the basic division of functions between the General Assembly and the Security Council. . . .

62. The Cause of Difficulty

SWEDISH REPRESENTATIVE

. . . 31. When the United Nations was established, it had been believed that the organization of collective security could be suc-

A statement by Mr. Vought, representative of Sweden, in a discussion of the report of the Collective Measures Committee in 1952, *General Assembly Official Records,* Sixth Session, First Committee, 476th Mtg., January 2, 1952, p. 123.

cessful only if the five great Powers were agreed upon any action against aggression, because they alone could provide the necessary superiority. Indeed, it was understood that the Organization could not take enforcement action against any great Power without leading to a major war. On that basis, the smaller States undertook to conform to the decisions of the Security Council and to that extent surrendered sovereignty while it was left to the great Powers to decide on their own participation. If the great Powers were not unanimous, other States would also retain freedom of action.

32. It was clear that a security system with such a basis was defective. However, no great Power would be prepared to abandon the right to decide upon its own participation nor would other States assume prior commitments to participate in collective measures which had been decided upon only by a majority. The difficulties arose from the disagreements amongst the great Powers.

33. Many States including Sweden were not prepared to undertake to participate in sanctions in a situation which might lead to a world war. A number of them had accordingly resorted to defensive treaties and alliances under Articles 51 and 52. Such arrangements were not surprising in view of the international situation and the capacities of the United Nations. . . .

63. The Charter: Ideal and Application

INIS L. CLAUDE, JR.

. . . The crucial element in the analysis is an understanding of the import of the veto rule which enables any of the five permanent members of the Security Council to block decisions on substantive matters in that organ—including the determination that aggression has taken place, the designation of the guilty party, and the decision

Inis L. Claude, Jr., "The Management of Power in the Changing United Nations," *International Organization*, Spring, 1961, pp. 219-235, at p. 225.

to resort to sanctions, military or otherwise, against the aggressor. Such decisions, be it noted, are fundamental to the operation of a collective security system. The veto rule clearly gives each of the great powers the capacity to prevent the operation of the United Nations enforcement system against itself, against any state which it chooses to support and protect, or in any other case in which it prefers not to participate or to have others participate in an enforcement venture under United Nations auspices. The veto provision, in short, renders collective security impossible in all the instances most vital to the preservation of world peace and order, and problematical in cases of lesser importance. . . .

64. A Rebuttal

RUTH B. RUSSELL

. . . As the Charter shows, the Great Powers would not accept any enforcement system not dependent on their voluntary accord. But an agreement *was* achieved that: 1) allowed a nascent collective security system to develop as fast as the precondition of Great Power co-operation might develop; 2) provided for a separate form of collective action to be organized outside the global agency, but within the framework of its nonaggressive security commitments, so long as the former was not able to handle matters itself (namely, collective self-defense); and 3) established sufficiently flexible machinery and procedures to permit considerable adaptation on the basis of experience. Rather than a "curious amalgam," the Charter seems to me to represent a rather practical amalgam of the possibilities in the circumstances of 1945. . . .

. . . We observe something of the old-fashioned balance of power in the relationships of the nuclear powers. We see a new-model

Ruth B. Russell, "The Management of Power and Political Organization," *International Organization,* Autumn, 1961, pp. 630-636, at pp. 634-636.

balance of power operation in the collective defense arrangements. We find several "extremely modest versions" of collective security actions under United Nations auspices, none of them, admittedly, of the type specifically foreseen in the Charter; but all of them, be it noted—from Korea, through Suez, to the Congo—representing operations carried out because there existed a sufficient degree of Great Power accord (either through acquiescence or abstinence) to enable them to work within their particular limitations, and because there was enough flexibility in the Charter to adapt to those limitations. We see also a new subversive form of international aggressive force in the Soviet and Chinese use of nationalist-communist groups, that so far has not shown itself very susceptible to either collective-security or balance-of-power forms of resistance. . . .

65. A Critical View of the General Assembly as a Collective Security Body

ERICH HULA

. . . The constitutional development of the United Nations reflects and is due to the political pressures brought to bear upon the organization by the two Cold Wars in which the members of the international community are engaged today, the one between the great powers and the one between the colonial and anticolonial powers.

According to the Charter, it was the Security Council, dominated by the great powers, that was to be the center of authority in the organization. Though its collective security functions were limited to minor conflicts, its legal powers within those limits were to be broad and its physical power sufficient to give them effect. When

Erich Hula, "The Evolution of Collective Security under the United Nations Charter," in Arnold Wolfers, editor, *Alliance Policy in the Cold War* (Baltimore: Johns Hopkins Press, 1959), pp. 75-102, at pp. 97-98. Reprinted by permission.

owing to the Cold War between East and West the concept of an executive concert of the great powers failed to materialize, we tried to shift the center of authority and power to a parliamentary concert of great and minor powers. It was hardly a realistic scheme from the beginning and became even less so when the extension of the collective security system to major conflicts was not followed by the establishment of military machinery commensurate in physical strength with the legal powers of the parliamentary concert. The claim of the General Assembly to speak on behalf of the organization as a whole rested exclusively on its moral authority as a democratic body. But the validity of that claim was not generally recognized; and moreover it was open to the objection that the Assembly was an essentially political body, acting in accordance with considerations of political expediency rather than of moral principles.

The expectation that the concentration of authority and power in a parliamentary concert would enable the United Nations to discharge its functions effectively as a collective security body was not well founded for yet another reason. As the scheme of Dumbarton Oaks and San Francisco was inspired and based upon the pattern of the Grand Alliance of World War II, so was the scheme of the "Uniting for Peace" resolution patterned upon the political constellation in the initial period of the Korean war. Not only was the democratic bloc in the Assembly at that time overwhelmingly strong numerically; it also seemed sufficiently coherent to serve as the foundation for a lasting system of collective security. However, the coherence actually was due rather to the fear of imminent Russian aggression than to a true community of views and interests. The Russian danger at that time overshadowed all other questions, even in the eyes of the anticolonial members of the United Nations. But this is no longer the case. On the contrary a growing number of member nations regards the United Nations today primarily as an instrument to further the emancipation of the colonial peoples and to eradicate the last vestiges of Western power and influence in the world. But quite apart from the colonial issue, the lines of the bipolar structure of the contemporary world are not as clear at the close of the fifties as they were at the beginning.

The weakening of the political coherence of the General Assembly forecloses the hope for an effective system of collective security built upon the Assembly that would permit great and small nations alike to dispense with the traditional devices of power-diplomacy. But it is not likely to end the sway of the collective security ideology and its successful use for diplomatic purposes. For instead of replacing traditional diplomacy, as it was hoped, collective security—or the idea of collective security—has itself become a diplomatic weapon in the struggle for power. This does not detract from the moral value of the idea, which is indeed inspired by man's eternal longing for a peaceful and just international order; it only means that the idea shares the fate of other lofty ideas, namely, employment for combative purposes. It has become part of the art of diplomacy to judge the adversary's actions in the inflexible terms of the idea of collective security while basing one's own actions on the more flexible law of collective security. . . .

66. "Uniting for Peace"

GENERAL ASSEMBLY RESOLUTION 377(V)

. . . 1. *Resolves* that if the Security Council, because of lack of unanimity of the permanent members, fails to exercise its primary responsibility for the maintenance of international peace and security in any case where there appears to be a threat to the peace, breach of the peace, or act of aggression, the General Assembly shall consider the matter immediately with a view to making appropriate recommendations to Members for collective measures, including in the case of a breach of the peace or act of aggression the use of armed force when necessary, to maintain or restore international peace and security. . . .

General Assembly Resolution 377(V), November 3, 1950, Resolutions Adopted by General Assembly during the Period September 19–December 15, 1950, *General Assembly Official Records,* Fifth Session, Supplement 20 (A/1775), pp. 10-12.

67. The Lebanese View of the Need

CHARLES MALIK

. . . 38. The policy of Lebanon, which was a member of the Arab League and of the United Nations, was to offset the meagreness of its resources for warding off aggression through participation in the regional collective security system of the Arab League and in the universal system of the United Nations. Accordingly it welcomed the development of any system of collective security measures under the Charter of the United Nations.

39. As a rule, an act of aggression would be determined by the Security Council in accordance with the provisions of Article 39 of the Charter. Clearly, however, if the five permanent members of the Security Council were unable to agree in determining an act of aggression, although in point of fact aggression had occurred and war was raging, the determination of such aggression must be done outside the Council, which meant by the General Assembly. That was the fundamental premise of the "Uniting for peace" resolution which the General Assembly had adopted at its fifth session. . . .

General Assembly Official Records, Sixth Session, First Committee, 480th Mtg., January 4, 1952, p. 140.

68. The Soviet Union's Position

ANDREI VYSHINSKY

. . . 22. However, the important element in the argument of the proponents of the joint draft resolution was the emphasis placed upon the necessity of strengthening the United Nations and re-

General Assembly Official Records, Fifth Session, First Committee, 357th Mtg., October 10, 1950, pp. 81-84.

moving organizational weaknesses which were supposed to have come to light. Unfortunately, those were only empty phrases. There could be no question of strengthening the United Nations by weakening the Security Council, which would be the inevitable result of the adoption of proposals like those contained in the joint draft resolution. The purpose of that draft was to relieve the Security Council of its primary responsibility, the maintenance of peace and security as stipulated in Article 24 of the Charter. There could be no strengthening of the United Nations if the cornerstone of the Organization, the organ which under the Charter had the exclusive right and power to fight against aggression, to forestall the threat of aggression, and to call upon forces not available to other organs under the Charter, was to be weakened. The proclaimed purpose of the sponsors of the joint draft resolution—the strengthening of the United Nations—would thus inevitably have a contrary result, through the implementation of measures which would weaken the Security Council. . . .

IMPLEMENTATION FOR WHAT PURPOSE?

69. An Early Example

JAMES T. SHOTWELL

. . . The Bulgarian account of the incident was a clear-cut statement in the note sent to the League of Nations appealing for intervention: "On the 19th instant, about three o'clock in the morning, Greek soldiers crossed the frontier and fired on a Bulgar-

James T. Shotwell, *A Balkan Mission* (New York: Columbia University Press, 1949), pp. 108-109. Reprinted by permission.

ian sentinel. . . . The Bulgarian sentinel returned the fire and killed the aggressor, whereupon a detachment of Greek soldiers under post orders advanced into Bulgarian territory to recover the Greek soldier's body. Soldiers of the Bulgarian post opposed this movement before the customary formalities had been fulfilled and a fusillade which lasted until the evening of the 20th instant commenced." The Bulgarian Government claimed that it had ordered its frontier garrisons to make no opposition to the invasion and that subsequently "Greek detachments were able to occupy a number of posts in the Struma Valley and Greek artillery hurled numerous bombs into the village of Petritch and the railway station at Marnopole . . . while a Greek airplane dropped bombs on the village of Levunovo wounding five Bulgarian soldiers."

The Bulgarian Government then appealed to the League of Nations under Article 10 of the Covenant, which guaranteed against external aggression, and Article 11, which empowered the Council to take any necessary action in case of war or the threat of it.

The Greek Government, on its part, held that the shooting had been begun by the Bulgarians and that it had been an unprovoked and flagrant aggression on their part, in the face of which their military commander had been authorized "to take measures he judged necessary for defense and clearing the national territory of which certain points were still occupied by Bulgarian regular troops."

In both countries the war spirit was immediately fanned by extremists. Refugees from sixty Macedonian villages came fleeing over the mountains with tales of the Greek invasion and memories of the horrors of past Balkan wars with all their atrocities. The situation was doubly difficult for Bulgaria because the country had been disarmed by the Treaty of Neuilly (its counterpart to the Treaty of Versailles), and its appeal to the League of Nations for help was all the more effective on that account.

By good fortune, the president of the Council at the time was M. Briand, whose moral authority was very high, and he, sensing the need for immediate action, telegraphed both governments reminding them of their obligation to submit their dispute to peaceful settlement and requesting them to keep their troops behind their frontiers. This appeal stopped a Greek offensive only two and a half hours before it had been scheduled to start. Thus an anxious weekend passed. The Council met on Monday, October 26, approved M. Briand's action, and sent a "stop-fight" order to both governments, with a demand that within twenty-four hours they issue orders for their troops to evacuate foreign soil inside sixty hours. The British, French, and Italian military attachés at Belgrade and Athens were sent by special trains to the scene of action, arriving there October 28 in the early afternoon. Then for the first time in history, the agents of an international body summoned the commanders of both armies and ordered them to carry out the League's instructions.

Eight hours before the expiration of the time limit, the Greeks were back on their frontier. Peace having been maintained, the League sent a five-man Commission of Inquiry to carry out investigations on the spot and determine responsibilities. Finally Greece was obliged to pay Bulgaria an award for damages amounting to about $210,000. . . .

70. Warning Devices against Preparations for Conventional Attack

UNITED STATES WORKING PAPER

ADVANCE NOTIFICATION

Purpose. Advance notification of major military movements and manoeuvres could provide additional opportunity for calm appraisal of military activities which might give rise to misinterpretation as threatening the imminent outbreak of hostilities. The ultimate character of such an appraisal would, of course, depend on

United States Working Paper: Reduction of the Risk of War Through Accident, Miscalculation, or Failure of Communication, December 12, 1962, *Documents on Disarmament, 1962,* Arms Control and Disarmament Agency Publication 19 (Washington, D.C.: Government Printing Office, 1963), Vol. II, pp. 1214-1225, at pp. 1217 and 1219.

many considerations in addition to the fact that advance notification had been provided. However, the establishment and use of procedures for advance notification could assist in reducing any hazard that detection of an unannounced activity of seemingly major proportions might induce a rapid and disproportionate military response. . . .

OBSERVATION POSTS

Purpose. Advance notification constitutes a potentially useful measure undertaken separately or in conjunction with other measures. A closely related measure would, in effect, represent an extension of the advance notification concept through the establishment of systems of ground observation posts at major transportation centers. The posts comprising such systems could receive such information relative to military activities in their vicinity as the host state might wish to provide and could, under agreed arrangements, observe the flow of military traffic and the general level of military activity on a local basis, thereby clarifying reports made pursuant to advance notification procedures.

Not only the capability of supplementing advance notification through direct observation but also the willingness of host states to co-operate in the establishment and operation of observation post systems could contribute further to the building of confidence and the improvement of reassurance in the relations of the states or groups of states concerned. . . .

71. The United Nations: A Punishing Organization?

ERICH HULA

. . . The spirit in which the enforcement system of the Charter was conceived is illustrated most strikingly by another feature of Article

---

Erich Hula, "The Evolution of Collective Security under the United Nations Charter," in Arnold Wolfers, editor, *Alliance Policy in the Cold War* (Baltimore: Johns Hopkins Press, 1959), pp. 75-102, at p. 87. Reprinted by permission.

39. It charges the Security Council with the determination of "an act of aggression" but not of the aggressor. The distinction would be too tenuous for any far-reaching conclusions if it had not, from the twenties onward, played a considerable role in the discussions on the definition of aggression. It is a distinction, in fact, to which two legal and political conceptions of collective security, the punitive and the diplomatic, must be related. While the allocation of the legal responsibility for an act of aggression is an essential function of the collective security organization according to the punitive school, the diplomatic school insists that it is not the proper task for an agency of collective security to perform. The restoration of peace, the chief purpose of collective action, and the adjustment of the dispute that has led to armed conflict, will be delayed and made more difficult if the organization assumes the role of prosecutor and judge in addition to its police functions and its conciliatory functions. The wording of Article 39 as well as other features of Chapter VII of the Charter prove that its authors were leaning in the direction of the diplomatic school. Far from constituting a criminal code, the rules of the Charter relating to the enforcement system of the United Nations could rather be called a mere legalization and formalization of the diplomatic conceptions and procedures characteristic of the concert system of collective intervention practiced by the European Pentarchy in the nineteenth century. . . .

72. The Importance of Repelling Aggression

WARREN R. AUSTIN

. . . 10. There was more important work ahead however than the post-mortem examination of dead hopes. What was needed was to build up collective security on so firm a basis that neither the

General Assembly Official Records, Fifth Session, First Committee, 426th Mtg., January 18, 1951, pp. 502-503. Footnote omitted.

Chinese communists nor any other aggressor could shake it. The fact should be faced squarely that aggression had taken place. A regime controlling vast manpower and vast territories had defied the United Nations. It was seeking to destroy a country that sought only the elementary right, guaranteed by the Charter, to live and be independent.

11. When the Charter was signed, the peoples of the United Nations, in their determination to reaffirm their faith in the equal rights of nations, large and small, decided to unite their strength to maintain international peace and security. The first responsibility of the United Nations was to take effective collective measures for the prevention or suppression of acts of aggression or other breaches of the peace. The Principles of the Organization established that all Members should settle their international disputes by peaceful means and should refrain from the threat or use of force against the territorial integrity or political independence of any State. The Charter also stipulated that Members should give the United Nations every assistance in any action it took in accordance with the Charter, and should refrain from giving assistance to any State against which the United Nations was taking preventive or enforcement action.

12. The time seemed to have come to recall the Purposes and Principles of the Charter and to examine them in the light of experience. The United Nations should take its decisions calmly and soberly, for the eyes of the world were upon it. There could not be two standards, two measures; the law should apply equally to aggressors, large and small.

13. No nation was strong enough to stand alone and unaided: the weak depended on the strong and the strong depended on the weak. Security was indivisible. The United Nations could not let one nation fall a victim to aggression and at the same time believe that it would be possible to protect another nation on the next occasion. If the Organization acted in that way, the very principle of collective security would be destroyed. The peoples of the world would not only turn away from the United Nations but would lose faith in the principle of the interdependence of nations.

14. On 25 June 1950 the United Nations had done what no

other world organization had ever done: it had taken legal and collective action to repel aggression. It had done so, not in order to wage war, but to fulfil its obligation to maintain the peace. That object could be obtained only by resolute and continuous effort. One of the fundamental principles of the Charter was the outlawing of aggression and it was therefore right that the United Nations should, by its determination, decisions and actions, prove that no Power could defy that principle with impunity. The whole world expected the United Nations to conform to that principle. The time for action had come, as any further delay might permanently destroy the unity of the Organization. . . .

16. . . . It was to be hoped that in the present case the United Nations would, by its firmness and unity, make the authors of the new aggression realize that to launch its armies against the Organization was, in the long run, neither prudent for the régime assuming that responsibility nor helpful to the welfare of the Chinese people.

17. In those circumstances, the United Nations should adopt a plan of action which would take into account the distribution and balance of power in the world and the imminence of the threat to collective security. The essential thing, in the view of the United States delegation, was that by opposing that threat the United Nations should discourage present or future aggressors. . . .

19. The facts were that the Peking régime had rejected all the efforts of the United Nations to bring about a cease-fire in Korea, had rejected the proposals for a peaceful settlement and had continued its invasion of Korea, and its attacks upon the United Nations forces. Hence, it was clear that the Peking régime had committed aggression and that the General Assembly should say so. It should call upon the Peking Government to cease its hostilities against the United Nations forces and to withdraw its troops from Korea; it should affirm the determination of the United Nations to continue its efforts to resist aggression in Korea and it should invite all States to assist the Organization and refrain from giving assistance to the aggressors.

20. By taking such action the United Nations would be deciding in principle that collective measures should be taken against the aggressor in Korea. . . .

73. The Question Posed

GLADWYN JEBB

. . . 25. It was, however, precisely on that question that the members of the Committee found themselves in a dilemma. Since all United Nations Members were determined to build up and maintain a strong system of collective security, no breach in the rules of the Charter could be overlooked. But some Members apparently thought that because a crime had been committed and because the culprit was apparent, there was no alternative but to proceed to condemnation and punishment; other Members, on the other hand, still thought it possible that the culprit might see the light and that the process of persuasion might prove fruitful. Either method, if successful, would have the effect of upholding the law. Was the Committee then to proceed by the method of penalties or by that of attempted reform? In pondering that difficult question it should be clearly understood that one of the principal objects of the Charter was to secure the rule of peace. While force might obviously be required, as it had been required in Korea itself, for the purpose of repressing aggression, no one would deny that the other method was preferable if it could be safely adopted. That general conception had been specifically restated recently in the statement issued by the Commonwealth Prime Minister.

26. Would the United Nations have to agree that the time had come to accept failure of a peaceful settlement in Korea and conclude that the Chinese people and government were irrevocably bent on a policy of militant aggression? While it was true that their recent acts inspired no feeling of confidence and gave grounds for that gloomy conclusion, a logical study of the recent communications on the subject of a cease-fire did appear to reveal some forms of advance. It might also be legitimately asked whether there might not have been some grave misunderstanding on the part of the Chinese of the real purpose of the United Nations in Korea. The Peking authorities had for some years been engaged in a life and death struggle in the course of which they had found themselves with hardly a friend in the world. They had had no representative

General Assembly Official Records, Fifth Session, First Committee, 431st Mtg., January 25, 1951, p. 546.

abroad, except in the USSR and countries in the Soviet orbit, and though they should be fully aware that their aggressive actions were inconsistent with the spirit which moved the rest of the free world, it was conceivable that they did not fully comprehend the deep emotions which their conduct had aroused and the dangerous precipice which had opened up before them. In view of the importance of the decision to be made, the United Kingdom delegation considered it would be wise, even essential, for the United Nations to continue its efforts to probe the intentions of the Peking Government.

27. The fluctuating fortunes of the United Nations troops and the apparent inability of the United Nations to bring to account the culprit had aroused so natural an indignation that to many almost any violent action seemed justifiable. That was an understandable emotion but, nevertheless, unwise. It was only natural that the United States, which was carrying the main burden in Korea, should feel the weight of the situation more than any other Member. It was also natural that, in considering further action, the United Nations should be largely guided by the effect it would have on its troops and by its determination to ensure that the sacrifice of those fighting men would not be made in vain. However, it would indeed be a poor return for those sacrifices if the Organization were to involve itself in a course which would lead to still further sacrifices, without having any clear conception of its objectives and the assurance that all possible means of peaceful negotiation had been tried out in order to limit those sacrifices and enable the bloodshed to come to an end. . . .

74. The Main Significance of the Security Council

DAG HAMMARSKJÖLD

. . . In the Charter, the right to the use of force is somewhat more extensive than may seem to be the case from a superficial reading

Secretary-General Dag Hammarskjöld's last *Annual Report, United Nations Review,* September, 1961, p. 14.

of the phrase "save in the common interest." Thus, apart from military action undertaken pursuant to a decision of the Security Council for repression of aggression—that is, for upholding the basic Charter principles—the Charter opens the door to the use of armed force by a nation in exercise of its inherent right to resist armed attack. This is a point on which, both in theory and in practice, the development of international law is still at a very early stage. As is well known, no agreement has been reached on a definition of aggression, beyond that found in Article 2, paragraph 4, of the Charter, and the Organization has several times had to face situations in which, therefore, the rights and wrongs in a specific case of conflict have not been clarified. It would be a vitally important step forward if wider agreement could be reached regarding the criteria to be applied in order to distinguish between legitimate and illegitimate use of force. History is only too rich in examples of armed aggression claimed as action in self-defence. How could it be otherwise, when most cases of armed conflict are so deeply rooted in a history of clashes of interests and rights, even if, up to the fatal moment of the first shot, those clashes have not involved recourse to the use of armed force?

In recognition of this situation and in the light of historical experience, the Charter makes yet another projection into international life of solutions to conflicts tested in national life, and establishes the final principle that the Organization shall "bring about by peaceful means and in conformity with the principles of justice and international law, adjustment or settlement of international disputes or situations which might lead to a breach of the peace." This principle, as quoted here from Article 1 of the Charter, is further developed specifically in Article 33, which requires parties to any dispute, the consequence of which is likely to endanger the maintenance of international peace and security, to "seek a solution by negotiation, inquiry, mediation, conciliation, arbitration, judicial settlement, resort to regional agencies or arrangements, or other peaceful means of their own choice." It is in this sphere that the Security Council has had, and is likely to continue to have, its main significance, both directly as a forum before which any dispute threatening peace and security can be brought up for debate and as an organ which directly, or through appropriate agents, may assist the parties in finding a way out and, by preventive diplomacy, may forestall the outbreak of an armed conflict. It seems appropriate here to draw attention especially to the right of the Security Council under Article 40 to "call upon the parties concerned to comply with such provisional measures as it deems necessary or desirable" for the prevention of any aggravation of a situation threatening peace and security, and to the obligation of members to comply with a decision on such measures. . . .

75. To Allow Time for Conciliation

U THANT

. . . Due partly to the lack of unanimity among the great powers ever since 1946 and partly to the radical change in the nature of war resulting from the development of atomic and hydrogen weapons, there has been a gradual change in thinking on questions of international security in the United Nations.

There has been a tacit transition from the concept of collective security, as set out in Chapter VII of the United Nations Charter, to a more realistic idea of peace-keeping. The idea that conventional military methods—or, to put it bluntly, war—can be used by or on behalf of the United Nations to counter aggression and secure the peace seems now to be rather impractical.

There has also been a change in emphasis from the use of the military forces of the great powers, as contemplated in the Charter, to the use, in practice, of the military resources of the smaller powers, which has the advantage of not entangling United Nations actions in the antagonisms of the cold war.

Although there has been one collective action under the aegis of the United Nations—Korea—and although in 1951 the Collective

"United Nations Stand-By Peace Force," Address of U Thant to the Harvard Alumni Association, June 13, 1963, *United Nations Review,* July, 1963, pp. 54-55.

Measures Committee, set up by the General Assembly under the Uniting for Peace resolution, actually published in its report a list of units earmarked by member states for service with the United Nations in actions to counter aggression, actual developments have in practice been in a rather different direction.

The nature of these developments is sometimes confused, wittingly or unwittingly, by an attempt to relate them to the use of force to counter aggression by the Security Council provided for in Chapter VII of the Charter. In fact, the peace-keeping forces I am about to describe are of a very different kind and have little in common with the forces foreseen in Chapter VII, but their existence is not in conflict with Chapter VII. They are essentially peace and not fighting forces, and they operate only with the consent of the parties directly concerned.

In this context, it is worth noting that all of the permanent members of the Security Council have, at one time or another in the past 15 years, voted in support of the creation of one or other of these forces, and that none of them has in any case gone further than to abstain from voting on them.

Since 1950, the United Nations has been called on to deal with a number of critical situations of varying urgency. The most urgent of these have been what are sometimes called "brush-fire wars," meaning, I take it, small conflagrations which, unless controlled, may all too easily ignite very much larger ones.

PRECEDENT AND PRACTICE

If we briefly look through the United Nations experience with this kind of operation, we can see that from small and informal beginnings a useful body of precedent and practice has grown up over the years of using military personnel of member states on peace-keeping operations. In Greece in 1947, the United Nations Special Committee on the Balkans found that professional military officers were invaluable as an observer group in assessing the highly complicated and fluctuating situation. The Security Council itself set up an observer group of military officers in India and Pakistan to watch over the Kashmir question. This observer group, which was set up in 1948, is still operating.

A much larger use of military observers by the United Nations was made when, in July 1948, the first truce agreements in the Palestine war were supervised on the ground by some 700 United Nations military observers working under the United Nations Mediator and the Chief of Staff. This team developed into the United Nations Truce Supervision Organization after the armistice agreements between Israel and her Arab neighbors were concluded in the period from February to July 1949.

This organization of officers from many countries still plays a vital role in keeping the peace in the Middle East and in reporting on and dealing with incidents which, though small in themselves, might all too easily become the cause of far larger disturbances if not dealt with. Its indefatigable members in their white jeeps are now a familiar and welcome part of the Middle Eastern landscape.

A peace-keeping organization of a different nature made its appearance as a result of the Suez crisis of October 1956. Confronted with a situation of the utmost urgency in which two of the permanent members of the Security Council were directly involved, the General Assembly voted for the urgent creation of a United Nations force. This was essentially not a force designed actively to fight against aggression.

It went to Egypt with the express consent of the Egyptian Government and after the other parties concerned had agreed to a cease-fire. It was designed not to fight but rather to allow those involved to disengage without further disturbance. It allowed for the peaceful resolution of one of the most dangerous crises which had faced the world since the Second World War. It also, incidentally, allowed for the clearance by the United Nations of the Suez Canal, which had been blocked during the previous military action.

NO WISH FOR REMOVAL

The United Nations Emergency Force in the Middle East has for six years watched over the borders of Israel with the United Arab Republic in the Gaza Strip and through the Sinai Desert. It also watches over the access to the Gulf of Aqaba and to the Israeli port of Elath. What was once a most troubled and terrorized frontier has become peaceful and prosperous on both sides, and the very presence of the United Nations Force is both an insurance against a resumption of trouble and a good excuse not to engage in it. It presents us with one serious problem. To maintain an army of over 5,000 men costs money, but at present the parties concerned have no wish to see it removed.

In 1958 another very tense situation, with quite different origins, occurred in Lebanon. After the success of UNEF, there were suggestions in many quarters that another United Nations force should be collected and dispatched to that country. Here, however, the problem, though aggravated by external factors, was essentially a domestic one.

The Security Council therefore set up a three-man observer group and left the Secretary-General considerable latitude as to the methods to be employed to make this group effective in watching over the possibilities of infiltration from outside. A highly mobile group of 600 officers was quickly organized to keep watch from ground and air, while the crisis itself was resolved by negotiation and discussion. By the end of 1958, it was possible to withdraw the United Nations Observer Group from the Lebanon altogether.

The greatest and most complex challenge to the United Nations in the peace-keeping field arose a few days after the Congo gained its independence from Belgium on June 30, 1960. The general proportions of this problem are sometimes obscured by a wealth of dramatic detail and are worth restating. Harassed by mutiny, lawlessness and the collapse of public order and services from within, and afflicted by foreign military intervention as well as by ominous threats of other forms of interference from without, the new Government of the Congo appealed to the United Nations for help.

The Security Council committed the United Nations to respond to this appeal and thus made the Organization not only the guarantor of law and order and the protector of the Congo against external interference from any source, but also the adviser and helper of a newly independent state which had had virtually no preparation for its independence.

By filling, in the space of a few hours, the very dangerous vacuum which existed in the Congo in July 1960, the urgent danger of a confrontation of the great powers in the heart of Africa was avoided and the territorial integrity of the Congo preserved. The new leaders of the Congo have been given at least a short breathing-spell in which to find their feet. Despite its shortcomings, which must be judged in the light of the fearsome complexity of the problem, the United Nations Operation in the Congo is, in my opinion, a most promising and encouraging experiment in international responsibility and action. . . .

76. A Comment on Shifting Objectives: Korea

LELAND M. GOODRICH

. . . At the time collective measures were being initiated, Secretary of State Acheson declared that the action was being taken "solely for the purpose of restoring the Republic of Korea to its status prior to the invasion from the north and of reestablishing the peace broken by that aggression."[28] This clearly excluded, as an objective of military action, the unification of Korea on the basis of the General Assembly's earlier recommendations, though the United Nations remained committed to this as the best solution of the Korean problem.

With the sudden and unexpected improvement of the military situation in Korea as the result of the Inchon landing of 15 September and the collapse of the North Korean military effort, the United States government appears to have substantially modified, if not reversed, its position. Speaking before the General Assembly's First Committee, Ambassador Austin urged that "the opportunities for new acts of aggression, of course, should be removed." It was not enough, he implied, to reestablish the peace that had been broken.

Faithful adherence to the United Nations objective of restoring international peace and security in the area counsels the taking of appropriate steps to eliminate the power and ability of the North Korean

[28] Department of State *Bulletin,* Vol. XXIII, No. 575 (10 July 1950), p. 46.

Leland M. Goodrich, "Collective Measures in Korea," *International Conciliation,* No. 494, October, 1953, pp. 172-174.

aggressor to launch future attacks. The aggressor's forces should not be permitted to have refuge behind an imaginary line because that would recreate the threat to the peace of Korea and of the world.[29]

With some reluctance, members of the General Assembly accepted this view by adopting on 7 October a resolution approving the idea that military operations should be pressed to the point where North Korean resistance to the implementation of the General Assembly's recommendation could be destroyed. The next day General MacArthur demanded the surrender of North Korean forces and announced his intention in the absence of a favorable response "to take such military action as may be necessary to enforce the decrees of the United Nations."[30] Thus, under the influence of military success and the prospect of complete military victory, the objective of military operations became merged with what had been the political objective of the United Nations since 1947.

The intervention of Chinese Communist armed forces, followed by the failure of General MacArthur's all-out offensive and the withdrawal of United Nations forces south of the thirty-eighth parallel, resulted in reconsideration of United Nations military objectives and return to a position close to that taken by Secretary Acheson in late June 1950. This position was later defined by Secretary Acheson in his testimony before the Senate Armed Services and Foreign Relations Committees in June 1951 in these words:

Our objective is to stop the attack, end the aggression on that government (Republic of Korea), restore peace, providing against the renewal of the aggression. These are the military purposes for which, as we understand it, the United Nations troops are fighting. The United Nations has since 1947 and the United States has since 1943 or 1944 stood for a unified, free and democratic Korea. That is still our purpose, and is still the purpose of the United Nations. I do not understand it to be a war aim. In other words, that is not sought to be achieved by fighting, but it is sought to be achieved by peaceful means, just as was being attempted before this aggression.[31]

---

[29] *Ibid.,* No. 588 (9 October 1950), p. 579.
[30] *The New York Times,* 9 October 1950, p. 2.
[31] *Military Situation in the Far East. . ., op. cit.,* Part 2, p. 1729.

This was the position consistently maintained by the United Nations Command throughout the armistice negotiations. Following the conclusion of the armistice, in the course of General Assembly debate, the Canadian Secretary of State for External Affairs, Lester B. Pearson, emphasized that the collective security action had been "for no other purpose than to help repel aggression" and he added, "we would be opposed to any attempt to interpret existing United Nations objectives as including the unification of Korea by force."[32]

[32] *The New York Times,* 24 September 1953, p. 1.

THE PROTECTION OF VITAL NATIONAL INTERESTS

77. Collective Action and the Protection of Vital Interests

CHARTER OF THE UNITED NATIONS

Article 51. Nothing in the present Charter shall impair the inherent right of individual or collective self-defense if an armed attack occurs against a Member of the United Nations, until the Security Council has taken measures necessary to maintain international peace and security. Measures taken by Members in the exercise of this right of self-defense shall be immediately reported to the Security Council and shall not in any way affect the authority and responsibility of the Security Council under the present Charter

Charter of the United Nations together with the Statute of the International Court of Justice, signed at the United Nations Conference on International Organization, San Francisco, California, June 26, 1945, Department of State Publication 2353, Conference Series 74 (Washington, D.C.: Government Printing Office, 1945).

to take at any time such action as it deems necessary in order to maintain or restore international peace and security.

78. Great Britain and the Suez Crisis

SELWYN LLOYD

. . . We have created a system of international law and order in which we have to face the fact that the Security Council is, first, frustrated by the veto and, secondly, that it cannot act immediately. In a sense, the policeman has his hands tied behind his back. He has to wait a long time before he is allowed to play his part.

I myself believe that, if you have accepted that system, you are only safe if you also retain the rights of individual countries to defend their own nationals and their own interests. . . .

We say that in the present international system, where the Security Council is subject to the veto, there must be the right for individual countries to intervene in an emergency to take action to defend their own nationals and their own interests. . . .

We have got to reserve to ourselves the right to take the necessary action in an emergency at the time we think fit. . . .

Statement of the British Foreign Secretary, Selwyn Lloyd, House of Commons, Debates, *Hansard,* Vol. 558, October 30, 1956, col. 1381.

79. French Interwar Policy

ARNOLD WOLFERS

Even if the League could have been successfully reserved to stop only German aggression, France would still have had reason to

From *Britain and France between Two Wars* by Arnold Wolfers, copyright, 1940, by Harcourt, Brace & World, Inc., and reprinted with their permission.

be troubled. Would pledges which were expressed in so general and universal a treaty as the Covenant prove reliable when assistance was actually needed? Many of the members of the League, such as the small neutral countries, would obviously never have agreed to pledge any assistance specifically to France or to one of her allies in Central Europe. Great Britain, even after having become a member of the League, resisted every attempt which was made to draw her into anything approximating an automatic commitment in the East, and refused consistently to make any specific pledges to countries in the integrity of which she was not vitally interested. At Locarno she drew a line between her readiness to assist France in the West and her attitude toward countries in the East. It would seem, therefore, that France and her friends were counting on obtaining these pledges through the back door of the League, apparently expecting that nations which would not have been willing to promise assistance to France or her small allies directly would be willing to assist them under the Covenant if they became "victims of aggression." This expectation was justified only if we accept the premise that the establishment of the League introduced a new element into the international situation which would induce countries to go further in their willingness to assist others than they would have been ready to do had they not been members of the League. In terms of the doctrine of "collective security," which we shall discuss later, the question was whether France could count on a new solidarity between nations, and on a new devotion to the enforcement of the law which would prompt countries to participate in League action against any violator of the Covenant.[58]

The French were inclined to be skeptical about all pledges, whatever the nature of the instrument into which they were incorporated. This accounted for what has been called France's "pactomania." Her skepticism, curiously enough, led her to seek pact after pact, promise after promise, as if a multiplicity of repetitious pledges would assure her of the much-desired security. . . .

---

[58] For criticism of any such expectations see James M. Spaight, *Pseudo-Security* (1928). Speaking of assistance in the air, he says, "The certainty and promptness of mutual assistance . . . must always be conditioned first by vicinage, secondly, by solidarity of vital interests" (p. 161).

It follows then that France had little basis for her hopes that the League Covenant would provide her with additional support against Germany. She would either have to deal with Conservative governments in other countries, which would only too readily evade their pledges by means of clever legal interpretations whenever the conflict appeared to them not to fall within the vital interests of their country; or she would be dealing with Liberal or Socialist governments, on whose devotion to the League she could count, but which would question the justice of the law she might wish to enforce. She would discover to her dismay that in the very cases most important to her (the territorial integrity of her Central European allies, Austrian independence, and the maintenance of the demilitarized zone on the Rhine) they would deny that the treaties deserved to be enforced, and would refuse to commit their countries to what appeared to them to be the prolongation of a regrettable *status quo*. The "Wilsonian principles" called for international solidarity and League sanctions in defense of victims of aggression, but they did not help a country seeking to preserve settlements which in so many respects violated the very principles of justice which Wilson had proclaimed.

From France's dilemma may be drawn a general conclusion. Even if for some reason the feeling of solidarity among nations should grow to the point where the nations would be willing in principle to participate in collective action against any "aggressor," no nation even then could rely on the assistance of the League unless it could convince the other members of the justice of its cause. The effectiveness of the League as an instrument of coercion would, therefore, depend not only on the existence of an adequate sense of solidarity among its members, but also on the justice of the law which was to be enforced. Since every law has to undergo change if it is to remain just, "revision" would be the *conditio sine qua non* of collective enforcement. While a League providing effectively for the redress of grievances and changes of the law may be imaginable only in a Utopia, it nevertheless serves as a standard against which to measure the Geneva League. . . .

ARE THE CONDITIONS ANOMALOUS?

80. The "Circular" Argument

WALTER SCHIFFER

. . . But the community in which this legal, nonpolitical method of compulsion was considered feasible appeared to require such a means of coercion because there was a constant risk of political disturbances among the same states which were expected, if necessary, to act together as guardians of the peace of the world. Thus the League concept was based on different assumptions which were not compatible with one another. The idea that a special machinery for the prevention of war was necessary implied the pessimistic assumption that the world's condition still was far from being perfect. But without the optimistic assumption that reason and good faith prevailed in the world, it could not be hoped that the new regime would work. It may be said that, as far as the prevention of war was concerned, the League's successful functioning depended on conditions which, if they had existed, would have made the organization unnecessary. . . .

. . . On the one hand, it was recognized that the unity of the global community still was disrupted by political conflicts which were the result of the antagonistic interests of states; under these circumstances the prevention of war constituted the most important international problem. On the other hand, the League was expected effectively to deal with this problem as if the peoples of the earth, united by nonpolitical interests, already had reached a degree of moral perfection and reasonableness which assured their peaceful coexistence.

Walter Schiffer, *The Legal Community of Mankind* (New York: Columbia University Press, 1954), pp. 199 and 201. Reprinted by permission.

81. A Kinder Appraisal

INIS L. CLAUDE, JR.

. . . The ideal of establishing collective security has been neither realized nor abandoned. The goal has been pursued more ardently and consistently in words than in deeds, and statesmen have regularly turned to other objectives when confronted with concrete situations of urgency. The world is very far from the satisfaction of the essential requirements for permitting the operation of a collective security system, and such a system, even if feasible, is in fact a less attractive ideal than it has often been considered. Nevertheless, this doctrine has achieved a major ideological significance, and it is probable that international organization will continue to pin its gaze upon the objective of collective security, while vacillating toward and away from it in actual policy.

If the analysis has suggested that the establishment of collective security would be a miracle, but that it would not work miracles if established, this point ought not to be taken too seriously. There are few if any doctrinal systems which can withstand the rigors of a maximalist analysis. Democracy, for instance, fares no better than collective security if subjected to a logic which pushes to the edges of its theoretical foundations. There is a logic of the practicable minimum, according to which systems are imperfectly established, and work moderately well, in defiance of the laws of logical gravity which should bring them tumbling down.

This happy rule of thumb in human affairs applies in the case of collective security. Some approximation of collective security action has been undertaken in two notable cases: the Italian invasion of Ethiopia in 1935, and the Communist assault upon South Korea in 1950. If the League's action in the former case was a failure, it was certainly not an unqualified failure, for it proved if anything the possible effectiveness of collective sanctions under better circumstances rather than the inherent unworkability of such an

---

enterprise. If the action of the United Nations in the latter case was a success, it was certainly not an unqualified success, for it did little to increase the probability that similar action—but action more fully compatible with the concept of collective security—would be forthcoming in future emergencies. Neither theoretical criticism nor practical experience has disposed of the possibility that the principles embodied in the doctrine of collective security may serve as elements contributing to the empirical development by international organization of a more effective approach to world order than has hitherto been realized. . . .

. . . It can be proved that collective security is a circular proposition, demanding the prior satisfaction of requirements which can be satisfied only after collective security has become successfully operative, and purporting to solve problems by means which assume that the problems have already been solved. It can be pointed out that a full-fledged collective security system cannot be achieved at one fell swoop, but that an incomplete and imperfect system may do more harm than good, by inducing states to rely upon it when it is unreliable, and by promoting the universalization of wars when it is in no position to achieve the collective frustration of aggression.

Yet, the point remains that the theory of collective security has inspired the growing recognition that war anywhere is a threat to order everywhere, has contributed to the maintenance of the realistic awareness that it is states which are the effective components of international society and which are consequently the essential objects of a system aiming at the control of international disorder, and has stimulated the rudimentary development of a sense of responsibility to a world community on the part of governments and peoples. As a doctrinaire formula for a global panacea, collective security is a snare as well as a delusion; as a formulation of the reality of global involvements and the ideal of global responsibilities, it may be a vital contribution to the evolutionary development of the conditions of peace through international organization. . . .

[VI]

Sanctions Open to a Collective Security Organization

What sanctions, if any, are open to a collective security organization for the purposes of preventing the disruption of peace or deterring aggression?

THE CONCEPTS OF SANCTIONS

The desire to "do something" to make aggression too costly is a perennial one: various suggestions have been made to carry it out, ranging from the "force of public opinion" (Reading 82), to the "outcast" concept (Reading 83), to the rigors of the economic boycott (Reading 84). The agent of the sanctions must also be considered (Reading 85).

THE APPLICATION OF SANCTIONS

Experience has, however, shown that the results of sanctions are largely unpredictable (Readings 86 and 87). Speculation about possible future sanctions continues (Readings 88 and 89).

THE CONCEPTS OF SANCTIONS

82. The "Force of Public Opinion" Concept

WOODROW WILSON

. . . Therefore, I want to call your attention, if you will turn to it when you go home, to Article XI, following Article X, of the

Woodrow Wilson, Speech at Indianapolis, September 4, 1919, *Addresses of President Wilson* (Western Tour, September 4-25, 1919), Senate Document No. 120, 66th Congress, 1st Session (Washington, D.C.: Government Printing Office, 1919), p. 26.

covenant of the league of nations. That article, let me say, is the favorite article in the treaty, so far as I am concerned. It says that every matter which is likely to affect the peace of the world is everybody's business; that it shall be the friendly right of any nation to call attention in the league to anything that is likely to affect the peace of the world or the good understanding between nations, upon which the peace of the world depends, whether that matter immediately concerns the nation drawing attention to it or not. In other words, at present we have to mind our own business. Under the covenant of the league of nations we can mind other peoples' business, and anything that affects the peace of the world, whether we are parties to it or not, can by our delegates be brought to the attention of mankind. We can force a nation on the other side of the globe to bring to that bar of mankind any wrong that is afoot in that part of the world which is likely to affect good understanding between nations, and we can oblige them to show cause why it should not be remedied. There is not an oppressed people in the world which can not henceforth get a hearing at that forum, and you know, my fellow citizens, what a hearing will mean if the cause of those people is just. The one thing that those who are doing injustice have most reason to dread is publicity and discussion, because if you are challenged to give a reason why you are doing a wrong thing it has to be an exceedingly good reason, and if you give a bad reason you confess [bad] judgment and the opinion of mankind goes against you. . . .

83. The "Outcast" Concept

WOODROW WILSON

. . . Let me remind you that every fighting nation in the world is going to belong to this league, because we are going to belong to it,

Woodrow Wilson, Speech at Des Moines, September 6, 1919, *Addresses of President Wilson* (Western Tour, September 4-25, 1919), Senate Document No. 120, 66th Congress, 1st Session (Washington, D.C.: Government Printing Office, 1919), p. 69.

and they all make this solemn engagement with each other, that they will not resort to war in the case of any controversy until they have done one or other of two things, until they have either submitted the question at issue to arbitration, in which case they promise to abide by the verdict whatever it may be, or, if they do not want to submit it to arbitration, have submitted it to discussion by the council of the league.

They agree to give the council six months to discuss the matter, to supply the council with all the pertinent facts regarding it, and that, after the opinion of the council is rendered, they will not then go to war if they are dissatisfied with the opinion until three more months have elapsed. They give nine months in which to spread the whole matter before the judgment of mankind, and if they violate this promise, if any one of them violates it, the covenant prescribes that that violation shall in itself constitute an act of war against the other members of the league. It does not provide that there shall be war. On the contrary, it provides for something very much more effective than war. It provides that that nation, that covenant-breaking nation, shall be absolutely cut off from intercourse of every kind with the other nations of the world; that no merchandise shall be shipped out of it or into it; that no postal messages shall go into it or come out of it; that no telegraphic messages shall cross its borders; and that the citizens of the other member States shall not be permitted to have any intercourse or transactions whatever with its citizens or its citizens with them. There is not a single nation in Europe that can stand that boycott for six months. There is not a single nation in Europe that is self-sufficing in its resources of food or anything else that can stand that for six months. And in those circumstances we are told that this covenant is a covenant of war. It is the most drastic covenant of peace that was ever conceived, and its processes are the processes of peace. The nation that does not abide by its covenants is sent to coventry, is taboo, is put out of the society of covenant-respecting nations. . . .

84. The Economic Boycott

WOODROW WILSON

. . . I want you to realize that this war was won not only by the armies of the world. It was won by economic means as well. Without the economic means the war would have been much longer continued. What happened was that Germany was shut off from the economic resources of the rest of the globe and she could not stand it. A nation that is boycotted is a nation that is in sight of surrender. Apply this economic, peaceful, silent, deadly remedy and there will be no need for force. It is a terrible remedy. It does not cost a life outside the nation boycotted, but it brings a pressure upon that nation which, in my judgment, no modern nation could resist. . . .

Woodrow Wilson, Speech at Indianapolis, September 4, 1919, *Addresses of President Wilson* (Western Tour, September 4-25, 1919), Senate Document No. 120, 66th Congress, 1st Session (Washington, D.C.: Government Printing Office, 1919), p. 22.

85. The Agents for Sanctions

WOODROW WILSON

. . . Let us go into particulars. These gentlemen say, "We do not want the United States drawn into every little European squabble." Of course, we do not, and under the league of nations it is entirely within our choice whether we will be or not. The normal processes of the action of the league are certainly to be this: When trouble arises in the Balkans, when somebody sets up a fire somewhere in

Woodrow Wilson, Address at Salt Lake City, September 23, 1919, *Addresses of President Wilson* (Western Tour, September 4-25, 1919), Senate Document No. 120, 66th Congress, 1st Session (Washington, D.C.: Government Printing Office, 1919), p. 324.

central Europe among those little nations, which are for the time being looking upon one another with a good deal of jealousy and suspicion, because the passions of the world have not cooled—whenever that happens, the council of the league will confer as to the best methods of putting out the fire. If you want to put out a fire in Utah, you do not send to Oklahoma for the fire engine. If you want to put out a fire in the Balkans, if you want to stamp out the smoldering flame in some part of central Europe, you do not send to the United States for troops. The council of the league selects the powers which are most ready, most available, most suitable, and selects them only at their own consent, so that the United States would in no such circumstances conceivably be drawn in unless the flame spread to the world. And would they then be left out, if they were not members of the league? You have seen the fire spread to the world once, and did not you go in? . . .

THE APPLICATION OF SANCTIONS

86. Attempts to Apply Sanctions: A Discussion

JOHN FOSTER DULLES

. . . We must in the international field look upon sanctions as adapted only to play a comparable role. They are not themselves a primary method of avoiding violence. This task is one to be achieved by the creation of a flexible and balanced form of world society. Until this is achieved it is premature to consider sanctions. When it is achieved, the role of sanctions will have shrunk to small

John Foster Dulles, *War, Peace and Change* (New York: Harper & Bros., 1939), pp. 96-99. Reprinted by permission.

dimensions and the problem of their form will be one of manageable proportions.

The premature development of sanctions has had definitely undesirable consequences. Most important is the fact that a procedure in itself meritorious has been discredited in many quarters by its improper use. Two other undesirable consequences seem worthy of note.

No people like to feel that their nation—personified as a hero—is subject to the coercion of others. In this respect nations are like individuals, who may accept coercion from an authority, as part of a balanced scheme of society, but who will bend every effort to be free of coercion by other individuals with whom they claim a status of equality.

To nations, the possibility of sanctions operates as a challenge to their independence. The immediate reaction is an effort to attain a status—military or economic—which will make them as immune as possible from coercion by sanctions. Thus the dynamic nations, feeling themselves to be the likely subject of sanctions by the *status quo* nations, are spurred on to build up their armament and attain economic self-sufficiency. They are unwilling that their internal economy should be so organized as to be dependent upon one or more other nations which are likely to apply sanctions. This explains such a fact as that Germany is relatively content to see prolonged the economic blockade which, when originally caused by the breakdown of her foreign exchange position, was regarded as a calamity. Now the economic independence thus forced upon her is welcomed as ending her vulnerability to economic sanctions. Other dynamic powers intensify their effort to control their own source of raw materials. Thus the potentiality of sanctions has tended to accentuate nationalism and the very policies which the sanction concept was designed to prevent.

In addition to the foregoing, it seems that the potentiality of sanctions is responsible, in some cases, for the tendency toward undeclared wars. Nations no longer feel bound to adhere to the classic procedure of "declaring" war. Hostilities, or the employment of force abroad, occur and may gradually expand in scope. Whether or not a "state of war" exists is left to individual judgments. There exists no formal criterion for fixing the moment when the external employment of force assumes the dignity of war. This tendency is dangerous. It permits subordinates, with local authority, to initiate a train of events having fateful consequences. There is lost a certain safeguard present when war involves a formal change of status which can be effected only by the solemn and deliberate decision of the highest authority. There are doubtless other causes operating to produce this trend toward undeclared wars. But one explanation is certainly the fact that this procedure renders awkward the invocation of sanctions, or of "neutrality" measures which have a similar effect. Neutral states, as a matter of friendliness or of domestic expediency, may close their eyes to operations which to others seem clearly to evidence a state of war. The possibility of cooperative neutral action is thus minimized.

* * *

The foregoing review permits of a generalization. Most peace efforts have only ephemeral results because they are limited to striking directly at an undesired manifestation. There is a failure to deal with causes which, if unaltered, inevitably produce that which we would avoid.

87. An Analysis of the "Economic Weapon" in Practice

RITA FALK TAUBENFELD AND HOWARD J. TAUBENFELD

. . . The revolutionary decision to employ sanctions against Italy in 1935 came after repeated failures of the League to take stringent action in the face of open aggression as, for example, with Japan in Manchuria. It was undertaken when there was still strong faith in the efficacy of economic measures, but it was circumscribed in many ways. . . .

Rita Falk Taubenfeld and Howard J. Taubenfeld, "The 'Economic Weapon': The League and the United Nations," *Proceedings of the American Society of International Law,* at its 58th Annual Meeting, April 23-25, 1964, pp. 183-204, at pp. 184-187. Reprinted by permission.

Actually, in the fall of 1935, the limited measures adopted were widely expected, at least as time went by, to make war so costly for Italy that a "reasonable" solution could be evolved. . . .

The belated and partial restrictions adopted did interfere with Italian trade to a substantial degree, but they did not interfere at all seriously with Italy's war-making potential or even with the comfort of her population. Italy had been able to build significant stockpiles of many essential products in the period from December, 1934, to September, 1935, while her intentions grew ever clearer. She was able to continue this process for at least a month and a half after the invasion, since, for coordination purposes, the effective date for many sanctions measures was November 18. The failure to ban important items, such as petroleum, and the failure to cut off shipments of banned items from non-Members and even from Members permitted Italian industry to function at high levels. Furthermore new or strengthened direct economic controls over the economy were employed by the Fascist government. Foreign exchange assets were marshaled. Imports and exports were controlled. The corporate system permitted informal controls on wages and many prices. There was some rationing. Autarchy was in any event a goal of Italy. Moreover, international opprobrium, rather than weakening the aggressor's government, was turned into a tool for uniting the Italian people behind the Fascists in defiance of the League.

With the measures of control over trade and over the economy which were adopted or strengthened, few of the hardships envisioned by the advocates of economic sanctions were in fact felt by the Italian people. Indeed, the build-up and war periods saw a substantial decline in Italy's unemployment problem. While wages rose little or not at all, many families saw over-all income rise as more members went to work or received Army pay. In the relatively brief period of the war, Italy was forced to draw heavily on her resources of gold and foreign exchange, and some sectors of the economy, the trade-dependent textile industry, for example, were seriously disturbed, but no shortages of *critical* raw materials developed either. Thanks to stockpiling, she would not in fact even have developed a shortage of that most vulnerable strategic need, petroleum, within the length of time of the actual warfare.

Paradoxically, the sharp rise in Italian trade which followed the end of sanctions was due, in large part, both to the eagerness of traders in former sanctionist countries to recover their positions in trade and to the futile attempts of several nations to regain Italy's valued friendship. It was largely financed by the former sanctionists. Since these credits went largely unhonored by Italy, they were in effect a form of reparations which compensated Italy for her temporary loss of international reserves. The resultant trade rapidly erased such shortages or diminished stockpiles as had been caused by sanctions and Italy's autarchical response. Sanctions had not caused Italy's stock of raw materials to dwindle to a dangerous level, but the possibility perhaps caused Italy to quicken her war efforts. As Haile Selassie told the League on June 30, 1936, the major effect of sanctions seemed to have been to cause Italy to use poison gas to hasten the conquest. While nuclear weapons are available at least to some nations, this hazard is implicit even in sanctions which are slowly succeeding, a point worth pondering when considering the usefulness of any program based exclusively on gradual deterrence.

It can be argued that the Italian case was no fair test of the concept of all-out economic sanctions. The nature of the Italian aggression was clear-cut. There was widespread public support in many countries for action by the League. Yet it was not possible for political, economic and, to a limited degree, technical reasons to make sanctions either as immediate or as comprehensive as the terms of Article 16 contemplated, or to obtain co-operation from all Members or from any major non-Member. Fear of war with Italy, fear of the loss of Italian political support against resurging Germany, fear of loss of markets, particularly to non-Members who were not even technically bound, and even sympathy with Italy's position imposed the real limits to the action taken. The nature of the victim, a country in a continent already largely occupied by major European Powers, led to a reluctance in some official circles, as in France, to risk much in her support.

The principal failures on the League's part, without consideration here of how politically inevitable these omissions were, can be summed up by that all too familiar phrase of the 1930's, "too little and too late." They include: (1) the long delay between the time Italy conceived and indeed openly avowed her project and the time sanctions went into effect, giving ample time for Italian stockpiling and military build-up; (2) the limited nature of the measures, involving a total refusal to consider seriously any measures that, by promising to succeed, might have offended Italy seriously enough to provoke retaliation in the form of war or even a "mad dog" attack on a base or ship. Thus, any move that might have involved or led to the use of even limited armed forces, such as closing the Suez Canal or embargoing *all* exports, including oil, to Italy or the giving of direct aid to Ethiopia was avoided. To these must be added: (3) the failure to obtain full compliance from all League Members, particularly Italy's neighbors, Austria and Hungary, with the measures adopted; (4) the failure to interfere, through persuasion or blockade, with Italy's provisioning by non-Members, particularly the United States and Germany; and later (5) the unwillingness to protract the crisis after the *fait accompli* by extending the duration of comprehensive measures for whatever period was necessary to bring Italy to the point where concessions would have been forthcoming.

At the same time that the League did not dare tip the scales decisively against Italy, other factors worked in Italy's favor. The disparity in the military strengths of the aggressor and the victim permitted a conquest in a far shorter time than the proponents of economic measures, used alone, would have sought for a test of this gradual weapon. The limited nature of the League's reaction itself in turn encouraged the later moves made by Hitler which, in turn, assured that sanctions would not be increased or continued indefinitely by nations far more anxious to have Mussolini's support against Germany than to save an African state.

In the U. N. Charter system, the Security Council, whose Members control most of the world's armed forces, can, under appropriate circumstances, take action for the maintenance of international peace and security, legally requiring that Members (and perhaps non-Members as well) participate in, or at least refrain from obstructing, the action ordered. While in both world wars economic measures formed only a support for comprehensive military operations, the second World War suggested anew certain potentialities of the increasingly sophisticated art of economic warfare. Article 41 of the Charter again gave the "easy" route of economic and financial sanctions a respectable place in the United Nations' arsenal, but only as a part of a sweeping plan of response to the problem of preserving peace. The General Assembly's Collective Measures Committee has also given detailed attention to economic measures, both as a normal adjunct to military action and, used alone, as an independent sanction, but the high hopes of the League were never revived after 1936. During the Korean conflict, major economic pressure was applied against the North Korean authorities in support of the vigorously applied but limited military sanctions used. The entry of Chinese Communist troops into the fighting was countered militarily, but initially drew only the additional measure of designation by the General Assembly of the Communist government as an aggressor, and it took until February 1, 1951, before several governments were reluctantly willing to go this far. The Soviet bloc openly refused co-operation. An embargo only on strategic materials was not recommended until May 18, 1951, and this fell far short in coverage of what the United States and other active participants had long since felt it essential to restrict in their own dealings with China during the war. The final political compromise aims of the participants were apparently even more modest than with Italy. This reflects the general desire to have widespread support and to avoid the risk of serious offense to the Soviet Union and to Communist China which might have extended the conflict. The limitations on the list of embargoed items and, particularly, the inevitable failure to cut off supplies and transshipments from Russia and Eastern Europe, assured that the U. N.'s economic recommendations could not seriously interfere with the Chinese economy. The net effect of the measures is unclear. While they reportedly slowed to some extent the building of a powerful Chinese economy, they may have spurred development by helping to mobilize the people's will to sacrifice. There was obviously little serious effect on China's war-making capacity. International opposition was used by the Communist government to build morale and to strengthen its already planned centralized controls. Moreover, after 1953 when the Korean truce became stabilized, United States insistence on the continued maintenance of the embargo brought it into sporadic conflict with its co-operating allies, who anxiously regarded China as a potential market. In 1957, these friends and allies abandoned special restrictions on trade with China and the United States officially ignored their "defection."

In a similar way, the more recent proposals for an embargo on trade with the Republic of South Africa, recommended by the General Assembly in November, 1962, have been ignored by South Africa's major trading partners, including the United States and Britain, which did not favor the resolution and abstained from approving it. The recommendation has also been largely ignored by most states which backed the embargo, including especially Albania, Czechoslovakia, Poland and Mexico, and South African exports in 1963 reached an all-time peak of $1.4 billion. As a recommendation only, no institutional organization for planning, sharing or policing the embargo was specified.

The admittedly limited forms of economic sanctions employed to date by general international organizations have failed to accomplish anything significant. Are these failures due to inherent weaknesses in the particular sets of measures chosen, or to the political circumstances under which such measures have been, and perhaps inevitably will be, adopted, or do they discredit the general potentialities of even the most comprehensive, well-administered economic measures? . . .

88. Economic Sanctions: Universal or Partial

AMELIA C. LEISS

It is obvious that the subject of collective economic measures and other economic pressures against South Africa contains a multitude of complexities and imponderables. While there are numerous un-

Amelia C. Leiss, editor, *Apartheid and United Nations Collective Measures, An Analysis* (New York: Carnegie Endowment for International Peace, 1965), p. 130.

certainties present, the greatest of all is the psychological response of white South Africans. Based on purely economic calculations and assuming determination on the part of the South African government to resist the measures taken, it becomes reasonably clear that no single economic measure would be likely to have a sufficiently powerful impact to force acquiescence. Indeed, South Africa could probably hold out against a complete boycott and embargo reasonably well for several years, possibly longer. Of great importance to those imposing measures are the elements of will and of unity, and the two are closely related. Without a nearly universal commitment to stringent measures, the will to sustain them is likely to dissipate; material effectiveness of any economic measures requires complete adherence, for any single developed nation could presumably replace whatever supplies were needed to keep the essential elements of the Republic economy in operation. Indeed, any nation that was prepared to transship the necessary items might destroy the material effectiveness of economic measures. . . .

. . . It does not necessarily follow that no measures should be applied or that none would be effective. The adoption of an increasing number of partial restrictions by a growing number of countries—these constricting moves taken as evidence of the moral condemnation of a larger and larger part of the world—might have just as effective psychological impact, at least over a number of months, as wholesale application of economic measures. Possible candidates for a partial approach include restrictions on new investment, discouragement of permanent migration to the Republic, boycotts on individual commodities such as wool and citrus fruit, continued denial of port, airport, and overflight privileges in Africa, and embargoes of specific exports to South Africa. It might even be possible to spread the burden and thus the acceptability of economic steps and measures through agreements by each trading partner to forego exports of some major item or to reduce exports and imports with South Africa by a given percentage. Such a strategy of partial and individual steps would have two advantages over more universal measures: imposition would not have to be postponed awaiting universal agreement that may never come, and it would give more time for South African opinion to adjust to the necessity for an accommodation. . . .

89. Speculation on South Africa

AMELIA C. LEISS

. . . The goals that are usually thought of as being sought through use of collective measures are repelling aggression, restoring a *status quo* threatened by force, or acting to thwart an imminent attack by one state on another. Even when UN action has been in response to aggression, the problems of achieving and maintaining consensus have proved formidable enough. In Korea, for example, the objective remained obscure throughout much of the period of UN action: Was the objective to throw the North Korean invaders back across the 38th parallel? Was it to implement earlier General Assembly resolutions calling for Korean unification? After Chinese intervention raised fears of a broadening of the hostilities, including possible Soviet involvement, did the objective shift to achievement of an honorable compromise? Can anyone state with assurance that there was any single objective generally agreed upon even at the beginning? In many respects, the objectives that many states appear to seek through the use of UN collective measures against the Republic of South Africa seem akin to aims often pursued in war, whether by individual nations or by coalitions: The principal objective appears to be to overturn the *status quo* there and replace it with one more in keeping with international standards. But it would be difficult to justify from history the contention that such war aims have been clear-cut, generally accepted, and stable over time.

Perhaps the nature of UN objectives in South Africa could be best understood in terms of the Congo operation, where, initially at least, a major problem was to restore order and the authority of the central government (with the crucial difference that in South Africa this might be the second task). In the Congo the problem of maintaining a consensus was perhaps the central one faced—both at UN Headquarters and in the field. Differing national ob-

Amelia C. Leiss, editor, *Apartheid and United Nations Collective Measures, An Analysis* (New York: Carnegie Endowment for International Peace, 1965), pp. 75-78. Footnotes omitted.

jectives became identified with the fate of competing groups within the country, at times gravely threatening the entire undertaking. This would almost certainly be the case in South Africa as well, particularly if the measures employed had been large-scale military ones, suggesting considerable political, social, and economic dislocation as well as the presence of military units of a number of different states.

CONSENSUS ON LIMITED GOALS

In the case of South Africa, the situation is complicated by the fact that there might be objectives limited only to South West Africa, or broader objectives that relate to the Republic of South Africa itself. A very difficult political situation could be created by a Security Council decision to use collective measures to compel South African compliance with a decision about South West Africa alone, if at the same time strong pressures were being exerted to persuade the Council to use such measures to compel a change in *apartheid* policies in the Republic as well. Presumably when the more limited South West African goals were achieved, the measures would be stopped. But the political pressure to maintain them in the pursuit of larger goals would be enormous. And, depending on how relations with the Republic had developed, much of the reluctance to do so might well evaporate in such circumstances. Furthermore if South Africa resisted to the full measure of its capacity measures aimed particularly at its South West African policy, the distinction between the partial and the larger goals could become largely academic.

Much the same could be said if the decision to take measures was based on some limited goal for the Republic itself—for example, the convening of a national convention to draw up a new non-racial constitution. A limited goal of this nature would pose the additional problem of whether the coercion should cease once the government agreed to call such a convention or whether the operation should continue—or be reimposed—if the majority in the UN were not satisfied either with the outcome or that the government was acting in good faith.

Another problem of a similar nature that is imaginable, if unlikely, is that the various elements in South Africa could agree on a solution to their problems that was not to the liking of a number of other states. For example, it was suggested in Chapter 3 that, under some circumstances, the Africans in South Africa might accept a restricted franchise now with the intention to press for a full franchise in future, although the only goal they at present say would be acceptable is full adult suffrage. Or perhaps still more unlikely, the groups in South Africa might agree to a partition—which again the Africans at present reject. Both of these compromise solutions have been vigorously attacked by the African and other members of the UN. Would they press to continue coercion until a one-man-one-vote unified South Africa was accepted? This could be a particularly difficult situation since there would doubtless be groups of Africans in the Republic and in exile who would also find the compromise unpalatable.

CONSENSUS UNDER PRESSURE

If it is important to be as clear as possible about the objectives being sought through collective measures, it is equally important to realize that the consensus may be influenced by the course of applying such measures themselves and by events unrelated to their application. The intervention of China in Korea clearly shook the consensus with which the UN Korean operation was undertaken. The Lumumba assassination and the Katanga secession effort strained the shifting consensus that underlay the UN's Congo operation. There are numerous ways in which a program of collective measures against the Republic of South Africa could be subjected to comparable pressures.

For example, were economic measures to be required for a longer period of time than had been anticipated, the strain on some of the participating states could become very severe. Or UN military forces might suffer temporary reverses that might shake the resolve of some participating states. Conceivably South Africa could itself exert economic or even military pressure on some of the states contiguous to it (the High Commission Territories may be particularly vulnerable, as will be suggested in Chapter 6).

One of the results of pressures of this sort could be to persuade some states to assist South Africa to evade a collective measures system—and indeed some states might do so in any event. The question would then arise whether to extend the collective measures to compel all states to cooperate. For example, should Portugal refuse to take the steps in Angola and Mozambique required to make certain economic measures effective, the result might be pressure to extend a blockade to those two territories, or to take measures against Portugal, or both. But states' willingness to take collective measures against Portugal may be far different from their willingness to do so against South Africa.

Finally, pressures on the consensus of those employing the measures could arise from unanticipated crises elsewhere. As an illustration, the problem for states using their naval units for a blockade could become difficult if a crisis elsewhere in the world demanded the use of those same units.

CONSENSUS AND FAILURE

It has already been suggested that it may not always be easy to agree on when UN objectives had been accomplished. Equally if not more difficult problems may be connected with deciding either that one form of measure had failed and that another more stringent measure should be imposed or that the entire undertaking had failed and should be terminated.

Failure in the first form would, in essence, entail decisions to abandon the effort or to "escalate" the level of measures. Preliminary analysis suggests that, aside from the initial decision to employ measures, the most difficult decisions would be to go from economic to military measures, and from a limited military measure such as blockade to larger-scale more direct military action. Consensus to employ fairly low-level measures may not imply consensus to take more stringent measures; indeed, it would probably imply the reverse, even though, as will be shown in Chapter 7, it might be desirable in some ways to have such agreement from the outset. However, once the collective measures door had been opened, it might be easier to obtain agreement to further measures than it was to agree to begin them at all.

CONSENSUS AND PARTICULAR STATES

Those who at present argue for collective measures against South Africa stress the central importance of British and American participation in them. And in terms of both economic and military measures, the analysis in Chapters 6 and 7 of this analysis will tend to support the same view. These two states would have, throughout most of the phases of a collective measures program, an overriding influence on the nature of consensus and on the decisions taken. Thus a U. S.-U. K. decision to terminate a blockade, whether because of success (as they would define it) or failure, would probably be decisive because they alone appear to possess the physical means of undertaking the blockade. Similarly, should collective measures ever reach the point of a large-scale amphibious landing, the same would probably apply. In the field of economic measures, their cooperation would be equally vital. This suggests two things: first, that consensus may crystallize at any one moment on what these two countries are prepared to do (even while pressure was exerted to do more) and, second, that regardless of what the majority wanted, the United States and the United Kingdom could, if they felt it necessary, prevent further action.

But looking over the entire spectrum of measures—from diplomatic, to more and more massive economic, to stronger and stronger military—there would come a point at which this was no longer true. Were a point to be reached of small-unit land fighting, for example, other states could supply and maintain a sizable operation.

[VII]

Collective Security and National Control of Power

A basic assumption of collective security is that the collective security organization will be able to muster sufficient power to deter or to deal successfully with any threat to, or breach of, the peace. The question arises whether this assumption can be generally realized when nations control power, especially military power, and the international organization does not independently control greater power. Would the possibilities for effective collective security be improved if nations reduced their arms significantly? Disarmed completely? Created an international military force under international control? Agreed to world government?

A STATEMENT OF GOALS

Disarmament, international peace-keeping forces, and collective security are linked. In February, 1960, Secretary of State Christian Herter (Reading 90) set forth the view which has since been incorporated into the basic United States position on disarmament, as evidenced in the United States Draft Outline for General and Complete Disarmament in a Peaceful World, of April, 1962.[1]

REACHING THE GOALS

1. *Is levitation possible?*

A discussion of a central paradox is found in Reading 91.

2. *Is political consensus an essential precondition for agreement on disarmament?*

In Reading 92, the argument is made that the most hopeful path along which to proceed is that of the separation of disarmament from problems of political consensus.

---

[1] For text, see *Documents on American Foreign Relations, 1962* (New York: Harper & Bros. for the Council on Foreign Relations, 1963), pp. 115-151.

3. *A caveat on the effects of disarmament.*

The author of Reading 93 argues that disarmament can never be *irreversible* and that this should be taken into account in any disarmament scheme.

SPECULATIONS ON AN INTERNATIONAL MILITARY FORCE

There is general agreement that disarmament would bring with it a need for some sort of international force capable of dealing in some way with the conflicts that would be bound to arise. There is, however, a wide variety of proposals as to the type of force this should be. To divide them in a very general sort of way, they fall into two broad rubrics: (1) those calling for some form of supranational organ with wide powers, and (2) the more moderate ones calling for a "deterring" or "balancing" force.

1. *Proposals for supranational forces.*

A call for a supranational force to be composed of individual volunteers and with careful safeguards against any undue proportion from any one nation is made in Reading 94. In Reading 95, a force under the control of the United Nations as a sovereign body is proposed.

2. *An international force as a deterring factor.*

An argument for an international force of a more modest character, to act as a "buffer" and as a deterrent is set forth in Reading 96. An international force of a modest policing nature is discussed in Reading 97.

A STATEMENT OF GOALS

90. The American Purpose

CHRISTIAN S. HERTER

. . . Speaking generally, we will have two major goals in the forthcoming negotiations:

Christian S. Herter, "National Security with Arms Limitation," *Department of State Bulletin,* March 7, 1960, pp. 354-358.

Urgently, to try to create a more stable military environment, which will curtail the risk of war and permit reductions in national armed forces and armaments.

Subsequently, to cut national armed forces and armaments further and to build up international peacekeeping machinery, to the point where aggression will be deterred by international rather than national force.

These two goals are equally important. I should like to discuss each of them. . . .

[Measures] to create a stable military environment would be the first stage in our approach to disarmament.

They would enhance our national security and reduce the danger of war.

They would also leave our essential national freedom of action and our relative national capabilities unimpaired. Since large national forces would thus still be under arms, national force—not international law—would still be the ultimate resort.

To assure a world of peaceful change, we should project a second stage of general disarmament. Our objective in this second stage should be twofold:

First, to create certain universally accepted rules of law which, if followed, would prevent all nations from attacking other nations. Such rules of law should be backed by a world court and by effective means of enforcement—that is, by international armed force.

Second, to reduce national armed forces, under safeguarded and verified arrangements, to the point where no single nation or group of nations could effectively oppose this enforcement of international law by international machinery.

Unless *both* these objectives are kept firmly in view, an agreement for general disarmament might lead to a world of anarchy. In the absence of effective international peacekeeping machinery, nations might violate the disarmament agreement with impunity and thus seek to gain a decisive headstart in building up their armaments. Moreover, since each state would be allowed to retain internal security forces, populous states would retain quite substantial forces which they might—in the absence of such peacekeeping machinery—use effectively against their smaller neighbors.

To guard against these dangers, we should, as general disarmament is approached, work toward effective international arrangements which will maintain peace and security and promote justice according to law....

REACHING THE GOALS

91. Is Levitation Possible?

LAWRENCE S. FINKELSTEIN

... When we begin to consider the long-range implications of disarmament, we encounter [a] ... central paradox. All those who address these problems seem to agree that, when disarmament proceeds far enough, the world will need new instruments for maintaining world order....

Where, you may ask, lies the paradox in this? It lies in the fact that we are introducing as important elements in the pattern of negotiations for disarmament questions which the world has never been able to solve and which we have little reason to believe it is now capable of solving. Why believe that a world which does not have enough consensus to reach international agreement on the limits of territorial waters can reach agreement on what amounts to world government? The paradox lies in the fact that the Soviet Government and the United States Government are advocating systems of international policing which depend on a very high degree of international consensus at a moment in history when discord prevails....

The formulation of goals for the future is, of course, an essential and desirable expression of human hopes and aspirations. There is no harm, it seems to me, in reminding ourselves that if our hopes

Lawrence S. Finkelstein, "Defense, Disarmament and World Order," Address, as reprinted in *Behind the Headlines,* periodical of the Canadian Institute of International Affairs, September, 1962, pp. 1-12, at pp. 8-10.

for disarmament are realized, we should expect to find, not that the world's problems have been solved, but that we have created new ones of equal difficulty and complexity. Probably, we shall not even have eliminated all the old ones. It is desirable for us to be turning our minds to the questions of this order which we hope some day to confront. . . .

However, I should be less than frank with you if I pretended that I believed that a disarmed well-organized world was likely to result from our efforts along these lines. It seems to me that, if such a world is ever to materialize, it will be because of drastic changes in the present international structure of ideologies, economics and politics—changes which we cannot now foresee and which, therefore, cannot be studied in the expectation that the studies will be operationally useful. There is, in short, very little evidence in recent history or in the contemporary scene to support the expectation that mankind has set foot on the road to utopia.

Why then do I believe it is desirable and useful to contemplate a future I do not expect to exist? The primary reason is that examination of the future as we would like it to be is an excellent way to understand the present as it is. It should also help us to identify the forks in the road from here to there which will pose for us crucial choices affecting our ability ultimately to arrive at our destination.

If we pursue these studies conscientiously and candidly, we are bound to be influenced by a central consideration. Disarmament and constructing a world order are not separable from the entire complex and contorted matrix of man's goals and values, political behaviour, and attitudes toward law and the other techniques for adjusting his relations with his fellow man. It is not irrelevant to our goals that communist purposes and methods conflict with ours in many areas of the globe. Some would say that this very conflict underscores the necessity to disarm and order the world. While agreeing with them, I fear that this conflict exemplifies the reasons why we cannot expect to succeed quickly in the effort. Soviet Deputy Premier Mikoyan dramatized the point when he said recently that "disarmament would strip the 'imperialists' of the means of 'resisting the revolutionary actions of the proletariat and the peasantry'." Mr. Mikoyan obviously expects the conflict between this world and ours to continue even after disarmament.

Even if the world were not rent by the dispute between communism and the West over who is to organize the world, do we have reason to believe that other differences—equally deep and equally central—would not arise to plague our efforts to construct a viable international order? We can see the outlines of such divisions already delineated in the differences between the northern and southern worlds, differences which find expression not only in a competition for the material benefits of contemporary technology, but also in far-reaching intellectual and ideological contests over the symbols of morality and the standards for the conduct of international relationships. . . .

The point of this is not that world order will never be achieved. It is that the road will be long and difficult and that we are very far from having established the conditions in which we can expect to achieve the end we seek. To me, it is more important to learn to live successfully with the problems of today and the near future than to rest our hopes on our ability to eliminate them. We should examine our vision of the future as a means to better understanding of our contemporary condition. We should not expect that we can, by some process of levitation, as it were, lift ourselves from today's quagmire to the pinnacle we hope to reach tomorrow. If we devote too much energy to the long range goals, the result may be to divert essential effort from the tasks that confront us now. In my judgment, the present tasks are both promising and difficult enough to be worthy of the best we have to give. . . .

92. Political Consensus: An Essential Precondition?

ARTHUR I. WASKOW

. . . It is also sometimes argued that no disarmament agreement will be reached unless and until the political climate in conflicting States

Arthur I. Waskow, *Quis Custodiet? Controlling the Police in a Disarmed World,* A Peace Research Institute Report Submitted under ACDA Grant ACDA/IR-8 (Washington, D.C.: Peace Research Institute, Inc., 1963), pp. 6-7. Reprinted by permission.

has changed so much that not only agreement on disarmament *per se* but adequate *political* agreements could be achieved sufficient to establish political institutions capable of controlling a "world army." This argument raises two questions: first, whether the achievement of disarmament *per se* is separable from settlement of political conflicts; and secondly, whether, if it is so separable, the United States should or should not be prepared to accept the one —disarmament—without the other.

The second question involves among others the problem of timing: that is, whether it is better to wait for disarmament until it can be achieved together with political agreements, or to accept disarmament *per se* if it is possible to get it. In any case, the question is outside the scope of this report.

The first question, however—may the achievement of disarmament be separable from political settlements?—lies near the heart of the problem being examined by this report. It is at least conceivable, taking into account the way in which various governments have during the last fifteen years distinguished the problem of arms control and disarmament from the pursuit of their national interests, that agreement on disarmament and political agreements are separable. *It may well be that many governments now regard disarmament not as a way of establishing a world order acceptable to all nations, but as a way of changing the means of independently pursuing the national interest.* This view of disarmament would assume that States had taken into account both the increasing danger involved in using military means of advancing the national interest, because of the scale of modern weaponry, and the increasing difficulty of actually using military means, because of the increasing deterrent effect of the large-scale weaponry. In other words, the interest in disarmament may have arisen from a growing acceptance of "the hypertrophy of war" as a *means,* rather than from a growing acceptance of world order as an *end.* In the event that this view has directed the attention of some governments to the possibility of achieving disarmament, *such governments may not regard it as necessary or desirable to change their political goals as a concomitant of changing from military to other means of pursuing those goals.*

If this view of disarmament as a means be taken by several or possibly even one of the major States, it is possible to see that agreement on disarmament could be made an issue separable from agreement on political settlements. And it is thus possible to imagine a situation in which neither as a prerequisite to nor as a result of a disarmament agreement is there any enlargement of the area of political consensus between States. In that case, to recapitulate the previous argument, the absence of sufficient political consensus may prevent the establishment of international political institutions capable of effectively controlling an armed force so large as to be a "world army." . . .

93. A Caveat on the Effects of Disarmament

THOMAS C. SCHELLING

. . . Total disarmament cannot make war impossible. Short of universal brain surgery, nothing can erase the memory of weapons and how to build them. Total disarmament would not preclude rearmament; it would not preclude the reconstruction of modern weapons in the event of primitive war. Primitive war itself may be large and destructive. Disarmament so total that, even without the reconstruction of modern weapons, war could not be waged is literally inconceivable.

If total disarmament makes war unlikely, and if it makes rearmament unlikely, it is not because it physically precludes war and rearmament, nor because it legally condemns them, but because it eliminates the incentives for rearmament and the incentives that lead to war or to its escalation and modernization.

Disarmament may slow the tempo of war and of military decisions; it may reduce the danger of precipitous decision and help to moderate war if war occurs. Disarmament may make it difficult

Thomas C. Schelling, *The Stability of Total Disarmament,* Study Memorandum I, Special Studies Group, (Washington, D.C.: Institute for Defense Analyses, October, 1961), pp. 1-4 and 50-51. Reprinted by permission.

to launch war without visible preparation—without warning—in time to permit countermeasures. Disarmament may make it difficult to rearm decisively, by making rearmament visible to other nations in time for their own rearmament or other countermeasures. Disarmament may thus be a situation in which war is deterred; or in which the enlargement of war, if war occurs, is deterred; or in which the resumption of the arms race is deterred. They may be deterred by an evident lack of advantage in initiating war, in initiating rearmament in the course of war, and in initiating rearmament in the absence of war. If so, disarmament meets the conditions sought in other proposals for arms control.

Disarmament may also reduce the destructiveness of war, if war occurs, by altering the character of war, the motives in war, or the timing of war. It cannot much reduce the *potential* capability for destruction; even primitive war can be long and destructive or can be modernized by rearmament.

These remarks do not disparage total or near-total disarmament. They remind us that there is no such thing as the general and complete elimination of all utensils with which nations might attack each other, much less a way to eliminate them *irreversibly*. . . .

We must not apply a double standard in comparing disarmament with the present world. It is sometimes argued that those who expect disarmed countries to be suspicious of each other, to have thoughts of cheating, or to seek advantage through war and threats of war or through rearmament and threats of rearmament, have a pessimistic, suspicious, and military orientation toward world affairs. But in this paper we shall be talking about disarmament in this world, with nations that now exist, and with governments not far separated in time from present governments. If there is now a genuine danger of war, because nations are suspicious, anxious, fearful for their security, nationalistic, tempted by military gains, or willing to take the risk of war on issues that divide them, and if this genuine danger of war motivates our interest in disarmament, we cannot base our hopes for the viability of disarmament on a denial of the very premise that makes disarmament attractive. If nations *do* suspect each other of contemplating *war,* we have to suppose that they might suspect each other of contemplating rearmament; if nations are willing to risk war, or to threaten it, they certainly might risk rearming or threatening to rearm; nations considered capable of being panicked into war might be capable of being panicked into rearmament. To suppose the contrary is to assume away the problem that disarmament is supposed to help us solve.

Nor should we suppose that acute crises, even some species of war itself, may not arise under disarmament, or that there will be no trouble makers, civil wars and revolutions, dissident countries, rearmament campaigns within countries, or bitter non-military rivalry, unless we assume international relationships of such tranquility that disarmament would be unnecessary for the foreseeable future. . . .

From some points of view there is an abrupt difference between some nuclear weapons and none at all, between maintaining deterrence and abandoning it for a disarmed world. Many people feel that an important advantage of "total" disarmment—an advantage it does not share with so-called "arms control"—is that it does away with military thinking, military planning, military preoccupations, and military establishments committed to indescribable punishment in response to attack. But this analysis of military security in a disarmed world has led us to suspect that disarmament and peace will be more durable if constant attention is paid to its "deterrent" structure, especially if the disarmament agreement permits the retention of some retaliatory weapons. If this attention is required, we may already have contaminated the "non-military" environment that many people hope for from disarmament. The character of the world and the organization of its security would not have changed as drastically as some people had hoped.

If our analysis is correct, this situation has to be acknowledged, even if reluctantly; and it would seem to require us to reconsider the original preference for "total disarmament." But although we began by assuming that a consciously stabilized deterrence had mutual advantages of a military sort, while total disarmament had advantages of a quite different sort, our analysis suggests that we should seek a controlled-deterrence system in any case, even under near-total disarmament. If so, we should be reconciled to it and do the best we can to design it effectively. Arguments that favor going *all* the way may not be good arguments for going *nearly* all the way toward total disarmament. Although this does not necessarily establish a presumption for large deterrence forces, it does deflate any presumption in favor of the smallest possible, if the smallest possible differs only in degree from other levels.

It may be argued that to perpetuate military deterrence is to settle for a peace based on fear. But the contrast with total disarmament is not persuasive. What deters rearmament in a disarmed world, or small wars that may escalate into rearmament and possibly war, is presumably the fear of a resumed arms race, and war. The point to be emphasized is that the "fear" involved in any arrangement—total disarmament, cooperatively established mutual deterrence, or anything else—is a function of confidence. If the consequences of transgression are plainly bad—bad for all parties, and little dependent on who transgresses first—we can take the consequences for granted and call it a "balance of prudence." What keeps me from stepping off a train before it stops is not "fear", I just know better.

Disarmament may make some of our military problems more manageable. It will not make them disappear.

SPECULATIONS ON AN INTERNATIONAL MILITARY FORCE

94. A Proportioned Supranational Force of Volunteers

GRENVILLE CLARK AND LOUIS B. SOHN

. . . This Annex contains a detailed plan for a world police force, to be called the United Nations Peace Force and to consist of two components, i.e., a full-time standing force with a strength of not

Reprinted by permission of the publishers from Grenville Clark and Louis Sohn, *World Peace through World Law*, rev. ed., Cambridge, Mass.: Harvard University Press, Copyright, 1960, by the President and Fellows of Harvard College.

less than 200,000 or more than 600,000 and a Peace Force Reserve with a strength of not less than 600,000 or more than 1,200,000. The standing force would be distributed throughout the world in its own bases and would include highly trained, mobile units ready to move at short notice; while the Reserve would be composed of partially trained individual reservists subject to call for service with the standing force in case of need. . . .

This plan rests on two basic assumptions. The first is that, in order to provide the nations of the world with adequate protection, a permanent and indisputably effective supranational force must be provided to take the place of national armaments.

It is true, as already stressed, that the problem of maintaining peace calls for more than national disarmament and a world police, and that workable world institutions are also required to enable peaceful change and to mitigate excessive economic disparities between different regions of the world. Nevertheless, the importance of a reliable world police as an absolutely indispensable element of world order cannot be exaggerated,—just as an adequate and respected police force is essential to the maintenance of order in a large city. It has been well said that "in every civilized community the members contribute toward the maintenance of a police force as an arm of law and order" and "only the society of nations has failed to apply this rudimentary principle of civilized life." The purpose of this Annex II is to apply that principle to the problem of world order through a detailed and practical plan.

The second basic assumption is that it would not be feasible to maintain an adequate world police force unless national disarmament is not only universal but also complete. While a world police force can and should be moderate in numbers, it must be strong enough to provide reliable protection against any foreseeable violation of world peace; and it would be clearly impracticable to maintain a world force of sufficient strength to supply the necessary confidence if any considerable national military forces remained in existence. For example, if we assume that in 1960 the strength of all national military forces on full-time duty is about fifteen million men, a reduction even by four fifths to three million would still make it impossible, as a practical matter, to maintain a world police that would unquestionably be superior to some possible military alliance. Theoretically it might seem feasible to reduce national military forces by nine tenths or more, to a point where even a strong alliance would not threaten a world police. In practice, however, it would probably be easier to agree on a complete elimination of national armaments than on a reduction to a very small fraction. And even if it were possible to reduce all the national forces of the world to one million men, the suspicion would still remain that they could be easily expanded and become dangerous in this age of new and appalling weapons. The practical fact is, therefore, that the problem of maintaining a world force capable of preventing or suppressing all international violence becomes manageable only under a regime of complete national disarmament.

With these considerations in mind, the proposed Annex I calls for absolutely complete national disarmament, thus making it practicable to provide in this Annex II for a United Nations military force sufficiently powerful promptly to suppress any threat to the world's peace. At the same time Annex II contains careful safeguards against the danger that any such world police force might itself threaten to dominate the world. . . .

Besides having the highest possible quality of personnel, the Peace Force should be equipped with excellent and up-to-date weapons. Moreover, in order to have a high degree of mobility so that the units of the standing component could be promptly concentrated, the Peace Force should be provided with fully adequate aircraft for troop transportation. Initially both components would be largely equipped by taking over arms and equipment discarded by national forces during the process of stage-by-stage disarmament. In later years, however, the Peace Force would need to be provided with newly manufactured arms and equipment; and to this end provision is made for their direct manufacture by the United Nations in its own plants under the management of a separate agency to be known as the United Nations Military Supply and Research Agency. The functions of this Agency would include research in new weapons and equipment, in order that the Peace Force shall at all times be equipped in the most modern manner. . . .

With regard to authority to order action by the Peace Force, care has been taken to limit such authority solely to the civilian authorities of the United Nations, i.e., the General Assembly itself or the Executive Council. Action by the Council would, however, be authorized only if the Assembly is not in session and special circumstances require immediate action, and there would be the additional safeguard that if the Council orders any such action, it must forthwith summon the Assembly in special session. These strict requirements would not, of course, prejudice the right of the Peace Force to defend itself in case of a possible direct attack against it.

Besides these safeguards as to authorizing any sort of action by the Peace Force, further safeguards are proposed as to the nature and extent of such action. In this regard, it is proposed that in ordering any action by the Peace Force to prevent or remove a threat to the peace, to suppress an act of aggression or to ensure compliance with the revised Charter, the General Assembly (or in case of an emergency the Executive Council) would be required to limit any such action to measures absolutely necessary to accomplish the desired end. For instance, in the event of threats to the peace of a minor sort, a mere demonstration by a few naval or air units of the Peace Force might well suffice to stop any further unlawful activity. Stronger measures would be required only in case of an actual aggression or serious resistance to United Nations authority; and even then any unnecessary destruction of life or property would be forbidden.

The solution proposed for the equipment of the Peace Force with nuclear weapons and their possible use is that the Force shall not be normally equipped with nuclear weapons at all, but that such weapons shall be held in reserve in the custody of the Nuclear Energy Authority, never to be used save by the order of the General Assembly itself and then only if such weapons have actually been used against the United Nations or such use is imminently threatened. While it would be possible to equip a world police force with these weapons of mass destruction so that it could crush forthwith any aggression by ruthless action, this is deemed no more consistent with the purpose of the Peace Force than it would be to equip a city police force with weapons which might tempt it to suppress a riot by the slaughter of thousands of citizens.

The Peace Force would, therefore, be so organized and equipped as to operate with the absolute minimum of force and destruction. On the other hand, while the possibility remains, as it would remain under the most effective inspection system, that somewhere or somehow nuclear weapons could be secretly concealed or manufactured, it seems necessary to make such counter-weapons available to the Peace Force in case of absolute need. The proposed precautions whereby these nuclear weapons would not ordinarily be in the possession of the Peace Force at all, but would be in charge of the Nuclear Energy Authority, subject only to release by order of the General Assembly itself, are intended to provide the maximum possible assurance against the misuse of these weapons.

During the period of actual disarmament (normally ten years) when the Peace Force would not as yet have achieved its full strength, the United Nations might perhaps need additional military forces if an emergency should arise. Since some national military forces would still exist during all of that period until the very end thereof, it is proposed to impose upon each member Nation the interim obligation to make available to the United Nations one tenth of the gradually diminishing strength of its military forces as they exist from time to time during the actual disarmament stage. The possible employment of such national contingents would be subject to various safeguards; and the General Assembly would have power to adopt laws and regulations to provide further guarantees that these forces would only be called upon and used for proper purposes.

By virtue of these carefully integrated measures, the United Nations should be able to suppress any attack by nation against nation or any possible revolt against its own authority with a minimum of destruction, either of life or property. At the same time, it is believed that the careful safeguards established in this Annex II would be sufficient to reduce to a minimum any risk that the Peace Force itself might seek to endanger the freedom of the world.

95. A Force under the Control of the United Nations

ROBERT E. OSGOOD

The military and political requirements of an effective UN Force designed to prevent threatening imbalances of military power, to deter and counter armed attacks, and to deter and rectify violations of the disarmament agreement, would be comparable to those of a powerful state like the United States in a world of unregulated arms.

To deter and redress violations of the disarmament agreement and to maintain a military equilibrium or a preponderance of force to deter or defeat military threats to the status quo, an international military force would have to be stronger than the force of any state or combination of states that might violate the disarmament treaty, upset the equilibrium, or violently upset the status quo. Even under complete national disarmament the international force would have to counterbalance the internal security forces and the war potentials of the major industrial nations. For this purpose it should be capable of expanding to offset rearmament by one or more states. To guard against the continual threat of militarily dangerous technological developments it would have to be backed by its own sizable research and development program. Against the threat of nuclear hiding or rearmament it should include a sufficient number and variety of nuclear weapons in its arsenal to deter a surprise nuclear attack. For the same reason it should have biological and chemical warfare weapons and production facilities. Against the threat of guerrilla warfare it should have special forces to assist local resistance to internal warfare supported from outside. The UN force should, of course, be continually ready for combat and capable of rapid action as soon as the need arose. It would have to have reliable logistics and financing and be trained, deployed, and utilized under a central com-

---

Robert E. Osgood, *An International Military Force in a Disarming and Disarmed World,* (Washington: Institute for Defense Analyses, 1963), pp. 45-50. Reprinted by permission.

mand. Because it might have to go into action at all levels of violence against numerous different states under a great variety of conditions in many parts of the world, it would require integrated strategic planning and training, diversified weapons systems, highly specialized troops and equipment, and a far-flung system of communications, depots, and bases—all under continual, reliable central command and control.

NEED FOR UN AUTHORITY AND DISCIPLINE

To serve its intended purpose of supplanting national with international force as the guarantor of security and order, the UN Peace Force should be subject to UN discipline and law and protected from national sanctions and restraints that might interfere with its activities. Moreover, it should be able to plan operations and make movements with some secrecy and stealth, keeping its multi-national personnel under effective security restrictions. Working closely with the international inspectorate, it should also be free to acquire intelligence of possible military significance without relying upon national governments.

All these military requirements are fraught with political significance. They impinge upon national interests in the most significant ways. Yet they could be met only if the international military force were controlled by a central authority that was not subject in its day-to-day peacetime or combat operations to national vetoes or even to a necessarily clumsy process of reaching majority decisions. In other words, the controlling body would have to have unprecedented executive powers. A reliable, responsive, integrated force would have to be a disciplined professional establishment with supreme loyalty to its global task of maintaining peace and order. It would have to be free from a variety of informal vetoes by states, such as obstruction of international recruitment and service, application of national discipline and sanctions, withdrawal of financial and logistic support, and denial or expropriation of international military and arms-production facilities.

The decisions to use the force in a particular circumstance, in a particular way, and for a particular purpose, would have to be determined by impartial application of some agreed standard of international order despite the opposition of even the most powerful states, which might, indeed, be the direct targets of such decisions. This would require the abolition of any great-power veto and, hence, the application of some scheme of majority voting in authorizing the employment of international force. . . .

THE UN AS A SOVEREIGN BODY

If particular states, on the other hand, were prevented from interfering with international military operations, there would be immense opportunities for the international body to interfere in their domestic as well as foreign affairs. The problem of an international force retaining reliable access to production, transportation, communications, depots, bases, and other military facilities located within state jurisdiction might be solved only if the UN owned these facilities; that is, *only if the UN itself became a sovereign political body*. In any case, the international operation of such facilities, like securing military intelligence or redressing violations of the disarmament agreement, would be a menace to the independence of states unless it were controlled by the most finely drawn legal and political directives, which were issued, executed, and adjudicated with scrupulous impartiality.

Clearly, none of these political conditions could be fulfilled unless a great majority of the UN and virtually all the states with a significant war potential were willing to collaborate actively with the UN military command and subordinate their peculiar national interests to UN authority, accepting judgments and actions adverse to their interests in order to preserve the cohesion and integrity of the international body. Otherwise a UN Peace Force would soon become, in effect, the instrument of a coalition of some nations with common interests against other nations who refused to accept their mandate. In other words, whatever their special interests might be, all militarily-significant nations would have to continue to share, and to be prepared to act upon, an overriding common interest in preserving the international political and military environment against any state action that was not in accord with universally agreed procedures, laws, and political decisions.

96. An International Force: Buffer and Deterrent

LINCOLN P. BLOOMFIELD

. . . To speak of these contingencies may seem contrary to the spirit of a disarmament agreement and a peace-keeping world military organization. The whole arrangement only makes sense if there are decent prospects for the cooperation of the major powers. To suppose that something like the present East-West struggle continues, or that other competing power blocs emerge to continue a cold war, and that some major country or bloc provokes the international force into action, may seem like imagining the worst. In fact, not just imagining the worst but contradicting the premise on which it is all established.

But we are discussing the "strategic problems" of the force. One may hope that the eventual actions of any such military force are purely ceremonial, that its strategic problems never become real. But to the extent that it is meant to be a real force, capable of handling actual problems, we have to ask what those problems might be.

Two tentative conclusions can be put forward. First, it is unlikely that an international strategic command would have a completely reliable, credible capability to intervene and to stop any rearmament of a major industrial power. Its "deterrent" against rearmament will certainly be subject to some doubt. It will suffer from some of the same disabilities as a national deterrence force. As a coercive military organization it will be quite imperfect.

Second, it would probably be unwise and unsafe to have it any less imperfect. The international force can itself be a threat to peace, even to disarmament, and surely to the freedom and independence of nations. The more nearly omnipotent it is, the less reassurance it would provide. The greater its military superiority

---

over individual nations, the more it can be viewed as a potential "enemy" by the nations that it is set up to guard. The more decisive its potential role, the more crucial becomes the capture of its political control or its disablement by those who cannot hope to control it.

If we are to have someday an international military force, we probably want one that is itself deterred. To create an instrument of painless world conquest, one that can overcome both passive and active resistance of national governments and national populations, might be to create extraordinary political instability. Indivisible, centralized, coherent power may be a good deal less conducive to peace and reassurance than a more diffuse, less decisive, less tempting instrument of control.

A world disarmament arrangement is unlikely to be viable if it requires a "perfect" strategic military force to deter violation and secession. Unless a quite imperfect deterrent can be believed adequate to forestall competitive violation, the arrangement should be abandoned or postponed.

Suppose an international strategic force were as likely to split apart as to stay together under crisis. Suppose it were believed appreciably vulnerable to various forms of sabotage. Suppose that individual nations could get hold of nuclear weapons and a capacity to deliver them on population centers. Suppose there were doubts whether the political arrangements were conducive to the force's timely action in a crisis—at least as many doubts as have ever been raised about American intervention on behalf of Europe. What is the consequence?

The consequence may be a significant deterrent, a deterrent based not on the certainty of decisive intervention but on a likelihood of intervention too great to ignore. A deterrent force does not have to *guarantee* that it can win the engagement.

This brings us back to the concept of "buffer." Instead of threatening to intervene against the rearming nation the force might be charged only with maintaining enough deterrence against war itself to permit other nations to take steps for their own protection. In the event of a rearmament race the international buffer force would try to ensure that no nation or group of nations could get a decisive headstart over its rivals.

Particularly since deterrence may depend on the absolute reprisal damage with which a nation can threaten an aggressor, not on just relative strengths, an international buffer might deter a rearming country's aggression long enough to permit other countries to develop at least "minimum deterrent forces" by themselves.

Under this concept the international force might even be authorized to assist in the laggards' rearmament. By simply threatening to facilitate the defensive, deterrent rearmament of the laggards (turning over its own production facilities to them, providing technical assistance, or giving some of its own weapons to them) the force might reduce the attractiveness to any nation of rushing back into an arms race. If this were the expected outcome of a rearmament race, there might appear little advantage in initiating such a race and no desperate haste to join a race that may or may not have begun.

How definitely and exactly can we hope to specify what the force is supposed to do? Can we rule out certain functions, such as its assisting laggards in their own rearmament? Can we make sure in advance that it will intervene (or that it will not intervene) in certain kinds of rearmament? Can we decide that it should engage in nuclear reprisal against a country that starts war, but not against a country that starts rearmament; or, choosing the opposite, can we guarantee that it will use nuclear weapons to deter or obstruct rearmament but not against a country that initiates conventional war?

I suppose we cannot. We can talk about the alternatives and can perhaps arrange weaponry, deployment, doctrine, political controls, and national military capabilities in a way that enhances the likelihood of certain decisions and reduces the likelihood of others. But no one can say in advance whether those who enjoy political control of the force will have the resolve, temerity, prudence, audacity, restraint, brutality, responsibility, or whatever else it takes, to launch war when they ought to, to threaten it credibly, to limit war properly if it occurs, or to abstain in the face of temptation. It is unlikely that we can deny the nations that politically control the force any ability to disband it, to redistribute its assets, or to charge it with grand new responsibilities that were never dreamed of before.

What could be decided in advance, and ought to be decided, is whether the force is to be viewed as an experiment in power politics or as a religious institution. If every war is a holy war, if the force cannot admit compromise or even occasional defeat, if every flaw in its strategy is to be construed as a doctrinal contradiction, if its leadership is to be considered the embodiment of disinterestedness and saintliness, and if any affront to the force is to be considered heresy, the demands on strategy will be exorbitant. The one thing we cannot do is to design a military force and strategy to support a doctrine of absolute self-righteousness.

97. An International Force of a Modest Policing Nature

ARTHUR I. WASKOW

The term "international police force" has become remarkably diverse in its meanings. It conjures up to different persons visions ranging anywhere from a large-size military force possessing all modern weapons to an observation corps of men wearing blue armbands. Particularly troublesome in discussions of an international police force has been the question whether it should be oriented to military activity—should be capable of acting like one of the present national armies of the world.

Indeed, in some discussions of a future disarmed world it has sometimes been assumed (rather than suggested or argued) that only a "world army" would be adequate to keep the peace, symbolize and support the agreed-upon international order, and punish nations that attempted to violate the agreements establishing that order. This assumption is frequently embodied in the phrase that in a disarmed world an international police force would need to have at its disposal such preponderant physical force "that no state could challenge it," in the words used by the United States

Arthur I. Waskow, *Quis Custodiet? Controlling the Police in a Disarmed World,* A Peace Research Institute Report Submitted under ACDA Grant ACDA/IR-8 (Washington, D.C.: Peace Research Institute, Inc., 1963), pp. 1 and 8-9. Reprinted by permission.

Treaty Outline on General and Complete Disarmament in a Peaceful World.

This assumption requires careful examination. At least two major problems present themselves in regard to such a "world army." First of all, there is serious doubt that agreements to create such a force would be forthcoming from present governments of present nation-states. This doubt of the world-wide political acceptability of a "world army" would not, however, seem so important in itself, if it were not for the underlying reason for the existence of such uneasiness on the part of some governments. After all, governments have changed their minds before on what was acceptable to them, and might do so on this point too.

But the reason that many governments fear the results of creating a "world army" is that *they fear such an army might prove to be uncontrollable.* They suggest that if naked and unanswerable physical power were to be made available to any institution it might soon become ungovernable and might begin to interfere in matters that it was not intended to affect—such as the domestic affairs of the various States.

In more exact terms, this fear of a "world army" is based on the assumption that such a sizeable force could only be controlled, financed, and supported by a true government or that alternatively, in order to finance and protect itself, the force would itself take on governmental attributes. . . .

THE NEW-MODEL POLICE

Because it is likely that none of these [more ambitious] outcomes would be acceptable to the United States and that each would be seen as a threat to American national interests, it is necessary to examine a version of an international police force that would be unlikely to result in such outcomes. For that reason, the remainder of this report will examine a possible version of an international police force that would not be equivalent to a "world army" and that would not possess the amount of concrete physical power "that no State could challenge." The questions to be examined are whether such non-"military" police forces could

(1) effectively enforce a world-wide disarmament agreement;
(2) prevent rearmament or a recourse to international war; and

(3) be susceptible of political control that would not require deep and broad political consensus among States.

In contradistinction to the kind of *military* force generally imagined, this report will proceed to discuss a force that might be constructed on the model of true *police* functions. Six basic assumptions concerning such a *police force* will be stated here in summary form, to be justified and discussed below in detail.

(1) If a Great Power should make a whole-hearted political decision and commitment to break the disarmament agreement, no presently imaginable international force could *suppress* such a whole-hearted violation.

(2) The task therefore is to create a kind of international police force that can *deter such a whole-hearted decision from being made.*

(3) The way to do this would be to create a series of graded deterrent responses to more and more serious violations, so that early in the process of violation the violator would be confronted with very small police-style detachments; as his violations grew the size of the force opposed to them would grow; etc. At each response step, the violator would have to reexamine the depth of his commitment to the violation and the repercussions of resisting the amount of force brought to bear by the international police force. At most levels, despite the increase in power brought to bear by the international police force, the violator would probably have the sheer physical force capable of resisting.

(4) The use of physical force to resist the international police force would be likely to increase the determination of other nations to present the violator with still higher levels of force. This increased determination would permit the international police force to bring larger levels of force into play. Thus police responses would be governed by the principle that *the more international consensus there came into being, the more force could be used.*

(5) The most effective way to present such a series of graded deterrent responses to a would-be violator *and at the same time make it unlikely that he would commit his own full prestige to the violation* (and thus make it an issue of national honor from which he could not retreat) would be to treat each violation *as if it were an act of private persons.*

(6) In addition to presenting "graduated deterrents" of the sort described to violators of a disarmament agreement, opportunity would be afforded them of pursuing their national interest by an extremely wide range of non-military techniques. In this fashon the "stick" of graduated deterrents would deflect nations away from risking violations of the disarmament agreement, while the "carrot" of wide opportunities to be achieved by other means would attract their energies to non-armed means of intense competition and conflict.

[VIII]

Evaluations of Collective Security

It is clear that collective security in the sense of an organized, quick, forceful reaction by the international community to aggression anywhere has not developed. There have been a number of explanations as to why it has not developed.

THE CONCEPT IS FLAWED

In addition to the argument that the concept deals unduly with abstractions, discussed in Reading 12, it has also been pointed out that the application of collective security would require a moral revolution (Reading 98). Reading 99 contains a summary of the flaws in the concept of collective security which have attracted the most attention among critics.

THE "BLANK CHEQUE"

No government can give a "blank cheque"; yet prior agreement as to goals and concrete actions has not been forthcoming. This dilemma is discussed in the light of League of Nations' experience in the Italo-Ethiopian conflict (Readings 100, 101, and 102).

COLLECTIVE SECURITY AS THE SUM OF THE GREAT POWERS

Readings 103 and 104 discuss whether collective security is anything more than the sum of the great powers.

RELUCTANCE TO ACT

States are often reluctant to act in a manner consistent with the demands of a collective security system (Reading 105).

COLLECTIVE SECURITY AND SMALL STATES

It is argued that an international organization will not by itself be able to eliminate war between small states (Reading 106).

COLLECTIVE SECURITY AND INTERNAL NATIONAL POLITICS

Security and internal political conditions are intimately connected. It can also be argued that this connection has been largely ignored (Readings 107 and 108).

CAN COLLECTIVE SECURITY SUCCEED?

Even with all of its flaws, is collective security "bound" to fail? The question is discussed in Reading 109. An empirical approach is presented in Reading 110.

THE CONCEPT IS FLAWED

98. A Moral Revolution

HANS J. MORGENTHAU

. . . The only question collective security is allowed to ask is: "Who has committed aggression?" Foreign policy cannot help asking: "What interest do I have in opposing this particular aggressor and what power with which to oppose him?"

Collective security, then, can succeed only on the further assumption that all or virtually all nations will come to the defense of the status quo, threatened in the security of a particular nation, even at the risk of war, regardless of whether they could justify such a policy in view of their own individual interests. In other words, what collective security demands of the individual nations is to forsake national egotisms and the national policies serving them. Collective security expects the policies of the individual nations to be inspired by the ideal of mutual assistance and a spirit of self-sacrifice which will not shrink even from the supreme sacrifice of war should it be required by that ideal.

This third assumption is really tantamount to the assumption of a moral revolution infinitely more fundamental than any moral change that has occurred in the history of Western civilization. It is a moral revolution not only in the actions of statesmen representing their countries but also in the actions of plain citizens. Not only are the latter expected to support national policies that are at times bound to run counter to the interests of the nation, they are also expected to be ready to lay down their lives and risk total destruction in a nuclear war for the security of any nation anywhere on the globe. It can be maintained that if men everywhere would feel and act that way, the lives of all men would be forever secure. The truth of the conclusion is as much beyond dispute as the hypothetical character of the premise.

Men generally do not feel and act, whether as individuals among themselves or as members of their nations with regard to other nations, as they ought to feel and act if collective security is to succeed. And there is, as we have tried to show, less chance today than there has been at any time in modern history that they would act in conformity with moral precepts of a supranational character if such action might be detrimental to the interests of their respective nations. . . .

99. A Summary of Flaws in the Concept of Collective Security

ROLAND N. STROMBERG

. . . It may therefore be suitable to conclude with a brief summary of the flaws in this idea which critics continue to find. One may find

Roland N. Stromberg, "The Riddle of Collective Security," in G. L. Anderson, editor, *Issues and Conflicts, Studies in 20th Century American Diplomacy* (Lawrence, Kansas: University of Kansas Press, 1959), pp. 147-167, at pp. 165-167. Reprinted by permission. Footnotes omitted.

them all stated in the debates of 1919-1920; they have been restated recently.

(1) The most succinct comment that can be made about collective security is, in words we borrow from a writer on another subject, that it is either so obvious as to be uninteresting or so wild as to be incredible. Because sovereign national states continue to exist and to act as they must, in defense of vital interests, a "league of force" becomes either an old-fashioned alliance or an old-fashioned conference under another name; it could be transformed into something different only if it could be a superstate. Deep confusions of thought went into the making of collective security; it was the result of strong emotions in hopeless conflict, of the desire to abolish war without relinquishing national interests.

(2) A successful collective security system would appear to presuppose the conditions it wishes to attain. It is workable only on at least some of the following assumptions: that the great powers are substantially in harmony, that the causes of serious conflict between them are relatively few and infrequent, that war is usually the result of an action that is patently "criminal" and without the least justification, and that states are capable of acting in an unselfish and disinterested manner. If these things were true, preventing war would not be much of a problem. Unhappily they are not, and so collective security fails us, as a panacea.

(3) If it merely failed us, it would have done no harm; but in failure it seems to threaten an even worse disease than it promised to cure, because it has in it an element of aggressive moralism which wants to exterminate war by waging it against the unrighteous. Its proponents have often declared in effect that war may be avoided by waging it. The dubious doctrine of preventive war is married to a dangerous gospel of moral self-righteousness in collective security at its worst. Nor is it necessarily true, as proponents of collective security take for granted, that the preventive war will always be a smaller one.

(4) While the above may be rather overdrawn, collective security as a type of moralistic and legalistic approach is likely to be rejected by realists on the ground that it ignores relations of power and the realities of particular situations. In recent thinking about foreign policy there has been a strong reaction away from the basing of policy on "broad moral principles." Doctrinaire, overrigid, and

averse to compromise, this sort of policy lacks the flexibility and delicacy necessary in diplomacy. And it is to diplomacy rather than to force that we must look to solve the problems of peace.

In brief, those who subscribe to a dictum of Sir Alfred Zimmern that war is more likely to be caused by muddled thinking than by human depravity, are apt to be suspicious of an idea as muddled if well-meaning as collective security. They will appreciate the force of Secretary Lansing's complaint that "it may be noble thinking, but it is not true thinking." A certain disillusionment is very widespread among those who have thought about the subject; the innocent hopes which blossomed among the Wilsonians and again during the Second World War are not any longer held by many. There remains a difference between those who would abandon the entire idea as mischievous and those who feel it can still be useful if tempered by greater wisdom and experience.

The last word has hardly been said. Let the last word in this paper be that of Sir Llewellyn Woodward, who has remarked in regard to the terrible question of war that the answers, if they are found, "will probably not be found in some grandiose act of state or some vast transformation of our political machinery. They are more likely to steal on us unawares. . . ."

THE "BLANK CHEQUE"

100. A Searching Analysis of the League of Nations Sanctions Experience

ROYAL INSTITUTE OF INTERNATIONAL AFFAIRS

. . . Is it possible, after the foregoing inquiry, to suggest certain conditions to which an effective system for the application of sanctions

International Sanctions (London: Oxford University Press under the auspices of the Royal Institute of International Affairs, 1938), pp. 210-212. Reprinted by permission. Footnote omitted. See Reading 80 for Schiffer's "circular argument."

should conform? The governing condition would appear to be the proviso that the efficacy of sanctions as a preventive of aggressive war or other international law-breaking depends upon the co-operation of all states, without serious exception, in enforcing them. Other conditions seem to emerge from our analysis. Sanctions should be immediate, applying the remedies the moment the ill is manifested. A disease which can be cured in its early stages must not be allowed to continue its ravages until the limb is mortified before treatment has begun. If law-breaking is to be stopped before it has done irreparable harm the reaction it provokes should be immediate.

The novelty in the post-War attempt to evolve a system of sanctions lay in the fact that it aimed at protecting a general principle which to the man in the street may often appear somewhat idealistic—the undesirability of war, especially aggressive war—rather than the direct, immediate and short-range interests of the parties to the Treaty. It was based on the fundamental assumption that the prevention of war overrides all other interests. The danger inherent in this attempt was that those states most interested in the aim of preserving peace might prove most reluctant to have recourse to the ultimate sanction of force. Being above all things lovers of peace for themselves, when the situation arose which sanctions were designed to meet, they might think, like Praed,

> Let Portugal have rulers twain,
> Let Greece go on with none,
> Let Popery sink or swim in Spain
> While we enjoy the fun;
> Let Turkey tremble at the knout,
> Let Algiers lose her Dey,
> Let Paris turn her Bourbons out—
> Bah! Take the sword away.

The danger of a break-down of the system thus arises if it appears that the nations are not sufficiently interested in the preservation of peace, apart from all other interests, to act up to their obligations when it comes to the point. Every failure to enforce the law or to make it wholly effective weakens the strength of the law and helps to render it eventually futile. The rule of law cannot afford to waive its sanctions, except in the event of submission to the threat of them, a submission not merely proposed verbally but substantiated by restitution for actions already done contrary to law.

If the enforcement of sanctions involves action by more than one state, their actions must be simultaneous. One of the obstacles to enforcement in these circumstances is the fact that the burden is unequally distributed between the enforcing states. Any delay by one or other of them increases the inequality of the burden. States which are the first to take action suffer its repercussions from the outset; those which act later not only avoid their burdens for a time at the expense of their collaborators, they may even make illegitimate economic gains thereby; and moreover, as already noted, the efficacy of sanctions is incomplete as long as there are abstainers amongst the states that should be enforcing them.

These conditions evidently entail that the whole process of applying sanctions should be worked out in detail beforehand, the machinery set up and the necessary powers assumed by the governments by which action will have to be taken, where they do not already possess such powers. The process and the machinery are elaborate. The occasion to use sanctions may well arise suddenly; they cannot be improvised on the spur of the moment. Even if the occasion can be foreseen, the eve of its use is not an appropriate time for the devising of machinery. Unless the process is worked out in detail beforehand, states cannot know to what they are committed and for what repercussions upon themselves they must be prepared when taking their part in the enforcement of law. No government can give a blank cheque; it must know its liabilities before it will assume them. Governments cannot take the necessary powers unless they have before them, not vaguely but clearly defined, the action required of them. Article XVI of the Covenant of the League of Nations has been left vague; it has never been fully supplemented by an inquiry into the actual measures that would be necessary in each state in order to put it into force. . . .

101. A Somewhat Different Evaluation of the League Sanctions Experience

JULIUS STONE

. . . For the student of international organisation, however, there are as yet only failures for his instruction; and, moreover, the final political failure of the League experiment conceals important gains in technique.

First, the Italo-Ethiopian affair was a full scale experiment in joint action by a preponderance of States to enforce treaty obligations not to resort to war. It would remain important even as a mere shadowy presage of gains to come in international organisation. In one sense, however, it still remains the only instance of enforcement which approximated to the pattern laid down in the operative instrument. Second, behind the overall failure, the techniques of reaching consensus, planning, coordination, supervision and implementation of enforcement measures, on both the international and municipal levels, registered pioneering successes. No later international organisation could afford to ignore these techniques, whereby the principal sanctions measures were worked out, drafted, agreed and dispatched to the various governments within a period of nine days, and came into effect for about fifty States within a month thereafter. Third, whatever the Italo-Ethiopian affair did *not* prove, it did at any rate show that the real difficulties of peace enforcement lie in the political and economic conflicts of States, not in the complexities of international or national administration, nor even in the difficulties of coordinating the wills and actions of many States. . . .

Julius Stone, *Legal Controls of International Conflict* (Sydney, Australia: Maitland Publishing Co., 1954), p. 183.

102. Basic Assumptions

ROLAND N. STROMBERG

... (a) It is claimed that, in 1931 or 1935 or 1937, a mere "warning" or show of force would have sufficed to cow the aggressor. Otherwise, one is forced to the absurd position of preventing one war by waging another. But the truth is that Japan in 1932 or 1937, Italy in 1935, Germany in 1938 were not to be halted by a mere warning. It was precisely the absurdity of waging war to prevent it—in all these cases, waging a big war to stop a small one—that was the chief stumbling block to action against the aggressor. If the theory concedes that war would have been necessary, then it may be argued that the time was then more favorable than later. But it is hardly true that the *status quo* powers were better equipped, physically and psychologically, to fight Japan in 1932 or 1937 than they were in 1941[1] or better able to fight Germany in 1938 than in 1939. It is true that from 1933 to 1936 they were stronger than Germany. But precisely for this reason, Hitler avoided "aggression."

(b) It is claimed that in all these cases, the fact of "aggression" was perfectly clear, that only a malevolent will could have doubted it. The truth is that, as we have indicated, Japan's action in Manchuria in 1931 did not appear to be a clear case, nor did Germany's action taken on her own soil in 1936. There is not often a crystal-clear case of aggression, dramatic enough to stir peoples to wage

[1] Ickes in his diary indicates that Secretary of Navy Swanson suggested war with Japan in 1937 but that Roosevelt simply remarked that he, Roosevelt, was "a pacifist." Obviously, public opinion, official opinion, and military preparation were far less ready for war in 1937 than in 1941. One of the principal reasons war came in 1939 and not 1938 (as M. Bonnet has pointed out with a wealth of evidence) is that the Allies were better prepared for it at the later date.

Collective Security and American Foreign Policy: From the League of Nations to NATO by Roland N. Stromberg, Frederick A. Praeger, Inc., Publishers, New York, 1963. Pp. 148-151.

war; even the German demands on Czechoslovakia were clouded by considerations of "self-determination."[2]

(c) In the collective police action, it is assumed, all the cooperating powers would have acted disinterestedly, as policemen should, and restored the *status quo*. But we know that a powerful deterrent to a League war against Germany, and to some extent against Japan, was the belief of experienced diplomats and statesmen that the Soviet Union would profit by the destruction of German and Japanese power and by the war to extend its power to a degree that would constitute a mortal danger to Europe and the world, the nature of Communist ideology a factor contributing to this view. It must also be recalled that Poland and Rumania constituted an obstacle to "collective security" with Russia because they refused to cooperate, preferring any other risk to the certainty of their fate if Soviet troops were granted access to their land. The real, though belated, efforts of France and Britain to reach an agreement with the Soviets stumbled over this powerful fact: The intended beneficiaries of collective security refused the offer because of their belief that the policeman was worse than the burglar. The price of Stalin's aid against Hitler was the delivering up to him of the Eastern European countries. In [an] article referred to, Mr. Swing was forced to rely on the hypothesis that Soviet policy in these years—the Litvinov period—was dominated by a concept of friendship and cooperation with the West and that only the hostility of the Western appeasers drove it into another mood. In this view, all that has happened since was the result of not trusting Russia sooner and more. Surely, this is incredible. Soviet Communism had not ceased to believe in its mission to overthrow Western-style democracy, despite its tactical desire for allies against Germany. It may be recalled that the fearsome purges in Russia at this time convinced the last independent minds in the West that Stalin's state was a murderous enemy of liberalism and democracy. Stalin's demand for territory as the price of an alliance is sufficient proof of his international ill will.

---

[2] Those who are endlessly indignant about what Chamberlain did to Czechoslovakia in 1938 might well consider what Churchill and Roosevelt did to Poland under very comparable circumstances in 1944-45; the two archenemies of "appeasement" managed to persuade themselves that turning this country over to the will of Stalin was the fulfillment of collective security.

(d) A further assumption is that force used against one aggressor would have discouraged the others. This is another argument that overlooks the realities of power in favor of a sort of vague moral analogy. It forgets the very lively possibility that, had the European states busied themselves in punishing Italy in Africa, the Rhineland gate would have been open wider for Hitler than it was or, if the European powers had committed their forces to the Far East in 1937-38, Hitler would have had an easier time in Europe. While the example of a determination to fight might have had some deterrent effect, the withdrawal of power would have more than counterbalanced it. It surpasses belief that Hitler would have been awed, shamed, or intimidated by the mere example; ruthless realist that he was, the tough little dictator itched for the right moment to begin war. It makes much more sense to urge that, imitating Hitler's realism, the democratic statesmen should have checked him by picking up Italy and Japan as allies, high though the price might have been.

In a crowning example of the loosely reasoned case for collective security, a publication of the United States Department of State (*Our Foreign Policy,* 1952, Publ. 4466) declares that the road to World War II was a result of the "disastrous decline" of the League of Nations "when its peace-loving members failed to stand up against the first *Axis* aggression in Manchuria and Ethiopia" (italics mine). The crude anachronism exemplifies the intellectual shoddiness of this line of thought. The "Axis" did not exist in 1931 or in 1935. Japan, Germany, and Italy did not form a band of war makers and criminals for all to see. Japan was not Germany's ally until 1940; Italy was indeed the ally of France and Britain in 1935, and, as we have seen, the chief *cause* of her becoming Germany's ally was the hostility of Britain and France in 1935 when they "stood up" against her aggression.

The list of dubious assumptions might be extended. A point of interest is that the heroes who supposedly had had the right answer all along do not turn out so well when one consults their contemporary records. It is clear that Stimson was an "appeaser" in 1931 and that Roosevelt and Hull were "appeasers" in 1935-38. Robert Vansittart's interesting memoirs (*The Mist Procession*) make it clear that Eden, Churchill, and Vansittart were seldom of one mind and that Sir Robert was an "appeaser" regarding Japan and Italy, for the great foe of Germany was not prepared to dissipate England's limited resources on other countries, who might be helpful in the anti-German cause. Indeed, an Englishman who had suggested fighting simultaneous wars against Italy, Germany, and Japan in 1936 or 1937 would have rightly been accounted mad. Mr. Eden, who led a temporary crusade against Italy in 1935, was impressed with the wisdom of calling it off when Hitler made his move, and Sir Anthony was wholeheartedly in favor of Japan's being punished, if at all, by somebody else.

Like all historical "might-have-beens," this theory of a preventable war can be neither proved nor disproved absolutely, but we must be suspicious of the confident assertions of relatively ignorant history in its behalf. At one point, it came close to reality: The Western powers (Italy was then included) thought seriously about intervening in Germany in 1933 and 1935. They probably should have done so. But the shallow interpretation we have been discussing ignores, typically, all the uncertainties about such a course, uncertainties that were referred to earlier and that, without the precious advantage of hindsight, must have seemed awesome. Perhaps, a preventive military action without an overt German act of aggression would have alienated American and world sympathy. (The state of American opinion at that time makes such a reaction quite plausible.) Perhaps, it would have made Germany's internal situation worse, not better. It might have assisted the spread of international Communism. The use of force, we may be reasonably sure, would not have provided a fundamental solution to the malaise of Germany and of Europe. For there is something to the remarks H. N. Brailsford and H. G. Wells were making about the League of Nations at about that time: that it was an organization for preventing war without removing its causes.[3]

[3] The above remarks should not be interpreted as meaning there is no case for resistance in 1936 or 1938. Good authority still holds that Munich was an error (see, e.g., Sir Charles Webster in *International Affairs,* April, 1961), though such a proposition could never be proved. It is against the theory of a conspiracy of all the "aggressors" from 1931 on and the other looser assumptions handled above that complaint must be lodged—as well as against the juvenile arrogance of the claim that anyone with decency and courage must have acted otherwise.

COLLECTIVE SECURITY AS THE SUM OF THE GREAT POWERS

103. Another Argument on the Locus of Power

ROLAND N. STROMBERG

. . . Here is no place to discuss the tangled history of interwar diplomacy, but some confusions of thought surrounding the League's rôle in that history ought to be clarified. It has become common to argue that the League system of collective security failed only because the powers lacked faith in the principle. "The reason why the League failed (to prevent World War II)," says Arnold Toynbee, "was that the enforcement of the Covenant had been backed by insufficient armed power and insufficient resolution to use such power as was available."[4] The statement is equally true, and much more to the point, if we substitute for the word "League" the words "British and French and American foreign policy" and for the words "enforcement of the Covenant" the words "their opposition to Germany and Japan." Their failure can be explained wholly without reference to the League. And indeed throughout the period the League played an obfuscating rôle, confusing the issues at every opportunity. It had frightened the United States away, and served as a convenient foil for American isolationists, and if British opinion was, as Mr. Toynbee concedes, hopelessly muddled in its thinking about foreign affairs, that was in part because of the illusions fostered by collective security. It was fatally easy to push the terrible burdens of national responsibility onto the shoulders of the League: let Collective Security do it, while Britain and France

[4] Survey of International Affairs, *The World in March 1939* (1952).

Roland N. Stromberg, "The Idea of Collective Security," *Journal of the History of Ideas,* April, 1956, pp. 250-263, at pp. 253-254. Reprinted by permission.

disarmed.[5] It is important to realize that nothing called collective security existed except as the sum of Britain and France and the United States, the great powers opposed to the Axis, and their ability to cooperate in particular policies. When realities of power are lost from view the result may be confusion and chaos in international affairs. We still read that the path to Nazi aggression was made possible by the failure of the League to coerce Japan in 1931 and Italy in 1935. We have the absurdity, to which collective security is always being reduced, of saying that war in 1931 would have prevented war in 1941. It is implied that had the Western states been fighting Japan in Asia they could have fought Germany better in Europe. The verdict of careful history might be that the ill-conceived effort to apply "sanctions" against Italy in 1935 weakened, not strengthened, the front against Germany, but collective security will have it exactly the opposite. The lamentable weakness of the powers opposed to Germany and Japan is of course the key to the period, but it has nothing to do with an abstraction called collective security. That dogma hardly helped them to find their way out of the darkness in the 1930s. On the contrary, it often enabled them to avoid their problems, and it sometimes increased their difficulties. At the end of its career the League of Nations was engaged in hurling moral thunderbolts at Russia, a power whose aid was vital in resisting Nazi Germany. . . .

[5] "Unfortunately the Locarno powers mistook their desires for verdicts and their verdicts for realities," M. François-Poncet observes in regard to Germany's remilitarization of the Rhineland in 1936, which was met by referring the problem to the League, as had also been done when Hitler announced rearmament in 1935. In his memoirs *The Fateful Years* the French diplomat makes clear his feeling that this amounted to a way of evading the issue.

104. Collective Security without Centralization of Authority

ROLAND N. STROMBERG

. . . We may safely predict that the abstract injunction to intervene where there is strife, just because it is strife, will never send a

Roland N. Stromberg, "The Idea of Collective Security," *Journal of the History of Ideas,* April, 1956, pp. 250-263, at p. 260. Reprinted by permission.

single soldier to war. National interest must still, as of old, determine action.

This is a profound point, because it involves collective security's confusion between nationalism and internationalism. If we are to expect nations to act in a disinterested and international way, we must expect them to cease to be nations. We imply the existence of that international community in which a resident of North America sees no difference in importance between those who live near him and those who live anywhere else in the world, politically and humanly speaking. If such a spirit existed, world government would be feasible. Since it does not, then it is doubtful whether collective security is more than occasionally and imperfectly feasible; better to say, doubtful whether it is anything more than a new name for a very old game, the game it thought rhetorically to condemn as "power politics" or "cynical nationalism." . . .

RELUCTANCE TO ACT

105. States' Reluctance to Act in a Collective Security Manner

ROBERT M. MACIVER

. . . [Most] of our studies give little or no attention to the specific provisions of Chapter VII of the Charter. And there is universal testimony for the view that the major function of the United Nations is the preparation and maintenance of the ways of international

---

Robert M. MacIver, *The Nations and the United Nations,* prepared for the Carnegie Endowment for International Peace (New York: Manhattan Publishing Co., 1959), pp. 90-94. Reprinted by permission.

peace and not the armed suppression of breaches of the peace. It is clear enough that the greater the armaments of the nations the less does the effective power to suppress aggression rest with the United Nations. Only in a world that has learned to control armaments to the minimum necessary for policing purposes can there be adequate assurance that the United Nations will fulfill its mission.

From different approaches the various nations shy away from the implementation of Chapter VII. India and the neutralist group in general regard the very concept of enforcement as out of place in an organization whose whole objective should be to advance the spirit of co-operation among the nations. The French study, like those of some other colonial powers, opposes any strengthening of the coercive authority of the Assembly as being unrealistic, out of relation to the facts and conditions of power, and likely to encourage the United Nations to meddle in matters rightly within the domestic jurisdiction of sovereign states. The British study expresses misgivings that the more promising and more significant responsibilities of the organization as an agency of conciliation might be adversely affected by over-ambitious efforts to become the armed guardian of the peace. The Danish volume holds that there is a clear incompatibility between the function of the United Nations as a mediator and its function as a coercive instrument of collective security. A similar idea is discussed in a study prepared for a US Senate Subcommittee set up to consider the UN Charter.[3]

More recent developments, however, show that there is a considerable body of UN members who will support, in certain situations, an employment of force that in important respects differs from that generally envisaged in Chapter VII of the Charter. The force in question is strictly a policing force, intended not to fight an aggressor but to keep the peace between antagonists who are at sword's point, are already committing acts of violence against one another, or are showing clear indications of undertaking warlike operations.

---

[3] U.S. Senate, 83rd Cong., 2nd Sess., Ctte. on Foreign Relations, Subctte. on the UN Charter, Staff Study No. 5, "Pacific Settlement of Disputes in the United Nations" (Washington: Govt. Printing Office, 1954), pp. 19-20.

While the need for a force of this kind has been voiced at various times by some UN members, it was the crisis culminating in the military action by Britain, France, and Israel against Egypt over the Suez Canal affair that brought it into being. It took the form of a UN Emergency Force set up under an Assembly resolution in November 1956 for the purpose of securing and supervising a cease-fire agreement. This force, organized by the Secretary-General in accordance with the resolution and improvised and dispatched with remarkable efficiency and speed, was highly effective in the achievement of its immediate objective. The situation was an extremely complicated one, and its later developments do not concern us here.

Nearly six years earlier, the "Uniting for Peace" resolution of the Assembly had declared that, under conditions where the purposes of the United Nations with respect to the maintenance of peace were frustrated by the inability of the Council to take the requisite action, the Assembly would, if necessary, recommend measures including the use of armed force and call upon the member states to take action accordingly. If not in session, the Assembly could for this purpose be called into emergency session by any seven members of the Council. This precedent—or this interpretation of the Charter—prepared the way for the steps taken by the Assembly in November 1956.

The resolution setting up the Emergency Force was spearheaded by Canada, which had on previous occasions advocated setting up an international force. The plan which required the consent of the nations directly involved was wholly an improvisation. It was stimulated by a double-barreled crisis, the conjuncture of the British and French military landings in Egypt with the strife between Israel and its Arab neighbors, particularly Egypt. How far the initial success it achieved provides an argument in favor of a permanently established UN international police system is a question beset by uncertainties, but the fact that the emergency measure did perform a most important service can hardly be denied.[4]

---

[4] For a study of the value of a permanent equivalent for the UN Emergency Force, see William R. Frye, *A United Nations Peace Force* (New York: Oceana Publications for the Carnegie Endowment for International Peace, 1957).

In sharp contrast to the attitude toward the Charter provisions for enforcement action, much stress is laid in a majority of our studies on the need for strengthening the procedures for pacific settlement laid down in Chapter VI of the Charter. Diplomatic negotiations aimed at the preservation of peace have been in practice since ancient times, but the machinery of the United Nations provides a much broader basis for such negotiations. World public opinion may thus be brought to bear on them. As the US study points out, the UN system gives official support to multilateral diplomacy, whereas old-time negotiations were generally confined by the two or more states directly involved in the dispute.

Various proposals, besides the removal of the veto right from this domain, which we discuss elsewhere, are offered. The Uruguay report wants the compulsory reference of all disputes, presumably those not otherwise settled, to the International Court of Justice or to an arbitration tribunal to be set up by the Security Council. This proposal would go further than the so-called General Act, originally formulated under the League of Nations and reactivated by the Assembly in 1949. Countries that accede to the act agree to submit to a conciliation process or to the International Court or other tribunal disputes not settled by diplomatic negotiation. But although the text of the Revised General Act was approved by a majority of 45 votes, only four countries—Belgium, Denmark, Norway, and Sweden—have actually signified their accession to it. A somewhat more promising proposal was made by Yugoslavia in 1950 for the establishment of a permanent UN commission of good offices as a subsidiary organ of the General Assembly.

Other proposals are addressed to improvements in the procedures of the Security Council for the settlement of disputes. One of these, advanced in the Japanese and Turkish reports, would extend the provision for the participation of non-member states in Council discussions, so that they would be invited to participate not only if they were parties to a *dispute* but also if they were involved in a *situation* being discussed by the Council. Another, which received the Assembly's approval, calls for the appointment of a conciliator or rapporteur, a member of the Council on whom the parties might agree, who might for a time be given a free hand in attempting to resolve a situation or dispute that had been brought to its attention.

In the evolution of the United Nations the Assembly has played an increasingly active part. It provides a much wider forum and has greater flexibility of action than does the Council. Its recommendations are made without the need to consider the interposition of a veto by any one member. In the realm of pacific settlement of disputes the recommendations of the Security Council have no more coercive authority back of them than those of the Assembly. In consequence various countries prefer to have their disputes or complaints brought before the Assembly. Several cases, including the Greek case and of course the Korean case, were taken over by the Assembly when for one reason or another the Council found itself unable to deal with them. This is in line with the sentiment expressed in the studies submitted by a number of the middle and smaller countries, which ask for a greater "democratization" of the United Nations. . . .

COLLECTIVE SECURITY AND SMALL STATES

106. Does the United Nations Play an Important Role in Small-State Conflict? A Negative View

RAYMOND ARON

. . . What is the U.N.'s function in the case of conflict between two small states, both independent, neither of which is attached to the Soviet camp? We are thinking, for example, of the conflict of India and Pakistan over Kashmir, or of the absence of a peace treaty

Raymond Aron, "Limits to the Powers of the United Nations," *Annals of the American Academy of Political and Social Sciences,* November, 1954, pp. 20-26, at pp. 24 and 26. Reprinted with permission.

between Israel and the Arab countries. One is hesitant to answer because it is by no means certain that events would take an essentially different course if the U.N. did not exist. Perhaps the intervention of the great powers to stop hostilities between India and Pakistan was facilitated through the use of the international organization as an intermediary. But the recommendations concerning a plebiscite made by a U.N. mediator have not been accepted by the state that fears the results of consulting the people's wishes. I believe after my experience in New Delhi, that basically the leaders of India do not consider themselves morally bound to subscribe to the results of a plebiscite. Strategic or geographic arguments seem to them to win out over the desires of the populations concerned. Quite obviously, no great power is interested in using coercion to make India and Pakistan comply with U.N. law. The matter will be decided locally in a manner determined by the facts and the relation of forces. Perhaps this is a deplorable conclusion, but it would be still more deplorable for us to give way to illusions dangerous for the values we profess to defend.

As for Israel and the Arab countries, peace between them will be established not by the U.N. but, sooner or later, by the pressure of Western countries, which are as anxious to pacify local disputes outside the Soviet zone as the U.S.S.R. is to inflame them.

THE REALISTIC REVOLUTION AGAINST WAR

Perhaps the preceding discussion will be judged cynical. Personally, I do not so regard it. To say that the establishment of the U.N. has not essentially changed international relations is a judgment of fact, not a value judgment. The critic of these views should prove that the judgment is false before accusing us of cynicism. If he admits that the judgment is true for the past, but holds that it must cease to be so in the future, it is incumbent upon him to show in what way we may modify the fundamental conditions of the present historical situation which limit the effectiveness of the U.N.

Real discussion, beyond these observations which are difficult to refute, should deal with the significance of this analysis. Can we conceive of an international system in which the U.N. would genuinely guarantee the security of all and every one? Would it be enough to change certain elements in the situation, or would it be necessary to change the essential characteristics of relations between states as we have known them for the past six thousand years?

Such a discussion would go beyond the scope of this short study. Permit us to advance, without demonstrating, the following hypothesis: the progress in arms of mass destruction or the spread of a world-wide empire will perhaps eliminate wars between states from history. I doubt whether an international organization will ever be capable of such a revolution. . . .

COLLECTIVE SECURITY AND INTERNAL NATIONAL POLITICS

107. A Sense of Responsibility

A. E. ZIMMERN

. . . Collective security involves an extension of the sense of social responsibility across the frontiers of the state. Such an enlargement of the social sense is only possible between states which are both constitutional and democratic. For if they are not constitutional, if their internal régime is despotic or lawless, their external relations will be tainted with the same spirit, so that there can be no basis for confidence and co-operation, still less for the beginnings of a common society. And if they are not democratic there will be an absence of that active sense of responsibility upon which the new

A. E. Zimmern, "The Problem of Collective Security," in Quincy Wright, editor, *Neutrality and Collective Security,* Harris Foundation Lectures (Chicago: University of Chicago Press, 1936), pp. 3-92, at pp. 30-31. Reprinted by permission.

social relationship must rest. Thus collective security, the safety of all by all, cannot, at the present stage of human history, be a policy for the world as a whole. It can only be brought into practical effect between the free peoples who, if they are sufficiently powerful, can form the nucleus of what, as the social and political advancement of mankind proceeds, will become an increasingly large and important political constellation. To the prospects of the formation and extension of such a society of states we will return in the next lecture. For the present it is enough to say that, whatever labels may be in use at Geneva or elsewhere, there is no other form of grouping which corresponds to the root-principle of collective security. . . .

108. Internal Stability and International Conflict

RICHARD N. ROSECRANCE

. . . War may occur in the absence of internal instability; internal friction may occur in the absence of war. In many of the chaotic international patterns of modern times, however, the two factors were associated. This tentative finding is averse to both doctrines and modes of analysis of certain previous theories.[19] The most venerable, and at the same time currently respectable contrary view is that the international system itself holds the keys to the cause of war and peace. Individual state policies are the product of international mandates and requirements. It is the system of international equilibrium, the balance of power system, or the mode of organizing international relationships which is decisive for peace

[19] See particularly Kenneth N. Waltz, *Man, the State, and War* (New York, 1959).

and tranquillity. If the formal organization of the system were changed, war might be exorcized. World government, a reformulated United Nations—these would successfully regulate international politics. At the extreme, drastic changes at the international level undoubtedly would work such a transformation; the difficulty with this prescription is that it is difficult to administer. Neither the League nor the United Nations was adequate to the task, and a more powerful world political organization is beyond our efforts. As Kenneth Waltz writes: "The remedy, though it may be unassailable in logic, is unattainable in practice."[20] The institutionalist theories of Leonard Woolf did not transform the system, and they blinded us to more important realities. World government will not be achieved without fundamental changes in the actors themselves.

The reaction against such internationalist views became overpowering after World War II. The institutional fallacies of the League, the abject reliance upon formal organizations as a substitute for policy, and the patent disharmonies of interest were stressed unendingly after the war. Institutions were not the remedies for conflict, for conflict was endemic in the nature of man and states. Motivational determinants, both individual and national, were pronounced the final bases of international action. According to a majority of scholars, power was the energizing motivation of individual and nation, and international relations was perforce "a struggle for power." In time, other motivational characteristics were adduced and the struggle for power had to make way for "purpose," "ideals," and competing ideologies. All seemed agreed, however, on the explanation of international politics in terms of fundamental human and social motivations. The problem of this line of theory, of course, was that it awaited a change in the nature of man. No policy scientist could alter the struggle for power or banish conflict from the international scene. Again, remedies could not be applied.

The present analysis calls attention to the internal organization of the state itself. In so doing it harks back to a tradition linking liberals and socialists, Kant, Wilson, and Mazzini. But unlike all of the above, it does not prescribe any particular political form or constitution. It does not favor republicanism over despotism or

---

[20] Waltz, *op. cit.*, p. 238.

liberalism over socialism, and certainly it does not prefer nationalism over dynasticism. It prescribes domestic stability and internal peace as the vehicle of international stability and external peace. This prescription is not easily filled. Domestic change is almost as chaotic as international change, and the arenas of action are almost numberless. Yet domestic governments exist; there are agencies to administer palliatives; there are bureaucracies to install reforms. Internal institutions are already formed. At the same time, the international supports for domestic stability can be mobilized, and international resources are available for the task.

In the final reckoning, however, one cannot be optimistic. Economic development may be an unsettling phenomenon in the net;[21] nationalist furor is scarcely stabilizing. And even stable domestic regimes are sometimes involved in war. Internal pacification and renovation may be both more vital and more simple than wholesale reorganization of the international environment, but that is little assurance that either will be accomplished in time.

[21] See S. M. Lipset, *Political Man* (London, 1959), pp. 68-70.

CAN COLLECTIVE SECURITY SUCCEED?

109. The "Inevitability" of a Collective Security Failure

JOHN H. HERZ

. . . In questions of "what might (or might not) be" or "what might (or might not) have been" there is always a danger of either sinning through overabstractness (distinguishing possibilities and impos-

John H. Herz, *International Politics in the Atomic Age* (New York: Columbia University Press, 1959), pp. 87-95. Reprinted by permission.

sibilities according to some abstract schemata) or falling into the trap of overconcreteness (believing that only what is, or has been, is or was possible). I believe that there is a middle approach, and that it is as necessary as it is important to distinguish obvious impossibilities from mere difficulties. For instance, if collective security by definition implies general commitments to counter aggression by force no matter who the aggressor is in any specific instance (that which we have referred to as the "anonymity of the aggressor"), its realization will be impracticable, that is, "impossible," if at a given moment there exists one overwhelmingly powerful (hegemonical) nation, because an "overwhelming powerful" anti-aggression coalition obviously could not be formed against it by the remainder of the states. This would be a clear case of incongruity. It is different where existing conditions *per se* are not in conflict with the basic prerequisites of a system. Congruity prevailed, for instance, between general conditions in the classical era of international relations and the balance system. It might have been, and frequently *was* difficult to maintain or restore a reasonable degree of stability to that equilibrium, but it was not impossible, and there were periods in which a relatively stable balance did prevail.

Taking these distinctions as a yardstick, I believe that for collective security the answers to the problem must differ according to the characteristics of the period under discussion. The still classical state system up to and including the period of the League of Nations must be distinguished from that of the post-Second World War era. At the time of the League there was yet in existence a plurality of territorial, impermeable states. Collective security then was aimed at the rationalization and legalization of power relations because power politics of the classical type had run into the vicious circle of increased insecurity owing to the decreased self-sufficiency of countries and the ensuing power competition and expansion.[11] The question was whether the difficulties in the path of such rationalization, which are obvious, were insurmountable. While it

[11] See my article "Power Politics and World Organization," *American Political Science Review,* 36: 1039 ff. (1942). I refer to this article also for a more detailed discussion of the problems dealt with in the following pages.

is always precarious procedure to indulge in "what might have been," I believe that actual trends in the interwar period were not quite as adverse to the realization of genuine collective security as current discussion, impressed by actual failure, is inclined to assert.

At a time when power was still quite widely distributed, that is, dispersed among half a dozen or more "big powers," which, moreover, were not yet too far removed in strength from a number of middle powers, the formation of the "grand coalition" against an aggressor which collective security calls for was still in the realm of the possible. In the "test cases" of the thirties, Japanese aggression against China and Italian aggression against Ethiopia, it would have been relatively easy, we now know, for the remainder of the powers, even just those who then were members of the collective security organization, to cope with the aggression by joint force. One needs only to compare the isolated condition of the aggressor nations then with the power they jointly commanded when they were nevertheless defeated in the Second World War.

With this example we also meet, at least partially, the argument concerning the "extension of local conflicts into general wars" with which collective security is frequently charged. That possibility of course exists. Under twentieth-century conditions local conflicts are likely to extend, and collective action then implies dealing with them at a point when they are still manageable. So far as the conditions of the thirties are concerned, there was also still present that "minimum of moral and political solidarity" among the powers to which one of the authors mentioned above refers as one of the prerequisites of collective security. To be sure, this requirement cannot mean identity of internal regimes and of political beliefs; rather, it refers to an identity of views on "international morality," which, in the interwar period, meant agreement on the necessity of "indivisibility of peace" and of the desirability of a system of "paix par le droit." Despite all their internal and ideological differences, the major nonaggressive powers, precisely in their opposition to the "aggressor nations," were inclined to agree on this required minimum of common attitude. It is immaterial in this connection that this happy congruence was in some cases (e.g., Russia's) motivated by pure self-interest, in others (e.g., the United State's) by a compelling wish to be "left alone," while in still others there existed a strong "internationalist" urge to establish once and for all a precedent for the impermissibility of any "breach of the peace."

Turning now to the problem of "status quo" and "peaceful change," it must be admitted that the difficulty is a very real one. No status quo can be perpetuated. It is hardly necessary to point out how damaging the connection between the League system and the status quo of Versailles and the related peace settlements turned out to be to the reputation of the collective security organization *qua* impartial organization for the maintenance of peace. But an even more fundamental question is: how can "just" settlements ever be attained when force is eliminated as a means of obtaining change? Indeed, if it be supposed that collective security should also provide for change through "fair" or "just" settlements of disputes, a solution may prove impossible, considering that views on what constitutes a "fair" solution ordinarily differ even among the parties not directly affected. But perhaps we are aiming too high if we expect change which is both "peaceful" and "just." All we can aim at is its "peacefulness," and it would not seem utopian to believe that such solutions could be had even where states no longer rely on the threat of individual force as *ultima ratio;* that is, to expect that even after a successful outlawry of force a status quo might be modified through the time-honored means of diplomacy which comprise pressures, compromise, accommodations, etc.[12] Thompson rightly points out how difficult it is to protect a status quo which itself remains ill-defined, but this argument highlights the opposite of the "peaceful change" argument, namely, the importance of first having a stable basis from which to proceed to solve outstanding issues. It is also true, as Schätzel states, that collective security means the separation of the procedural aspects

[12] At a time when I still believed that postwar conditions might lend themselves to the establishment of a functioning collective security system (in 1942), I wrote: "The fundamental issue would be nothing less than finding rational solutions for what rarely, so far, has been regulated in other than irrational ways. It would be more than optimistic to hope that 'inherent justice' rather than compromise would be the main device in the adjustment of still clashing interests of still more and less influential stronger and weaker, parties, at least for a long time to come. This will, then, still be an age of relative fallibility, not of accomplished rightfulness" (*ibid.*, p. 1052).

of international conflicts (maintenance of the given status by prohibition of "breach of the peace") from the substantive issues (the underlying conflict which leads to the breach of the peace). But must one assume that the anti-aggression countries, as a result of their "possessory" action, will necessarily try to "get something" from the aggressor? Collective security means the restoration of the status quo *ante,* independent of the question of the merits. All one has to "get" from the aggressor is what *he* has gotten through aggression.[13]

Whether such separation of issues is possible constitutes the core of the really vital problem: the relation between "national interests" and the "common interest" in preventing aggression. One argument described above, with all its seeming logic, is not convincing. That collective security is based on trust and distrust simultaneously is true, but this is only an apparent paradox. All law is based on the possibility (and actuality) of law violation. It expects the citizen to be law-minded, knowing that there will be instances where the expectation fails. Without that failure law would be superfluous; with too much failure, however, it would be ineffective, because unenforceable. Law, as a functioning institution, is suspended between a certain minimum and a certain maximum of "effectivity."[14] The really decisive question, internationally, has been whether a "minimum" of effectivity could have been obtained under collective security law; that is, whether at a time when the power system had become world-wide, powers, and particularly the big ones, might have been made to realize that their overriding "national" or "self-interest" existed in opposing the use of force as a means of individual national policy wherever and on the part of whomever it might occur. Most discussants now tend to be skeptical on this point. But it is at least imaginable that the degree of "rationality"

[13] Confusion about this was apparent in connection with the Korean case (whether or not one considers the Korean action as "genuine" collective security action). Those who wanted to see North Korea thrown back behind the 38th Parallel were motivated by the idea of the "possessorium," while those who wished to solve the problem by going up to the Yalu River and thus unifying Korea had the "merits" in mind. See in this respect Hula's more pessimistic conclusions for our age on "wars for righteousness" ("Fundamentals of Collective Security," *Social Research,* 24: 1 ff. [1957-58]).

[14] As Hans Kelsen has pointed out in many of his writings.

in foreign policy which such realization demands is attainable once more and more states and groups within states become aware to what extent the individual nations' own security has become intermingled with the general security (in the sense of peace) in a world where conflicts usually can no longer be "localized" and aggression eventually tends to affect the most remote. I believe it is incorrect to assume that what is "natural" in the behavior and attitudes of nations must perennially follow one and the same pattern, namely, the one set by "national interests" as conceived in the classical age of their individual and individualistic pursuance. Such an assumption is implied in terms like the one that refers to collective action as "war against nature." Why should not a more rational attitude, distinguishing between short-range and long-range interest, become "second nature" to nations?[15]

If one studies the Ethiopian case in detail, the alleged "inevitability" of failure becomes a bit doubtful. One gains the impression that it was not insurmountable resistance in countries like France or Britain which defeated the "sanctions experiment"; rather, there was a precarious balance of forces which might as easily have turned in favor of adoption of the decisive "oil and steel sanctions" which were at issue as it actually tipped against them. There are situations in international affairs in which several "might-be's" are almost equally close to becoming "are's," and where a very slight difference in actual trends and events tips the scale. In the early thirties there did exist a growing awareness in various countries all over the world, and in a growing number of groups within countries, that peace was "indivisible" and that a precedent, once set, to make this clear to all, might become a firm basis for future collective security. If everything hinged on so (relatively) small a detail as the implementation of certain embargoes against a country so relatively unimportant in international trade as Italy in 1935-36, it is at least imaginable that the outcome might have been different, that is, successful. And if actual success was that close in the case of the League, would it be entirely chimerical to assume that a really universal organization, with all of the then "big powers"

[15] More on the relation between "security" and "national interest," in our day and in the classical era, will be found, in subsequent chapters.

represented on its council, might have succeeded where the predominantly European League of Nations failed?

It is one of the supreme paradoxes of the postwar period that when countries belatedly realized what they should have realized in the interwar period, namely, the identity of national and common interests in an indivisible peace, they did so (and even tried to act) when the preconditions for a genuine security system had vanished. At the time of the Korean war at least three essential prerequisites were no longer extant. First, the new bipolar concentration of power had rendered the idea of marshaling preponderant force on one side nugatory. In the split world of today East and West are so finely balanced that "overwhelming coalitions" against isolated aggressors, the basic requirement of collective security in action, can no longer be formed.[16] What appears in the guise of collective action then is either bloc action or majority action by the international organization; but majorities and minorities mean little where the chief antagonists have thermonuclear weapons. If collective security is predicated upon deterrence as one of its prime instrumentalities, that security is of course unobtainable where preponderance of collective strength is no longer available as a deterrent.

In the second place, the ideological split in today's world would render the functioning of a collective security system impossible even if there still were a plural rather than a bipolar distribution of power. "Domestic" creeds and ideologies in disagreement with those in other countries would not concern a collective security organization so long as there was general agreement on the necessity to suppress aggression. As long as the Soviet Union agreed with the Western democracies on this, or at least subordinated its

[16] Such equally balanced blocs can of course occur in a system of plural powers as well; however, in it there is at least the possibility of preponderant coalition. On the other hand, bipolarity does not preclude collective action where the big powers agree. This means collective security in regard to smaller powers and their conflicts. However, the area in which the big powers do not clash is shrinking. That the United Nations itself was not based on the idea of collective security among the big powers is clear from its structure and charter, especially the veto principle. Korean action was possible only because of the historical joke of the Soviets' temporary absence from the Security Council.

own views on world relations to the practical necessity of checking fascist-totalitarian expansion, a common basis for enforcement of the peace against the aggressor nations did exist. Today, Communist and non-Communist regimes clash over what is exactly one essential collective security definition, namely, what constitutes aggression.[17] Even such a disagreement would not matter so much if the "deviator" was an isolated minority of one (or a few) as against the "overwhelming" opinion of all or most of the others (as in, for instance, the case of Italy in 1935). It matters very much where what looks like "aggression" to one half of the world appears as "defense" to the other half. In that event voting majorities of 55:5 or similar ones merely indicate that one side has managed to rally a majority of organization members to its point of view, while the other side still asserts that a majority of the actual population of the world was on its side.[18] Ideological bipolarity is as much a block to collective security as is the bipolarity of power.

Third, the final and, perhaps, most serious obstacle to collective security today is in the new nature and destructiveness of war itself. How the atomic bomb and related developments affect power and power relations among states will be discussed in subsequent chapters. So far as collective security is concerned, it means that the power which possession of the new weapons conveys is such that the rallying of overwhelming power against it is impossible. Nuclear power *per se* is "overwhelming." At the same time the vulnerability of a country exposed to the new weapons is such that only split-second retaliation could counter them, with no time left for discussion, voting, and similar decision making in and by a security organization.[19] Whether, under these circumstances, such

---

[17] On this problem more will be said below.

[18] Something which might easily happen in the East-West conflict if India and a few other Asian countries should side with Communist China and the Soviet Union. The Western powers, of course, might then in turn maintain that populations under totalitarian rule are not free to voice their opinions. And so forth, *ad infin.*

[19] Mr. Eban, addressing the United Nations commemorative meeting at San Francisco, rightly stated: "The grotesque potency of military force is reducing the military argument to impotence, even in the domain of collective enforcement" (New York *Times,* June 22, 1955).

an organization could still have some other sort of useful purpose is, of course, quite another question.

The foregoing consideration of trends, possibilities, and impossibilities of collective security has already touched upon the fundamental change in the structure of international relations which occurred at what may be called the end of the classical era. We now have to study more systematically the factors which have caused this change.

110. An Empirical and Practical Approach

KENNETH W. THOMPSON

. . . Clearly the moral is that collective security as a means of achieving world peace is no more an absolute than arbitration or disarmament or the outlawry of war. Its positive value may sometimes be very great, but this will depend on a whole series of specific variables which cannot be brought under the control of any fixed theoretical concept. It is unhappily the case that however persistently men may seek for some blanket code of procedural rules, compliance with a code would automatically do away with such realities as the immense variety of the human family, the inescapable conflicts of its members as they seek influence and power, and the fact that human behavior is only partially calculable by man himself, by reason of the fact that he lacks both the means and the moral courage fully to understand himself.

If collective security is insufficient as a theory of international relations, it may nonetheless have its place if applied judiciously and with immense reserve and self-restraint. It can be a means of organizing and making legitimate the network of mutual interests

Kenneth W. Thompson, "Isolationism and Collective Security: The Uses and Limits of Two Theories of International Relations," in Alexander DeConde, editor, *Isolation and Security* (Durham: Duke University Press, 1957), pp. 159-183, at pp. 182-183. Reprinted by permission.

of a "free-world" coalition, especially if the task of preserving the tenuous ties among them is taken seriously. This calls for the best arts of statecraft and diplomacy, arts which antedate collective security by centuries. I have suggested in another connection that

> Perhaps the supreme paradox of American foreign policy today is the necessity placed upon us to seize and employ the essentially utopian instruments of collective security in a brutally realistic power struggle. Its agencies furnish a political framework through which the broad coalition of the free world can be strengthened and a more stable equilibrium of world power be restored. Britain and France and the free powers of Asia are more likely to play their part and contribute to the restoration of a balance of power in Asia if we assure them support through mutual guarantees and create confidence by discussion in the halls and anterooms of the United Nations.

Three years later I would add only that for every concrete policy, the value of the consolidation of the "free world" must be measured coolly and dispassionately against the effects on our ties with the neutral and uncommitted nations. In certain cases they may yearn more for economic aid or political recognition than mutual guarantees. Thus an empirical and pragmatic approach, as against a legalistic and punitive view of collective security, finds uses more modest and limited than the ardent advocates assume. It is but one variable among many. It aims at the institutionalizing of force but perhaps must settle for the facilitating of a more stable balance of power. Today's realities are such that it should be played in a minor key as against economic growth, peaceful change, and the harmonizing of differences. Tomorrow's facts could call for new estimates and insights. Until then perhaps we should safeguard and preserve the recurring truths we find at the heart of isolationism and collective security, however inadequate, until we have a more inclusive and recognized body of theory for American foreign policy.

[IX]

The Future and Collective Security

An Essay

MARINA S. FINKELSTEIN AND
LAWRENCE S. FINKELSTEIN

Collective security is like a mirage. It beckons on the horizon. It seems full of promise. But it remains unattainable. It remains unattainable because the basic requirement of collective security—that nations subordinate their conflicting purposes and interests to collective action for the suppression of prohibited acts no matter how or where they may occur—has remained an illusion. Since the will to act collectively in specific instances in support of this very general purpose is the essence of collective security, it has simply remained unrealized.

Experience has shown that collective security is dependent, at the very least, on a firm nucleus of great power agreement. The United Nations Charter came close to an accurate reflection of the irreducible, the essential "collective will," in its requirement for great power unanimity as the condition for Security Council decisions on all but procedural matters. In spite of the storm of criticism at San Francisco of the "concurring votes" provision of Article 27, there was also recognition that collective security would be impossible without great power unanimity. Of course the smaller powers resented the privileged voting position of the five permanent members of the Security Council. At the same time, however, they recognized that when the "Big Five" were able to agree on what they wanted, it was in the interest of the smaller states to accept that agreement. In 1945, besides, to oppose the great powers meant to risk not having any Charter at all. In addition, it was recognized that the Charter represented an advance over the Covenant in that it substituted "for the rule of complete unanimity of the League Council a system of qualified majority voting in the Security Council." [1]

However, the hoped-for great power unanimity failed to materialize in the face of bitter ideological and political schism and military confrontation between the Soviet Union and the non-Communist permanent members of the Security Council. The United Nations, in spite of its many significant activities in the field of security, has not been an instrument of collective security.

The United Nations has, however, been put to the service of collective defense. In the Korean case, for example, the fact of North Korean aggression was clearly authenticated by a United Nations agency, and the United Nations majority which resisted the aggression was thus able to enjoy the legal umbrella of United Nations authority. What took place was war, with the special moral and legal cachet that derives from the ability to command "legitimatization" by the international organization. In the words of a recent paper, the United Nations has certain "obvious advantages for playing the role of custodian of the seals of international approval and disapproval. While the voice of the United Nations may not be the authentic voice of mankind, it is clearly the best available facsimile thereof. . . ." [2]

At a different level, regional agencies have given legitimacy, of a somewhat different sort, to collective defense measures or arrangements. For example, the Organization of American States gave its blessing to the actions of the United States in the Cuban missiles crisis of 1962. The potentialities for competitive legiti-

---

[1] *Report to the President on the Results of the San Francisco Conference,* by the Chairman of the United States Delegation, the Secretary of State, June 26, 1945, Department of State Publication 2349, Conference Series 71 (Washington, D.C.: Government Printing Office, 1945), p. 75.

[2] Inis L. Claude, Jr., "Collective Legitimization as a Political Function of the U.N.," Study Group on International Organization, European Centre of the Carnegie Endowment for International Peace, Geneva, 1965, mimeo., OI 12.65, p. 9.

mization of military collective defense measures by the NATO and Warsaw Pact organizations in mutual conflict have, fortunately, not been put to the test.

It is sometimes argued that collective security may have a better chance in the regional organizations, because to a significant degree each such organization may represent a common cultural or religious heritage or a common historical experience of its members. However, such bonds of themselves do not ensure a common view on foreign affairs. Thus, the Arab League and the Organization of African Unity are, in different degrees, riven by disputes over ideological and political influence, over boundaries, questions of leadership, and various points of concrete foreign policy. The Organization of American States, which is the only regional organization to include formal collective security obligations in its constitutional documents, and which has on occasion been able to carry out collective security policies, is also subject to pulls in different directions. Fear of intervention by the northern "colossus" vies thus with the concept of collective security, with the outcome in any given instance unpredictable.

PEACE-KEEPING AS AN ALTERNATIVE TO COLLECTIVE SECURITY

In the United Nations, the frustration of the early hopes has produced various efforts to improvise effective means of dealing with the threats to peace posed in the decades since 1945. On the whole, the United Nations has proved remarkably resilient and surprisingly able to devise new responses to evolving needs, within the limits imposed by the fact that, through much of this period, the world was polarized around two great power centers in conflict.

In this history, Korea marked a turning point. In the early years of the United Nations, until the Korean War, the organization was able to perform two important peace and security functions. The first was to act as a forum for mobilizing resistance to Communist expansion, with a consequent legitimizing of the contingent threat that United States power would be applied in any given instance. One example was the Security Council's role in the issue posed by the continued presence of Soviet troops in Iranian

Azerbaijan.[3] Another was the Greek case, in which it was possible to set up partially effective means of observation and border patrols, intended to cut off the illicit flow of arms into Greece for the use of Communist-supported guerrillas.[4] In Korea, as has already been pointed out, the presence of the United Nations Commission on the spot was fortuitously decisive in the determination of aggression when it occurred in 1950.

Experience until 1950 even led to the belief, expressed in the "Uniting for Peace" Resolution of November, 1950, that the United Nations might be developed into an effective instrument of collective defense. After all, in spite of all the difficulties and conflicts, the United Nations had been able to perform some collective defense functions. The Soviet Union had at least tolerated this use of the organization, most markedly when it did not withdraw from the United Nations despite its role in blocking achievement of Soviet goals in Korea. All this inspired the belief that the veto could be evaded by relying on the General Assembly's powers to recommend actions to members. It was of course recognized that the General Assembly, unlike the Security Council, could not require members to act.

Throughout this early period the United Nations had also been playing another role, that of dealing, and with some success, with threats to the peace that did not directly involve the two hostile blocs. There had, in other words, proved to be enough consensus, even if sometimes of a tacit nature, to enable the United Nations to intervene effectively in a number of instances.

Thus in 1947 the United Nations began its intervention in the Palestine problem.[5] In 1948 the dispute between Pakistan and India as to the future status of Kashmir came before the Security Council. Although no agreement on the future of the area proved possible, a United Nations military presence was interposed and is still stationed at the disputed border to supervise the carrying

[3] See Richard W. Van Wagenen, *The Iranian Case, 1946* (New York: Carnegie Endowment for International Peace, 1952).

[4] See C. E. Black, "Greece and the United Nations," *Political Science Quarterly*, December, 1948, pp. 551-568.

[5] For an early discussion, see L. Larry Leonard, "The United Nations and Palestine," *International Conciliation*, No. 454, October, 1949, pp. 603-785.

out of truce arrangements.[6] In the Indonesian case the United Nations had a more positive success, the international organization being able through its good offices to help the Dutch colony achieve independent status (1947-1949).[7]

However, even in this period, it was clear that the United Nations could be relevant to the central sphere of great power conflict only in a marginal way. This does not mean that matters concerning the peace settlements and the future of Europe did not appear on the agenda. They did. Various aspects of the German problem, Trieste, the Corfu Channel case, peace treaty violations by the East European satellites, all these did find their place before United Nations bodies. Indeed, the United Nations even provided the venue for the opening of negotiations leading to the settlement of the intense crisis over Berlin (1948-1949). However, this experience only underlined the fact that lack of agreement, coupled with the importance of the issues to the two blocs, made it impossible for the United Nations to have a determining role in these issues. The main response of the West to the need for a mobilization of collective defense took place not in the United Nations but in the Brussels Pact of 1948 and in the North Atlantic Treaty of 1949.

As has already been mentioned, Korea marked a turning point in a number of ways. From this time on, the United Nations' role as a forum to mobilize against Communist expansion declined while its role as a peace-keeper in "third world" conflicts became more prominent. There were a number of reasons which help to explain why the attention of the organization shifted in this way. First of all, the Soviet atomic explosion of 1949 had introduced a new element into the international power equation, one which seemed to many to offset United States predominance and thus to make its "lead" less compelling. Second, the emergence of Communist China as an important actor of considerable power on the international scene injected an increasing element of caution into the policies of a number of nations.

[6] See Joseph Korbel, *Danger in Kashmir* (Princeton: Princeton University Press, 1954).

[7] Foster Collins, "The United Nations and Indonesia," *International Conciliation,* No. 459, March, 1950, pp. 115-200.

The results flowing from these changes were reinforced by later developments. First of all, Stalin's death in 1953 and the consequent evolution of Soviet foreign policies seemed to decrease the likelihood of dangerous threats from the Soviet Union and, by reducing fear of such Soviet initiatives, reduced willingness to engage in political controversy within the United Nations. Europe seemed to be entering a period of increased political stability. In 1955, in a surprising turnabout, the Soviet government agreed to sign the Austrian Peace Treaty. Even the ruthless Soviet suppression of the Hungarian Revolution in 1956, though it served as a jolt for many, did not reverse this trend. Bolstering this reluctance to react forcefully was a second factor: the development of a concept of nonalignment, first among Asian members and then among the rapidly growing group of African members. This introduced an almost professional "middle man" role, first significantly exhibited in the Indian mediation during the Korean crisis.

To sum up: a lessening of the United States predominance in some eyes, a seeming "softening" of Soviet policy, and the development of nonalignment—all these contributed to make it increasingly difficult, and perhaps also less necessary, to mobilize majorities for a vigorous United Nations role in bloc conflicts.

What was possible became therefore more limited. It also became more significant, as the movement of colonial areas into independence added a new dimension to the problems of the "third world." In this setting, the United Nations combined old and new devices to produce somewhat different patterns for preventing the breakdown of order under certain special circumstances. The process began with the Suez crisis of 1956-1957. What has emerged has been labeled "peace-keeping."

The purpose of peace-keeping is to prevent the breakdown of international order, or to mitigate it, should it already have taken place. Taken this far and no further, peace-keeping may seem identical with collective security. In actuality, however, the two are very different. Collective security is intended to apply against any threat to international peace, no matter where or by whom posed; it calls for universal participation; and its aim is to strike down the aggressor, the law-breaker, and to enforce the decision of the international community. Peace-keeping, on the other hand, is limited in application, posits no "enemy," and is essentially voluntary.

Thus, peace-keeping is not intended to operate against threats to the peace anywhere in the world and without regard to the states involved. It is intended to operate in areas which do not fall within the spheres of great power interest, and especially where there is a risk that the great powers might be drawn into a mutual confrontation in such areas. Where such a situation is shaping up, the United Nations may be called on by its members to intervene with the consent of the parties, in a number of different ways: to prevent bloodshed, to supervise truces or cease-fire arrangements, to investigate, to perform pacifying missions of observation or patrol, or to give a new government a chance to survive and establish itself.[8] To achieve these ends, United Nations forces have been mobilized from national units voluntarily contributed through individual national decision. The permanent members of the Security Council do not normally contribute men to such United Nations forces. However, in practical terms, their role in the formation of the guiding United Nations resolutions, and their role, or the role of some of them, in terms of money, supplies, and equipment may be of crucial importance to the success of any peace-keeping operation. Nevertheless, it is possible to say that in a sense, instead of supplying security as the Charter envisioned, the great powers now consume it. Finally it should be pointed out that in peace-keeping operations, a special guiding responsibility has fallen to the Secretary-General, in the context of the members' interests and policies.

As was stated earlier, peace-keeping operates under rather special conditions. It involves functions and powers which were not specifically contemplated in the Charter. In purpose and character, such functions and powers seem more closely related to the Security Council's role with respect to the pacific settlement of

[8] Since 1956 such operations have taken place in the Middle East to patrol the lines between Israel and its neighbors (1956—); in Lebanon (1958); in the Congo (1960-1964), as well as in West Irian (1962-1963), Yemen (1963), and on Cyprus (1964—).

disputes or situations which might lead to international friction or give rise to disputes, than to its powers of enforcement after it has determined "the existence of any threat to the peace, breach of the peace or act of aggression." In other words, peace-keeping seems more closely related to Chapter VI of the Charter than to Chapter VII.[9]

A number of consequences flow from this constitutional interpretation. Because peace-keeping is based on Chapter VI and not on Chapter VII, it assumes no "enemy" as such and seeks to "defeat" no one. As Ralph Bunche, United Nations Under-Secretary, put it in discussing the operation of the United Nations Force (UNF) in the Congo,

> The United Nations in the Congo has neither sought to replace the Congo Government nor to make it a captive. The UNF is in the Congo as a friend and partner, not as an army of occupation.[10]

On this basis, United Nations forces as a rule are instructed not to use armed force except in self-defense, and many of their functions can be likened more to policing functions than to traditional military ones.

Since peace-keeping is based on the United Nations' enforcement powers under Chapter VII, it follows that peace-keeping must be voluntary. Therefore, it cannot start without the consent of the parties or without the permission of the government or governments on whose territory it is to take place. Nor can the decision to engage in a peace-keeping operation create any obligations on United Nations members to contribute forces or supplies or give permission for the use of any facilities. Impressed by the difficulties which arise from the ad hoc nature of peace-keeping as it has developed so far, some nations have decided to "earmark" units of their own forces for future peace-keeping service but these have been national, voluntary decisions and the actual use of such units is subject to national decision each time.

The argument which has developed in the United Nations as to

[9] For a discussion, see Ambassador Francis T. P. Plimpton's remarks, "War/Peace Conference on the Future of the United Nations," April 20, 1965, *War/Peace Report,* June, 1965, p. 10.

[10] *Security Council Official Records,* Fifteenth Year, Supplement for July, August, September, 1960, Doc. S/4451 (August 21, 1960), pp. 114-115.

the proper way to finance such operations centers on whether the financing of voluntary operations should also be voluntary or whether it should be governed by the provisions of Article 17, which give the General Assembly the power to "consider and approve" the budget and which state further that "the expenses of the Organization shall be borne by the Members as apportioned by the General Assembly." The argument arises out of a Charter ambiguity, the fact that Article 17 gives the General Assembly a power of compulsory assessment while the only other compulsory power is assigned to the Security Council under Chapter VII. The Soviet Union and France lead those who argue that financing of peace-keeping should not be compulsory; the United States leads those who advocate the principle of collective responsibility, which was supported by the International Court of Justice in an advisory opinion in 1962. As things developed in 1964 and 1965, it would seem that the principle of collective financial responsibility does not enjoy the support of a large enough majority to make it stick. Underlying this issue is the fact that national policies may differ—as in the Congo—concerning the objectives to be pursued and the sharing of control to reflect national influence in peace-keeping operations. The Soviet Union, for example, has been insisting that only the Security Council can undertake operations involving the deployment of military force for any purpose, obviously because of interest in strengthening Russian influence over peace-keeping decisions through its "veto" in the Security Council.

At the same time, even though the principle of collective financial responsibility does not seem to have wide support, the principle of peace-keeping does have large majority support. Therefore, while it may not now be possible to agree on the general principle of peace-keeping financing or on general guidelines for future peace-keeping decisions, it does seem likely that future "third world" crises which are not dealt with satisfactorily in other ways will precipitate enough agreement to make United Nations ad hoc intervention possible. Even so, this may depend on whether the great powers, the United States and the Soviet Union in particular, will be able to agree, at least tacitly, that prevention of crisis escalation to avoid the risk of a mutual encounter (or of Communist

Chinese gain) is more important than the independent pursuit of competitive interests.

Just what the decision would be in such instances is not at all clear. Independent Soviet action in the Congo, the appearance of Soviet weapons on Cyprus, United States insistence on the right to support governments which request its help as in Vietnam, intervention in the Dominican Republic in 1965, great power inability to agree on the financing of peace-keeping operations or on the general guidelines for the initiation of such operations in the future—all these suggest that the great powers may have conflicts in the "third world" which may make it difficult for them to agree on impartial peace-keeping measures when crises arise. It is at least probable, however, that in individual situations the interest of the majority in avoiding the deterioration of a tense situation will press the great powers toward the minimal agreement necessary to achieve the limited goal of insulating the crisis. In this connection it may be worthwhile to recall that it is possible for a permanent member of the Security Council to abstain from casting a yes or no vote. Since the Iranian case in 1946, it has been considered that a permanent member's abstention does not count as a veto. The Security Council may thus act without the concurrence of a great power, provided that it shows acquiescence by abstaining.

In this connection it may also be worth mentioning the Soviet complaint that "Socialist" members of the United Nations have been excluded from both direction of and participation in peace-keeping efforts. This may be important. In the future it may become necessary to find some accommodation in this matter if peace-keeping operations are to continue on the basis of adequate great power consensus. If the development of polycentric tendencies in Eastern Europe continues, it may become less undesirable to do so. Also significant has been the Soviet emphasis during the spring of 1965 on the possibility of revitalizing the Military Staff Committee, perhaps with an enlarged membership, as a means of strengthening the Security Council's capacity to control peace-keeping operations.

In short, the future development of the peace-keeping function may come to depend on a mutual effort to find a consensus through some degree of mutual accommodation. Progress toward such consensus might be eased if the United Nations majority were to press for a limitation on the use of the veto in order to reduce the temptation for great powers, especially the Soviet Union, to hamstring the Security Council capriciously. In particular, limiting the use of the veto to issues specifically stated by a permanent member to be a matter of "vital importance, taking into account the interests of the United Nations as a whole,"[11] might be a useful approach, consistent with the expectations in 1945 as to the purposes for which the veto might be employed. In May, 1965, the permanent representative of Pakistan to the United Nations advocated a similar standard when he suggested that:

> . . . the Security Council would be restored to its full authority if the permanent members undertook to refrain from using the veto in the case of disputes in which they are not directly involved or on which the General Assembly had made recommendations under Article 10 of the Charter. . . .[12]

Whether it will be possible to arrive at necessary accommodation will depend, of course, on great power willingness to forego competitive advantage in "third world" crises and to arrive at "ground rules" limiting national intervention in such crises to make impartial intervention both possible and necessary. It may then become possible to make the Security Council work as originally intended. If this is not possible, there will have to be at least enough consensus to enable the General Assembly to perform the peace-keeping function without causing the breakup of the organization.

The development of peace-keeping was unplanned and unexpected. It is a promising development. However, it does not amount to collective security since it involves interposition with the consent of all concerned and not the imposition of a collective will on a recalcitrant state.

PROSPECTS OF DEVELOPING COLLECTIVE SECURITY UNDER THE UNITED NATIONS

The next question to ask is obviously whether there might develop a consensus which could support collective security ac-

---

[11] General Assembly Resolution 267 (III), April 14, 1949.

[12] Ambassador Amjad Ali, Special Committee on Peace-Keeping, Prov. SR of 6th Mtg., May 6, 1965, A/AC.121/SR.6, May 11, 1965, pp. 4-5.

tivities as well as peace-keeping. The answer is by no means self-evident.

It may be quite reasonable to assume that, if the United States and the Soviet Union should find enough consensus to lead them to support a peace-keeping operation, that consensus may stretch to support collective security enforcement measures if they should become necessary. As Paul H. Nitze, later to become Secretary of the Navy, put it in 1957,

> As the destructive power of the weapons systems possessed by the major powers approaches the absolute, these systems cannot be invoked except in support of absolute and unlimited objectives. Any involvement of the forces of the major powers, even limited forces in support of limited objectives, may involve an intolerable risk that the objectives and means employed will spread as a result of the military and political interaction of a war situation. The risks involved are of vital concern not just to the major powers but to the world as a whole. A growing realization of this situation among the politically effective masses of mankind can in the long run lay the foundation on which the necessary political consensus which is the pre-condition for a functioning United Nations force can be expected to arise.[13]

In other words, the argument here runs that the nuclear "balance of terror," in however uncertain a fashion, deters both major powers from taking intolerable risks and that this situation may be laying the basis for the development, however haltingly, of that political consensus which is the prerequisite for functioning international forces of an undefined character. Though not denying the very real possibility that the Soviet Union may elect to sow dissension, to ship its arms to tense areas for the use of one side or the other, and otherwise to create chaos, it is assumed in the following pages that such consensus should be helped to grow, at least in situations in which the so-called "vital and direct" interests of the powers are not immediately involved. If this point is correctly taken, then it should be a guideline of United States policy to seek to impress on all its desire to move toward a situation in which the

---

[13] Paul H. Nitze, "When and Under What Circumstances Might a United Nations Police Force Be Useful in the Future," in William R. Frye, *A United Nations Peace Force* (New York: Oceana, 1957), pp. 119-121, at p. 121.

enforcement provisions of the United Nations Charter in this area can be carried out as they were intended and to show how existing peace-keeping procedures might best be developed to their fullest usefulness in this area.

There is an obvious inconsistency in the proposition stated in the preceding paragraph. The inconsistency lies in the effort to pursue simultaneously the goal of seeking to establish enough great power consensus to enable the Security Council to work and pressing for Security Council intervention in individual cases, when to do so may obviously appear to be directed against the interests of a reluctant great power, especially the Soviet Union. There is no solution to this dilemma. However, a great deal might depend on the selection of issues to be pressed in the Security Council. Obviously, for the very reasons that make a veto power necessary, caution should be shown with respect to issues that directly affect what may be legitimately considered vital interests of a great power. Thus, to put it in more specific though hypothetical terms, the United States should not press for enforcement measures in the Warsaw Pact area and should resist proposals for United Nations enforcement measures in the NATO or OAS areas but should be willing to press for such intervention in Africa, the Middle East, and South and Southeast Asia.

From the above it is clear that collective security is not likely to operate in areas in which the great powers are directly or vitally concerned. This conclusion implies a certain risk of disagreement between the great powers and the rest of the members, already foreshadowed in the remarks of the Mauritanian delegate on the final day of the abortive nineteenth session of the General Assembly:

> We do not want to entrust to five great Powers or to two great Powers the task of deciding . . . what our common destiny will be. . . .[14]

However, this is not a new argument but an old one, already hotly contested at San Francisco in 1945. Although the marked change in United Nations membership since that time makes it difficult to predict exactly how a discussion over relations in the organization

[14] UN Document A/PV.1330, p. 47.

between greater and lesser powers would come out now, a different conclusion seems unlikely. When the great powers agree that intervention is needed to prevent a breakdown of the peace, it is still probable that the other United Nations members will find it in their interest to agree or at least to acquiesce.

Recent events even evoke a question which has hitherto been unthinkable. As has been pointed out, United Nations history underscores the obvious conclusion that whatever role the United Nations may develop, that role is unlikely to be relevant to zones of most direct great power interest—Eastern Europe, the North Atlantic, and Latin America. Now, however, one can begin to speculate about a question which is no doubt remote but nevertheless of interest, namely, whether we can begin to detect any signs that the weakening of alliance ties and of leadership from Washington and Moscow may not point, however tentatively, to a day when United Nations intervention may become possible even in some parts of these sanctuaries. Thus it might be pointed out that in the Cuban missile crisis and in the Dominican crisis of 1965 the United Nations accepted responsibilities in relation to a problem of peace and security in Latin America.

Obviously enough, one cannot predict that United Nations collective security or even a peace-keeping function will become possible in these areas. But for the first time since the Potsdam Conference of 1945 it becomes possible to speculate as to whether such a role might become possible. In Eastern Europe and in Latin America new stresses and strains may create uncertainties regarding the roles of the great powers. It may be that relations within the areas and with interested great powers may be worked out with relative calm and without outside intervention. On the other hand, it is perhaps more likely that changes within the areas may bring serious hazards to world peace, which may lead to threatening great power confrontations or to new needs for intervention to stabilize difficult situations. These might involve roles for the United Nations.

Whether such roles will actually be possible is unclear. One possibility is that the great powers will extend to these areas any consensus they may develop in other parts of the world to permit impartial intervention as an alternative to their direct intervention.

Or, on the other hand, the great powers might pose such severe threats to each other over these especially important areas that they and the rest of the world might welcome rescue by the world organization. In such circumstances, there might be a limited and transitory agreement to avoid a severe threat of catastrophe.

One should pause briefly at the question of the role of Communist China in this context. While it is not impossible to conceive of peace-keeping operations and in some instances even of collective security operations in areas close to the periphery of Communist China without strong opposition from Peking, it is very difficult to believe that Peking would readily acquiesce in such measures. Moreover, China's influence in other parts of the world may grow. It is clear that a "consensus" which does not include that country is a limited consensus. Nations within the reach of Communist Chinese influence may not be anxious to become involved in international operations close to that country against its opposition. It is likely that Communist Chinese influence will grow rather than decrease, barring some drastic change. Therefore, it is essential to keep in mind that any discussion of collective security or peacekeeping actions on the periphery of Communist China, in areas in which that country has expressed an interest, would start out under a strong inhibition. The consensus of which we talk here thus remains limited, though if it were to come about, it would be significant.

COLLECTIVE SECURITY AND DISARMAMENT

Thus far, this analysis of collective security possibilities has been concerned with a world slowly evolving from today's baseline, a world heavily armed, organized in competing major coalitions and with a large neutral or nonaligned floating vote. Beset by new uncertainties, this world also confronts new opportunities arising out of the loosening of the binding cement in the major alliance systems.

However, one should also ask what would be the implications for collective security of a quantum jump, in the nature of major progress in disarmament. That there is a close connection has been well established. Secretary of State Herter, for example, in February, 1960, defined the United States task as the double one of trying to "create a more stable military environment" and of subsequently trying

> to cut national armed forces and armaments further and to build up international peace-keeping machinery, to the point where aggression will be deterred by international rather than national forces.[15]

The point crops up also in varying forms in the proposals of both the United States and the Soviet Union for general and complete disarmament.

In the first place, it is important to recognize that there is a point of demarcation, hard to identify and perhaps never precisely measurable, between a projection of *today's world* in which the main contemporary assumptions still apply even though national armaments have been reduced and a *new world* in which the reduction of armaments has proceeded so far that new measures for policing world order may be necessary. It seems reasonable to speculate that in a world of thermonuclear weapons, the transition point is more likely to be encountered late in the disarmament scale rather than early.

It is only when the great powers' nuclear capacity to deter each other and to dominate other powers has been brought into question that a thoroughly new situation will have been created. That point will probably not have been reached before disarmament has progressed well into the third of the three Stages of the United States Draft Outline of 1962. While the Draft Outline calls for United Nations peace-keeping capabilities to be built up prior to that stage and, in fact, makes transition to the third Stage contingent on prior success in this regard, it is clear that United Nations peace forces can only be subsidiary to great power strength and dependent upon great power collaboration, as is true today, until reduction of arms has destroyed great power dominance. Put this way, the argument is virtually tautological.

The contrary argument, that United Nations capabilities can be built up so that they dominate great power strength, even while the great powers remain very strong, or at least provide a new balanc-

[15] February 18, 1960, Address at National Press Club, *Department of State Bulletin,* March 7, 1960, pp. 354-358.

ing force, postulates a degree of great power consensus as to the goals, methods, and control of a United Nations force which it is virtually impossible to conceive of. Such vague generalizing as the Soviet Union and the United States have been willing to indulge in so far on this subject indicates that they are poles apart in their conceptions of what United Nations forces in the context of a disarming world might be like. And Communist China has not yet joined the dialogue, such as it is. It is difficult, nay virtually impossible, to conceive of the powers bridging their differences, short of such a complete resolution of all their differences as would make complete or near-complete disarmament possible.

There is, however, a school of thought which urges that the thing to do is to divorce both disarmament and world policing from ideological, political, economic, or social questions. The notion that a regime in which ultimate power is vested in some peace-keeping authority can be based on a common interest in controlling the risks of national armaments and the hazards of war is an attractive one. As one author put the argument,

> *It may well be that many governments now regard disarmament not as a way of establishing world order acceptable to all nations, but as a way of changing the means of independently pursuing the national interest.* . . . In other words, the interest in disarmament may have arisen from a growing acceptance of 'the hypertrophy of war' as a *means*, rather than from a growing acceptance of world order as an *end*.[16]

Attractive this argument is. But it is also totally unreal. In a world in which important differences persist and the risk of international conflict continues so that a world peace authority is thought necessary, how likely is it that states with vital interests at stake will entrust decisive power to a mechanism which must in these circumstances itself be an important object of competition? The point is really quite simple. Defense of important interests in such circumstances would depend on ability to control the world peace authority. How can such a world peace authority be set up by

---

[16] Arthur I. Waskow, *Quis Custodiet? Controlling the Police in a Disarmed World,* A Peace Research Institute Report Submitted under ACDA Grant ACDA/IR-8 (Washington, D.C.: Peace Research Institute, Inc., 1963), pp. 6-7.

nations which do not have substantial ideological and political consensus? Without such consensus, how can they agree on arrangements to control the authority? And if they cannot agree on such arrangements, can they really be expected to agree in the first place on the disarmament which would make the authority necessary? The argument, it will be urged, is circular. The charge is correct because the problem is circular. Disarmament, collective security, and political consensus, like love and marriage in the popular song, are inseparable: "You can't have one without the other."

Another approach to the problem leads to the same conclusion. One of the central dilemmas confronted by those who have been concerned with schemes for maintaining world peace and security has been the relationship of arrangements to keep the peace to the nature of the peace that is to be kept. To say that a peace and security system can maintain peaceful procedures in a world in which important states or many states and their populations are not satisfied by the existing distribution of the world's territory, assets, or justice, and by the procedures on which agreement can be reached to alter that distribution is like saying that the lid can be kept on a kettle full of boiling water. Security and justice are intimately related. Where there is strong dissatisfaction, the maintenance of peace depends on the existence of agreed procedures to change the state of affairs. A complete system of peace and security must, therefore, include arrangements for what has been called "peaceful change." Perhaps it might have to come to include a so-called "legislative power." It is clear that any agreement on such procedures would require a high degree of consensus to start with.

In sum, disarmament, world policing, and peaceful change are not separable phenomena but part of one tightly knit package. All of them depend on the existence of a willingness among nations to subordinate their individual interests to agreed procedures for resolving their differences. That is a large order. It involves more consensus by a good deal than exists in today's world.

CONCLUSIONS

It is striking that, however the question of collective security is approached, the lesson appears to be the same. Change, whether in the short-term task of peace-keeping, in the longer-term development of collective security under the United Nations, or in movement toward the ultimate vision of a world peace authority, depends on the development of consensus. There is no short cut here.

Our recent experiences with the Soviet Union are instructive. There appears to be a minimum though not too certain consensus today. In part it has developed by chance. The death of Stalin marked an important turning point. President Kennedy's appearance on the national scene in the United States had a good deal to do with it also. In part, it may be a response to the deterioration of Sino-Soviet relations, and it may be debatable whether the world is in balance better off as a result of the developments in Chinese doctrine which played an important part in that split. But in considerable measure the United States-Soviet consensus is undoubtedly the result of confrontation and tension over a long period. Through this experience the two countries have learned to fear and respect each other as adversaries. Their disproportionate strength puts limits on their desire to fight each other. Out of this amalgam of circumstance, context, and constraint has come a degree of agreement which offers some hope of a better future relationship.

Fortunately, the United Nations exists as a forum in which to strive to reach broader accommodations, both with the Soviet Union and other nations. All powers which seek disarmament and world order as their ultimate goals should seek to engage in the United Nations in a process of accommodating their differences through dialogue and tension. Out of the crucible may emerge an evolving consensus which will enable the world to move by stages to a higher degree of collective policing capability on the part of the organized international community.

Selected Bibliography

The purpose of this bibliography is to help the student to find his way around in the literature dealing with collective security. It is confined primarily to books in the field, touching only very lightly on periodical material. For the latter, the reader is directed to consult the *Reader's Guide to Periodical Literature* and the *International Index to Periodicals*. More specifically, his attention is drawn to the files of *International Organization, Foreign Affairs,* the *Department of State Bulletin,* and the *United Nations Review.*

For further information concerning books in the field, the student should look at current issues of *Foreign Affairs* and should consult the *Foreign Affairs Bibliography* volumes, which cover the literature in ten-year spans, beginning with 1919.

For documentary material, a good starting point is to be found in the annual volumes published by the Council on Foreign Relations, entitled *Documents on American Foreign Relations.* Although not as up-to-date, the series published by the Royal Institute of International Affairs, in London, entitled *Documents on International Affairs,* is also recommended.

Bourquin, Maurice, ed., *Collective Security,* A Record of the Seventh and Eighth International Studies Conferences, Paris, 1934, and London, 1935. Paris, International Institute of Intellectual Cooperation, 1936.

Cecil, Viscount, *The Great Experiment*. London, Jonathan Cape, 1941.

The Charter of the United Nations, Hearings before the Committee on Foreign Relations, U.S. Senate, 79th Congress, 1st Session. Washington, Government Printing Office, 1945.

Clark, Grenville, and Louis B. Sohn, *World Peace through World Law,* 2nd ed., rev. Cambridge, Harvard University Press, 1960.

Claude, Inis L., Jr., *Power and International Relations.* New York, Random House, 1962.

———, *Swords into Plowshares,* 3rd ed., rev. New York, Random House, 1964.

Commission to Study the Organization of Peace, *Preliminary Report.* New York, 1940.

———, *The United Nations and the Organization of Peace,* Third Report. New York, February, 1943.

DeConde, Alexander, ed., *Isolation and Security.* Durham, Duke University Press, 1957.

Frydenberg, Per, *Peace-Keeping, Experience and Evaluation,* The Oslo Papers. Oslo, The Norwegian Institute of International Affairs, 1964.

Goodrich, Leland M., *Korea: A Study of United States Policy in the United Nations.* Washington, The Brookings Institution, 1957.

———, and Anne P. Simons, *The United Nations and the Maintenance of International Peace and Security.* Washington, The Brookings Institution, 1955.

Haas, Ernst B., "Types of Collective Security: An Examination of Operational Concepts." *American Political Science Review* (March, 1955), pp. 40-62.

Hemleben, Sylvester J., *Plans for Peace through Six Centuries.* Chicago, University of Chicago Press, 1943.

Herz, John H., *International Politics in the Atomic Age.* New York, Columbia University Press, 1959.

Highley, A. E., *The First Sanctions Experiment.* Geneva, Geneva Research Centre, 1938.

Hinsley, F. H., *Power and the Pursuit of Peace.* Cambridge, Cambridge University Press, 1963.

Introduction to the Annual Report of the Secretary-General on the Work of the Organization, 16 June 1959-15 June 1960. General Assembly, *Official Records,* 15th Session, Supplement No. 1A.

Liska, George, *International Equilibrium.* Cambridge, Harvard University Press, 1957.

Mitrany, David, *The Problem of International Sanctions.* London, Oxford University Press, 1925.

Morgenthau, Hans J., *Politics Among Nations,* 3rd ed. New York, A. A. Knopf, 1960.

Morley, Felix, *The Society of Nations.* Washington, The Brookings Institution, 1932.

National Studies on International Organization, a series of over 20 volumes, published under the auspices of the Carnegie Endowment for International Peace, New York City, from 1952 and still in process, with special attention to Robert M. MacIver, *The Nations and the United Nations,* New York, Manhattan, for the Carnegie Endowment for International Peace, 1959.

Nicholas, H. G., *The United Nations as a Political Institution.* London, Oxford University Press, 1959.

Nicolson, Sir Harold, *The Congress of Vienna: A Study in Allied Unity, 1812-1822.* New York, Harcourt, Brace and Co., 1946.

Phillips, Walter Alison, *The Confederation of Europe.* London, Longmans, Green and Co., 1914.

Rappard, William E., *The Quest for Peace.* Cambridge, Harvard University Press, 1940.

Report to the President on the Results of the San Francisco Conference, by the Chairman of the United States Delegation, the Secretary of State, Department of State Publication 2349, Conference Series 71. Washington, Government Printing Office, 1945.

Reves, Emery, *The Anatomy of Peace,* New York, Harper and Bros., 1945.

Review of the United Nations Charter: A Collection of Documents, Senate Doc. No. 87, 83rd Congress, 2nd Session, Washington, Government Printing Office, 1954.

Review of the United Nations Charter, Final Report of the Committee on Foreign Relations, Subcommittee on the United Nations Charter, Senate Report No. 1797, 84th Congress, 2nd Session. Washington, Government Printing Office, 1956.

Royal Institute of International Affairs, *International Sanctions.* London, Oxford University Press, 1938.

Russell, Ruth B., and Jeannette E. Muther, *A History of the United Nations Charter. Washington,* The Brookings Institution, 1958.

Schiffer, Walter, *The Legal Community of Mankind.* New York, Columbia University Press, 1954.

Shotwell, James T., *On the Rim of the Abyss.* New York, The Macmillan Co., 1936.

Stromberg, Roland N., *Collective Security and American Foreign Policy.* New York, F. Praeger, 1963.

Symposium on World Organization. *Yale Law Journal* (August, 1946), Vol. 55, No. 5.

Thompson, Kenneth W., "Collective Security Re-examined." *American Political Science Review* (September, 1953), pp. 753-772.

"The United Nations: Peace and Security," A Symposium. *American Political Science Review* (October, 1945).

Walters, F. P., *A History of the League of Nations*. London, Oxford University Press, 1952.

Wilcox, Frances O., and Carl M. Marcy, *Proposals for Changes in the United Nations*. Washington, The Brookings Institution, 1955.

Wolfers, Arnold, ed., *Alliance Policy in the Cold War*. Baltimore, Johns Hopkins Press, 1959.

———, *Britain and France between Two Wars*. New York, Harcourt Brace, 1940.

———, *Discord and Collaboration*. Baltimore, Johns Hopkins Press, 1962.

Wright, Quincy, ed., *Neutrality and Collective Security*. Chicago, University of Chicago Press, for the Harris Foundation, 1936.

———, *The Study of International Relations*. New York, Appleton-Century-Crofts, 1955.

Zimmern, Sir Alfred E., *The League of Nations and the Rule of Law, 1918-1935*. New York, The Macmillan Co., 1939.